D0295775

ESCAPE TO PAGAN

Brian Devereux

John Michael Devereux
Army no: 6284273
Sergeant 1st Battalion Royal Scots
RSM 2nd Battalion Royal Scots
Born 1912, Haslingden, Lancashire
Died 1962, Uxbridge, Middlesex

CASEMATE
uk
Oxford & Philadelphia

Published in Great Britain and
the United States of America in 2016 by
CASEMATE PUBLISHERS
10 Hythe Bridge Street, Oxford OX1 2EW, UK
and
1950 Lawrence Road, Havertown, PA 19083, USA

Hardcover Edition: ISBN 978-1-61200-373-3
Digital Edition: ISBN 978-1-61200-374-0

A CIP record for this book is available from the British Library

Printed in the United Kingdom by TJ International

For a complete list of Casemate titles, please contact:

CASEMATE PUBLISHERS (UK)
Telephone (01865) 241249
Fax (01865) 794449
Email: casemate-uk@casematepublishers.co.uk
www.casematepublishers.co.uk

CASEMATE PUBLISHERS (US)
Telephone (610) 853-9131
Fax (610) 853-9146
Email: casemate@casematepublishing.com
www.casematepublishing.com

Contents

🪷 denotes a change in narration between Brian Devereux and his mother Kate.

Foreword

I was very pleased when Dad decided to put down on paper our family's history. My grandma Kathleen Devereux was a great storyteller managing to narrate her past in a special way thus lightening even the saddest and most awful events. Many of the stories she had heard from my grandad, RSM Jack Devereux who rarely discussed his war experiences except with his ex-comrades and Jim Durant, my maternal grandmother Eileen's husband. Jim also served in Burma. It is this fortitude and strength of spirit that are a testament to all the men and women of that generation, which somehow enabled them to endure the life changing circumstances of the War in the Far East.

My great grandmother Harriet was also an exceptional woman and was key to their survival throughout their dangerous journey to evade captivity during the occupation of Burma. Grandad spent a lot of time with his grandchildren and gave us " … much chocolate … !" Sadly, he died when we were very young. Grandma was a devout catholic and I feel it was her unswerving faith that helped her through the difficult war years and enabled her to forgive her captors. She loved her whisky and her love of animals was also renowned as was her particular attention to personal hygiene which extended to daily showers for poor 'Chummy', the family dog.

When I think of grandma I recall the beautiful scent of roses which were her pride and joy. She had an exquisite smile that warmed you instantly and first and foremost she saw the good in everyone. She loved her children, their families and her grandchildren with all her heart. She touched our lives with her kindness.

Kim von Heintze

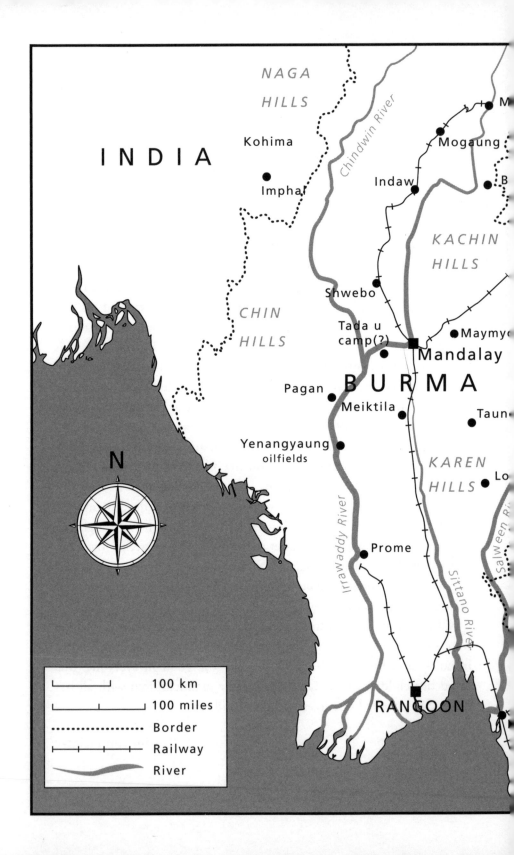

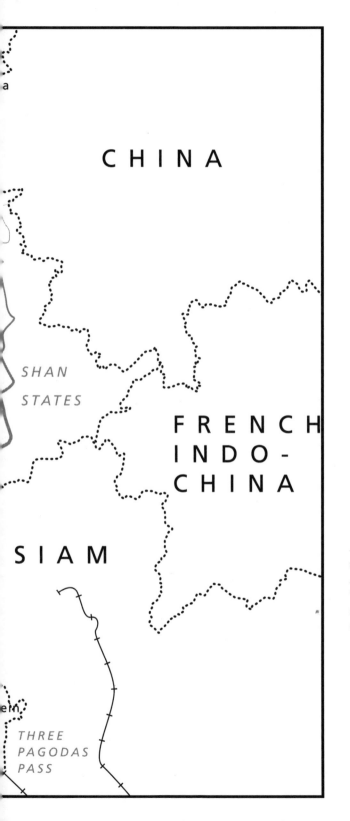

a

CHINA

SHAN
STATES

FRENCH
INDO-
CHINA

SIAM

THREE
PAGODAS
PASS

A map of Burma and surrounding territories. A potential location for Tada-u, determined from research undertaken by the publisher, is indicated.

CHAPTER 1

The Temple Bells of Pagan

BURMA

To my dear departed Mother

> After an infinite time I met my dear Mother; she looked as
> I first remembered, young and nimble, smiling always caring
> *"Son – how old and tired you seem,"* she said, as if surprised
> Yes Mother, the years have been unkind, unjust – unsparing
> *"Never mind Son,"* she answered – as if in her distant dreams
> She gently stroked my old grey head, *"soon – you will be my*
> *Little boy again – I will chase you laughing – like I used to*
> *As on baby legs you ran while I delighted in your joyful screams."*
> Forgive me my dearest Mother, I wish I had been a better son.

At the beginning of her story Mother would always pause, narrowing
her eyes as if protecting them from a burning Burmese sun while
she scanned some dusty, jungle fringed bullock track. Maybe she
was searching for the first front-line Nipponese soldiers we were
suddenly confronted with all those years ago. The Japanese soldiers'
sudden appearance shocked both mother and daughter, yet they found
themselves strangely curious; the fast approaching warriors looked
medieval. Perhaps in her distant mind's eye she was peering into a
remote stilted Burmese village surrounded by tall graceful palms and
sheltered in the dapple-shade of mango trees. She may have been

looking for the red face of her mother in the colourful milling crowd of villagers, or her young child running naked, laughing with the village children. Perhaps Mother was searching for a fleeting glimpse of her tall, handsome young husband looking dashing in his Glengarry and tartan trews on their wedding day.

I would wait while Mother searched for a particular indelible memory of her past. All she had to do was find the correct location and the correct bookmark. Only then would she smile and begin.

Meeting the enemy for the first time was one of her favourite stories, for now the terror of that moment has faded with the passing years. I would always listen, even though I had heard the story many times since the age of seven, for the re-telling gave Mother pleasure. I was the only one left, the only one there. Once the images and locations were established, her flow of words would increase. When in full flow she did not like me interrupting.

"How do you spell the name of that village, Mum? What direction were we travelling?" I would ask. Mother would stop and give me one of her long looks, regardless of my age.

※

"Do you want to learn the story of our survival, our hardships, or how to spell the names of Burmese villages? I just followed my mother. There were too many other worries: your father, escaping, the dangerous wild animals, poisonous snakes and you. You kept running away.

"At night we were vulnerable. Human corpses lay everywhere; many bodies had been half eaten by wild animals. Lying on the ground at night was tempting providence. I was also terrified of dangerous snakes as they killed so many people in Burma. As the sun sank below the horizon jackals began calling. Their eerie calls always frightened me. These were the things I was concerned with not the spelling of Burmese villages, now stop interrupting me!"

※

The warriors of Dai Nippon swept away all before them like an unstoppable Asiatic tsunami. Unlike the Mongol invasion centuries past, these warriors came from the east, out of the rising sun, from islands scattered like a handful of pearls in the cold waters of the East China Sea.

Looking back as an adult, I can now describe these images that I witnessed as a child, images that impressed my receptive young romantic mind; the Japanese were the first soldiers I had ever seen. Each Nipponese soldier was loaded down like a pack-animal, their faces contorted by the pain of their burdens. They marched at a desperate speed with their Havelock's bouncing on their shoulders like ancient chain-mail. They marched with their overlong bayonets exposed, blades that stabbed upwards to a cloudless sky, a sky dominated only by their Sun Goddess Amaterasu-o-mikami; a goddess that had smiled down favourably on her warrior sons as reward for worshipping her image and emblazoning it on their national flags and also for revering a close relative of hers; their Emperor, a son of heaven. These fighting men on the march gave the impression that they had come from another bygone age or perhaps even another distant planet.

Without my dear, wise, matriarchal grandmother, my mother and I would not have survived the many attending dangers of the jungle. Serious diseases, parasitic infestations and snakebite, were only some of the dangers we faced. This is the true story of our survival that took place in that far off land of green-domed pagodas now called Myanmar.

The dreaded meeting

In the distant shimmering heat haze stands the mystic spectacle of Pagan, a city of a thousand ornate red and white green domed pagodas. Temples devoutly built by the placid hands of Buddhists centuries long past, long forgotten. Pagan now stands lonely surrounded by wildness on the burning red ochre plains of central Burma.

When the shadows of the pagodas lengthen, a balmy wild jasmine fragrant breeze blows in from the far off purple tinged mountains. This scented zephyr seems to whisper ancient secrets to the thousands of small temple bells that hang idly during the still heat of the day. The lazy temple bells slowly begin to stir and tinkle tranquil sutras to their many listening Buddhas that guard each pagoda.

This ancient city of Buddhist temples is now surrounded by wilderness. On still moonlit nights only the solitary hamadryad and skulking hyena wander there cautiously, for Pagan (it is said) is a place where spirits still linger.

The once prosperous British Devereux family, Kate, her mother Harriet and young son were now destitute, making their way towards Pagan alone. At night as they slept on the ground, they shivered with cold and fear of attack by wild animals. It was somewhere near Pagan that the first dreaded encounter with the invaders occurred.

⚜

"We were walking along a lonely cactus and prickly-pear bordered bullock track that had been previously used by the retreating and ravenous Chinese Army; we could tell this by the litter they had dropped. Our slow exhausted steps were watched with hostile intent by the white-bleached skulls of village dogs that littered the ashes at the side of the track. Each skull had been picked clean by eager chopsticks. My mother said the starving Chinese soldiers favoured dog flesh above pork to fill their shrunken stomachs, for dog flesh is red and contains no rich fat.

"We feared the Chinese soldiers and Burmese dacoits only second to the Japanese. Pagan was my mother's intended destination of our escape. She decided we would be safer in the less populated rural countryside away from the Japanese Air Force. At one point, she wanted to reach some villages on the other side of Pagan. Mother believed we could get food in these villages and hide in one of the pagodas. My brother Harry Talbot used to camp near these villages while out hunting and knew the headmen. He always helped when a predator became a danger to livestock or the villagers; he also gave them the excess meat. Harry was a well known sportsman in Burma and popular with the Buddhist pongee monks who supported the football team he played for [it was Mandalay or Rangoon]. My mother believed the headmen of these villages would help with food and shelter without betraying us. The invaders called themselves 'The Warrior Gods of Dai Nippon' in their propaganda pamphlets, dropped by their shiny silver planes. We had secrets to hide from a suspicious and paranoid race who dealt harshly with suspected spies. Jack and my brother Harry Talbot were both in the British Army.

"My mother and I were now exhausted and so thirsty; we also had you to care for. We had now been walking for many days and nights, sleeping in the open. I hated the eerie calls of the jackals as they heralded the night. My mother always chose the site where we bedded down before the sun disappeared below the horizon. She knew the safest places least likely to be visited by venomous snakes, but we were never really safe. We always placed a waterproof sheet on the ground first then a blanket to lie on and one to cover us. Despite the heat of the day, the nights were so cold. You slept between us for safety; we had heard many stories of wild animals running off with children in rural Burma.

"Occasionally we could hear the distant sawing call of a leopard, sometimes the alarm calls of barking deer that terrified me and kept me awake, particularly if their calls seemed to be coming closer; we had no walls to protect us. After an hour of total darkness, the moon and the stars appeared. To reassure me, Mother always told me that dangerous wild animals would be frightened off by the noise of the fighting and bombing. I did not believe her: something was eating the dead. At night I just stared into the shadows of the jungle that surrounded our hard earthen bed. Cold dawn always took an eternity to appear.

"On our way to Pagan, we could hear sounds of heavy fighting and see plumes of smoke rising behind us *[possibly the oilfields]*. It was on this bullock track that we would soon encounter a column of Japanese soldiers. This unexpected meeting came as a terrible shock to my mother and me. China was just over the border from our new home in Taunggyi; we had heard news of the atrocities at Nanking. We were also afraid that copies of my marriage certificate were still in the town hall at Taunggyi. The Japanese were convinced that the British had left spies behind. To be suspected of spying meant torture and death by the Kempeitai.

"It was now April. This was the hottest time of the year in Burma. On that particular day, we were very thirsty and tired. We needed to find water and shade to rest. When your mouth and throat are parched there is no hunger, you cannot swallow, and fear and trauma adds to your thirst. All you have is an overwhelming desire for any kind of liquid. Before rounding a bend in the bullock track, both my mother and I as if by instinct, turned around and were shocked to see a column of marching Japanese soldiers behind us. I could feel my heart pounding. We just stood there rooted to the spot, watching them closing the distance. Even though we were terrified, we were also strangely curious. These soldiers looked so primitive and untidy. As they approached, we could hear them all making a soft grunting sound; they seemed to be chanting a single repeated word. We stood aside; Mother could speak Nippon Go but decided not to communicate. 'Stay calm, Kate, and keep your mouth shut,' whispered my mother. 'Don't you dare start bawling – they are unpredictable when their blood is hot.' She said this just before the column of Japanese troops approached us. They looked so intimidating with their long fixed bayonets. They were marching so quickly, hardly making a sound in the dust. We just stood still; my heart was pounding as I held your hand.

"They were led by an officer riding a Shan pony. The faces of the troops were screwed up with fatigue, their uniforms covered in red dust; some soldiers were pulling a kind of big gun. One of the Japs marching in front held the red and white sun flag of Japan aloft. The officer on the horse studied us without expression. The marching soldiers paid us little attention. Each Japanese soldier was loaded down with equipment; they carried big packs on their backs, packs festooned with leaves and grass, they looked so different from our own British troops. We wondered how soldiers that looked medieval and had to pull their own guns could have beaten the proud British Army so quickly. After the Japanese troops had passed us, we noticed strange cloven-hoof foot prints in the red dust and a slight fragrant smell."

🪷

The "slight fragrant smell" left behind by the marching Japanese troops matches other similar descriptions; an American officer fighting with the Chinese described the smell as "tooth-powder", while an Australian Officer recalled the scent of a passing Japanese patrol as "not unpleasant". After the surrender of the British in Hong Kong, Japanese officers often placed handkerchiefs over their noses when approaching their British counterparts.

✿

"The last column of soldiers had not long passed when there was a guttural shout and the marching column of Japanese soldiers suddenly stopped. Turning, they looked straight in our direction.

"'My God!' I whispered. 'They have changed their minds and are going to bayonet us.'

"'Shut up Kate!' said my mother. Her face was flushed red. We just stood silent; I hoped they would kill us quickly. We soon realized the enemy troops were not looking at us but up at the sky over our heads. We then heard aircraft approaching. There was nothing we could do. If the planes were British and attacked, we would also be killed as we were so close to the Japanese soldiers. If we ran, the Japs might shoot us. There was nowhere to hide. The cactus plants and prickly pear that surrounded us were covered in long needle-sharp thorns and offered little protection. Suddenly two Japanese planes came in low; we could see the red sun symbol and the pilot's faces.

"The Jap soldier with the big flag began waving it and the rest of the soldiers took out small white handkerchiefs and also began waving them at the planes. The Japanese fighters left. The enemy soldiers continued their march. We did not move until they were out of sight. We quickly learned to identify the different sounds of the planes; Japanese aircraft had a higher pitched tinnier sound than the British and American fighters. With the possibility that more Japanese soldiers would use this bullock track heading in the direction of Pagan, my mother decided to leave the track and enter the scrub jungle where we would be safe and less visible. We could see green hills in the distance, so we headed north away from Pagan."

✿

It is also true, as Mother states, that the warriors of Dai Nippon in marching order, always had a certain medieval appearance; their light cloven-hoofed split toed rubber boots (tabi), were ideal for tree climbing and jungle warfare. The local Burmese often referred to Japanese soldiers as the "Monkey People" because of their habit of nimbly climbing trees at every opportunity in order to scout their surroundings. Their outdated long bayonets and swords, flashed in the bright tropical sunlight and searing heat. In the van they carried their striking sun flag (the Hinomaru), always proudly held aloft like a feudal banner. This was the banner of their eternal Emperor warlord: a living God. These wispy whiskered hardy soldiers pulled, pushed and carried their artillery like draught animals, softly grunting the same single inaudible word. Their dusty sweat streaked faces twisted with total exhaustion no western fighting man would be expected to have endured. These were frugal, sturdy, olive-skinned men with muscular puttied bound calves. Their hungry, alert eyes constantly scanned the sky and their surroundings with the caution and suspicion of peasants. These men who grew rice (the food of the gods) and fished the deep cold waters that surround their cherry blossom islands, were the hardy warriors from Dai Nippon Teikoku (The Empire of Great Nippon). They were Shinto and Zen Buddhist; rice and fish eaters, who could force-march thirty-five miles in a day. Like all fighting men they marched towards the sounds of battle. But unlike other soldiers who fought to live the warriors of Yamato fought to die. They had already taken their final leave of their loved ones in a "haiku" (a farewell poem).

> "Sayonara, sayonara, when
> The cherry blossoms fall I will return
> Look for me at Yasukuni Shrine Mother."

Nipponese soldiers also loved their mothers.

❧

"My mother and I carried all that we possessed. To add to the difficulty of our situation you had the habit of bolting. We were so tired and got fed up of chasing you and calling you all kinds of names, for our shouting could give our position away to anyone nearby. God knows how many dangerous wild animals were in the vicinity that could have snatched you."

☙

Being deeply religious my grandmother and mother never swore at me in English. Swearing in Burmese, it seems, was not a sin: "Come here you little ..." or "wait till I get my hands on you – you little ..." When older, I began to understand Burmese swear words, and then realized what they were calling me. It still makes me smile.

☙

"Apart from the advancing enemy, another immediate danger to us was trying to avoid the desperate locust-like retreating Chinese Army. They would take everything we had as they were starving themselves, poor men. These ravenous Chinese soldiers left a trail of their own dead in burnt out Burmese villages.

"When our small group passed through such a destroyed village, the fire blackened skulls looked evil in the half light of evening. My mother could always recognize the skulls of Chinese soldiers by the worn v-shaped gap between their front teeth due to a lifetime habit of cracking open dried salted pumpkin seeds. Their dead were placed in huts which became their funeral pyres. We were now alone, two women and a child hoping to avoid capture. My mother led us deeper into the wild ..."

☙

CHAPTER 2

Golden Hill

MAINLAND CHINA

Sergeant Jack Devereux lay prone and semi-conscious on the Golden Hill battlefield. He had been shot through the head by an explosive or hollow-point bullet fired from the standard Japanese 6.5 calibre Arisaka rifle. The bullet had entered his left temple exiting from the back of his neck, leaving a gaping wound and many small fragments. Every now and then his body twitched and periodically went into violent spasm as the shattered and torn nerves in his head and neck struggled to function. From the corner of his right eye he glimpsed a single stray dog wandering among the dead and dying. The Sergeant could taste stale congealed blood in his mouth.

A sound slowly began to seep into Sergeant Devereux's pain-ridden thoughts; it slowly began to awaken him from his dreams of oblivion. The sound grew louder, a humming drone, the pitch of which rose and fell lingering around his shattered throbbing head. His brain was still numb from the impact of the Japanese bullet and struggled to analyze the sound and the reason he could no longer control his once strong body. Other thoughts also troubled him. Where was D Company? Where was Lieutenant Ford? Why was he alone? They had both led the counter-attack on Golden Hill.

These questions would remain unanswered; he could not move his head and look around. If he could, he would see the droning sound was coming from clouds of glinting, swollen green flies who were attending him. He had become the lord of the flies. As his body was paralyzed he was unaware of them crawling over his deep head and neck wounds. The flies were paying him homage while laying their eggs; for the maggots of some species prefer helpless living tissue over rotting dead flesh.

Sometimes he heard the voice of a human being groaning in despair and pain; he later realized the sounds were coming from his own parched throat. He craved water. The Sergeant continued to study the same few inches of Chinese real estate that his one open eye could see; instead of grass, he saw a glutinous mess of congealed blood and pieces of his own raw flesh, framed by small splinters of white bone from his shattered skull and jaw. His thoughts drifted to his young wife Kate still living peacefully in their home in Taunggyi, capital of the Shan States of Burma: At least she was safe. He would never see her again.

Perhaps it was for the best that the Sergeant did not know at that very moment that the long tentacles of the Japanese Imperial Army were slowly reaching out towards the borders of Burma from Thailand. Or that his wife, mother-in-law and young son, whom he had yet to meet, would shortly be wandering the dangerous jungles of Burma, without shelter or protection. The Sergeant began slipping back into a dark chasm that beckoned him. It was tempting him to enter its painless oblivion. On the Golden Hill battlefield, the sun was now only a hands breath from the horizon, night was falling. The Sergeant began to shiver.

࿇

"Jack told me that he and Lieutenant Ford led a counter-attack to clear the Japanese soldiers from Golden Hill when he was wounded. The battlefield was now quiet. Jack was paralyzed and unconscious but every now and then his body jerked in spasm. Unfortunately, these spasms indicated he was still alive.

"When Jack awoke early the following day he felt so cold, his uniform was wet with dew. He longed for the warmth of a blanket and something hot to drink. Soon he found he could move his right arm and his fingers. His left arm was trapped under his chest *[the Sergeant was left-handed]*, the fingers of his trapped hand still clutched his service revolver; its barrel was pointing towards his stomach. After the war, he told me that thoughts of ending his suffering entered his numbed brain; all he had to do was to pull the trigger but the revolver barrel was positioned under his stomach and he did not have the strength to force the barrel higher towards his heart. He knew a stomach wound would only prolong and increase his suffering. He pushed the idea from his mind: he was dying anyway.

"Jack lay wounded on the battlefield for several days drifting in and out of consciousness. Hong Kong as yet had not fallen; he could hear the sound of artillery in the distance. Jack managed to lift his throbbing head; looking around the battlefield he began to hallucinate. Suddenly he saw his mother slowly walking towards him with a cup of tea and a blanket. He hoped she was also bringing him cigarettes. Jack was always a very heavy smoker, he needed a last smoke so badly. He could see his mother's dark shadow approaching but why was she moving so slowly? She seemed to be stopping and looking down at the dead as if studying the bodies at her feet. Perhaps she was looking for him? He wanted to call out to her but his vocal cords did not respond.

"Suddenly his mother's shadow was standing over him, he waited for her to speak; she remained silent. It was then he felt a heavy blow to the back of his neck followed by a sharp pain; fresh warm blood trickled down into his mouth. It was not his mother.

"The dark shadow standing over him slowly bent down and gripped his right arm roughly. The shadow then began to pull him over several dead bodies that lay nearby. Jack began lifting his stiff bloodied neck and shattered head and could see a pair of shiny black, riding boots covered with splashes of blood. The riding boots were occasionally obliterated by a flash of gleaming metal reflecting the weak early morning sunlight. Jacks stunned and pain ridden mind soon awoke to the reality: he was being dragged by an enemy officer to a more convenient place of execution."

The flashing metal object was a naked sword held in a smooth brown hand.

Anger welled up in the Sergeant's shattered head; he could be a volatile man when roused. His wounded brain struggled back to consciousness. He desperately wanted to extend his life even for a few moments longer, despite the pain of his wounds; for such is human nature and our fear of the unknown.

The Japanese officer hesitated and stopped pulling his victim, this tall man was heavy. A sixth sense perhaps or the sound of a revolver being cocked made him turn his head. He instantly knew he had made a foolish mistake. It was the severity of his victim's head wound that had initially fooled him. The lucky Buddhas around his neck, given to him by his mother before he left Japan, had deserted him. Almost immediately two heavy blows hit his back. One bullet passed straight through him, the second bullet shattered the young Japanese officer's spine. Even before his body hit the ground, his spirit had quickly ascended and began the long flight back to the misty islands of Dai Nippon to the sacred shrine at Yasukuna to become a falling cherry blossom every spring.

The sergeant would soon learn the name of his would-be executioner: a name he would never forget. The Japanese officer's details became known when his body was searched later by a Japanese speaking doctor from the military hospital who was a resident of Hong Kong.

Earlier that morning the young 2nd Lieutenant Nakamura, attached to Lt General Takashi Sakai Headquarters, had spent the morning running around tending to the senior officer's demands and getting his face slapped. Despite coming from a rich family (judging by the quality of his sword) he had first to serve eight months as the lowest of low, a Second Class Private. He was treated brutally by his NCOs and comrades with longer service which was as good as rank in the Imperial Japanese Army. Face-slapping was the least of his problems that day; he had not as yet personally blooded the sacred family blade, proudly handed down to him by his father. During three months in China the opportunity had never arisen. The letter home was long overdue. To save time he had already gone through the vital ritual of purifying the ancient blade with water that morning; a blade tempered and beaten over 700 times by a craftsman.

That morning General Takashi Sakai wanted his Headquarters closer to the front, the General left with his senior staff. It fell to the young 2nd Lieutenant Nakamura to organize the move of the headquarters, allowing him the opportunity to search the Golden Hill battlefield. He was now walking through the battlefield seeking life among the dead. The crimson spray needs to be driven by a live pumping heart; beheading a corpse was beneath the dignity of a Samurai. The act is an artistic form of beauty to a warrior of Nippon.

The young enemy officer's eyes fell on Sergeant Jack Devereux whose body he noticed twitched periodically in spasm. It is also possible he may have recognized the tall sergeant from his observations, while squatting (in that position westerners find most uncomfortable) under camouflage a few hundred yards to the front of D Company, the day before the attack. The Allies, during the early stages of the war, had not as yet appreciated the enemy's skill at camouflaging their positions.

The men who later found the Sergeant assumed that the young Japanese officer was blooding his sword; it is also possible the enemy officer was administrating the coup de grâce known to his race as a "warrior's compassion".

⚜

"Jack said that the exertion of lifting his arm and pulling the trigger of his revolver made him feel faint; the noise of the two revolver shots made his head wound throb in agony. He passed out again. Jack welcomed the oblivion as it divorced him from the pain and his raging thirst. When he awoke the flies had gone, leaving only maggots to take their place. He could now feel them in his head eager to burrow deeper into his living flesh, into the dark depths to escape from the hot sun.

"The following day while foraging amongst the dead for medical supplies, a group of Royal Scots and a medical officer who was fluent in Chinese and Japanese came across Jack and found him still alive, thank God. The dead Japanese Officer's body was lying nearby and was searched. The search revealed the young Japanese Officer belonged to the 38th Regiments Headquarters. There was also a diary and some pictures of his family. This doctor knew Jack well and had been treating members of the Royal Scots who had just been discharged from hospital, still suffering from malaria. I would meet him in Alexander Military Hospital Singapore, where Glenis was born after the war. He saved Jack's life.

"The documents and diary found on the dead Japanese officer gave his name, rank and that he had been in a surveillance party observing the Gin Drinkers' Line before the attack. Having seen what the enemy did with soldiers who were captured and found in possession of Japanese souvenirs, Jack's comrades left the beautiful sword. The men took Jack back to their hideout in Nathan Road. They intended to escape. Poor Jack, the deep sword wound and the bullet's exit hole on the back of his neck caused him much pain during the cold winter months. All the nerves on the right side of his face had been damaged. Fragments of the bullet remained in his head, too near the brain to remove despite two facelifts and operations at Roehampton Military Hospital. He never complained. Thank God Jack was lying awkwardly; the sword blade must have been obstructed by something on the ground."

☙

Lt General Takashi Sakai was executed by firing squad in 1946.

Hong Kong

Meanwhile in the distance, the battle for Hong Kong Island was coming to a premature conclusion. It would be the first of many humiliating defeats.

A few days before the Japanese attack, the 2nd Battalion Royal Scots had taken up position on the Gin Drinkers' Line. Sergeant Devereux and D Company under the command of Lieutenant Ford were working on improving their defensive positions. Many of the Scots were new recruits, others like the Sergeant were regulars and veterans transferred from the 1st Battalion Royal Scots who had seen active service protecting the flank at Dunkirk.

As the soldiers anticipated the coming attack, they must have taken comfort from the many negative intelligence reports concerning the Japanese soldiers. According to British Intelligence, the Japanese soldiers were afraid of the dark and British cold steel. It was claimed that the Japanese were rotten shots because of the shape of their eyes. The truth was simple; Japanese recruits were given little or no practice on the firing range: "Practice on the enemy" was the advice. Their long bayonets constantly attached to the end of their Arisaka rifles did not encourage good marksmanship.

Good intelligence was ignored. General Wavell appeared in Hong Kong and chanted his favourite mantra: "The Japs are useless!" According to some modern historians, he was the worst offender in underestimating the Nipponese Army. Wavell's opinion of the enemy germinated when he saw a scruffy group of Jap soldiers lounging on a bridge in China. He was disgusted; all the Jap soldiers had their flies undone (a popular habit on hot days). The General concluded: "The Japs were an absolute shower and when they saw smart Tommy Atkins and his shiny brass buttons would mess their baggy cotton trousers and scarper on bandy legs back to the embraces of their weeping, sloe-eyed mothers. That is of course if the Japs had the stamina to run considering their protein deficient rice diet.

After the war the Sergeant and his old comrades (when in their cups) always smiled when they spoke of the other rumours they had heard (and presumably believed at that time) concerning the Nipponese soldier: "Japs had no sense of balance because they were carried on their mother's backs. When they charged, they were likely to fall over and impale themselves on their over long 15in Meiji type bayonets or the even longer Meiji Type 30 sword bayonets at 20in."

It was also claimed that Japanese soldiers were obsessed with pornography; another reason for their poor eyesight and lack of stamina. The thought of scattering the approaches to the Gin Drinkers' Line in advance with hard porn (there were no anti-personnel mines available in Hong Kong) must have occurred to some of the soldiers; it would surely cause large groups of porn-loving, myopic Japanese infantry to closely congregate around a particularly desirable beauty making a fine target for British machine guns?

Air Marshal Sir Robert Brooke-Popham was more ambiguous in his opinions of the enemy's air force; he told his pilots that the Jap airmen could not fly in the dark. You have to presume he meant Japanese pilots weren't nocturnal, but most damming of all he stated: "Jap pilots are dirty!" This must have begged the question, did the Air Marshal mean dirty in personal habits? Dirty in uniform? Or perhaps dirty minded? It is possible he meant all three. The Nipponese are in fact a scrupulously clean and hygienic race and do not hold the monopoly among fighting men for an interest in porn.

Gin Drinkers' Line, Mainland China

When the Japanese attack came early on the morning of the 8th December 1941, it fell on the Royal Scots and came as a total surprise to the men of the 2nd Battalion. British anti-personnel mines, had they been available, would have provided a warning while taking a toll on the enemy. The ferocity and determination of the Japanese attack also surprised the Scots. The Japanese infantry had crept silently to within grenade throwing range under the cover of low lying ground mists. It must also have come as a nasty surprise to the Scots that the attacking Japanese preferred to throw real hand grenades instead of firecrackers (as rumoured). The Japanese fragmentation grenades (type 97) were packed with dynamite.

Most surprising of all was that the Japanese soldiers showed no fear of the bayonet. In fact, the bayonet was part of the Japanese samurai tradition and the art of bayonet fighting techniques were regularly practised under the sharp eye of an instructing Sergeant who held a wooden pole (for punishment). Both combatants were protected by kendo armour in these violent and realistic contests. Japanese front line troops had another advantage over Allied troops; they were well acquainted with the vulnerability of the vital organs in the human body and knew exactly where to push their blades. The soldiers of the Emperor did not practice their thrusts on straw filled dummies but on live and bound Chinese prisoners with real working organs and active vocal cords. Furthermore, as an aid to close quarter fighting, the Japanese bayonet came with a built-in hand guard (J shaped) that with skilled handling could lock onto a British or American bayonet; then with a strong twist wrench the rifle out of their opponent's hands. The longer Japanese bayonet addressed its owner's height and reach disadvantage. Practicing on living organs gave them a wider range of targets. Another advantage was that the Japanese bayonet was always fixed, always at hand; his western counterpart usually had to wait for the order "fix bayonets."

Back on the Gin Drinkers' Line, hand to hand fighting had begun as the enemy got into the Scots positions. Though shocked by the suddenness and ferocity of the Japanese attack, the brave Royal Scots managed to repulse the initial onslaughts.

While evicting the enemy dead from their trenches, the Scots noticed that their foes were not "small-boned myopic dwarfs", but fine examples of muscle and bone, despite being short in stature. And to the defenders' surprise not a single pair of pebble spectacles or buck-teeth were to be seen.

Then, adding to the trauma of battle, the young inexperienced recruits were subjected to heavy and accurate artillery fire from British guns at the rear. This was the last straw for some soldiers. Men had to be restrained from retreating by their officers and NCOs. This however did not stop some soldiers deserting their posts in the confusion. The experienced soldiers just cursed the gunners and their ancestors, the British artillery had months to range their guns.

Another shock awaited D Company. While tending their dead they found the body of one of the new arrivals from Maryhill Barracks (the best piper in the Regiment): he had been decapitated. Nearby, his pale severed head stared up at the sky, his blue eyes wide open; his face had a surprised expression according to two of dad's comrades. The reality of seeing the headless body of a comrade confirmed they were fighting a savage Asiatic enemy a long way from home.

It was during a brief lull in the battle that Captain Pinkerton observed a large body of enemy troops with field artillery ascending Golden Hill. Once in place, the enemy artillery could fire down on their positions. Lieutenant Ford and Sergeant Devereux of D Company were ordered to attack the enemy and eliminate this danger.

The men of D Company, approximately 120 soldiers, began their steep climb. The soldiers were exhausted; no rations had reached the Royal Scots during the last 24 hours. Water for drinking and cooling the Vickers machine guns was in short supply. Added to this many of the soldiers were still suffering from the strength sapping after effects of malaria. So exhausted were these men that they were forced to crawl up Golden Hill on their hands and knees dragging heavy equipment and arms behind them.

Gaining the high ground, D Company attacked the Japanese and cleared them from the summit only to be counter attacked by superior numbers.

⚜

"Jack remembered a group of Japanese struggling to pull a big gun uphill with ropes. D Company attacked these enemy soldiers but despite their losses, the enemy did not let the big gun roll back down the hill. It was there near the summit that Jack was suddenly shot, he did not realize that the bullet had passed straight through his head, all he felt was a blow to his temple. Jack desperately tried to remain lucid at this vital moment but lost consciousness. The men believed Jack was dead because of his terrible head wound. D Company was ordered to retreat.

"The remnants of D Company fell back to their ill prepared positions on The Gin Drinkers' Line. They arrived just before the enemy appeared in strength. The attacks lasted most of the night. The Gin Drinkers' Line fell sometime during the next morning.

"Luckily, after several days and nights of slipping in and out of consciousness Jack was found by some Royal Scots and a British medical doctor, who missed the withdrawal. By now the battle for Hong Kong was raging.

"The group of men, who had found Jack, carried him to a large multi-storeyed building in Nathan Road. The soldiers knew this area well. Here, the wound at the back of Jack's neck was cleaned of maggots and the rotting flesh was cut away with an old razor blade. Ointment was applied and the gaping wound at the back of his neck was filled with gauze and stitched with needle and cotton. He was given all the remaining painkillers. Jack was then given a cigarette; he could not live without tobacco and often said if it was not for me and nicotine, he would not have survived.

These men of the Royal Scots were hoping to escape into China. Once his wounds were tended, Jack was taken to another block of flats where other soldiers were hiding. These men had collected a liberal supply of alcohol and tinned food, but water was always difficult to find. The only safe available water came from draining the taps. Several of the soldiers were constantly drunk.

"Jack was given water and some hot food but chewing was excruciating; he could feel and hear the torn cartilage and bones in his head making strange crunching noises. The food made him feel stronger but his deep head wound was throbbing as the painkillers began to wear off: the pain was unbearable. Luckily new arrivals brought medical equipment and painkillers allowing him some relief and rest. Jack was still very weak from the loss of blood. But now it must have been a comfort and blessing to him that he was back among men he knew."

❦

In the streets below, drunken Japanese troops celebrated their victories with looting and rape. Executions of Chinese civilians became commonplace. All these indulgences were collectively referred to as "the fruits of victory." If Sergeant Devereux believed that his worst problems were over, he was greatly mistaken. The *Lisbon Maru*, the sharks of the South China Sea, the coal mines of Nagasaki and the atom bomb still awaited his presence.

The Royal Scots suffered the highest losses of officers and men during the battle on mainland China defending the Gin Drinkers' Line. General Maltby wanted them to hold out for seven days while the islands defences were improved. Yet months had been wasted.

After the mainland fell so rapidly, the defenders of Hong Kong Island braced themselves for the coming attack. Confusion reigned, troops were scattered in penny packets; the most obvious crossing point was only lightly defended. The two commanding officers entered their deep bomb-proof bunkers and stayed put. They remained out of touch when the battle above began. On the 15th December before attacking Hong Kong, the Japanese began a heavy bombardment of the islands north shore. Demands for surrender were made on December 13th and December 17th. When these demands were refused, the Japanese successfully forced a crossing from the mainland, suffering few casualties.

During that night the Japanese massacred 22 gunners who had surrendered. Soon after this there was another massacre of medical staff at an aid station. At the hospital, patients were bayoneted in their beds, doctors and surgeons shot out of hand and the nurses repeatedly raped.

The poorly trained and equipped Canadians gave a good account of themselves, one of their numbers receiving a VC. The Japanese had cut the water supply after capturing the islands reservoirs. Hong Kong surrendered: shades of Singapore.

Before the fall of Hong Kong, Tam and Willie (two of dads' fellow NCOs and lifelong friends) had safely crossed the bay. The Royal Scots were now in a position above and not far from the harbour at North Point. Their view of the enemy landings and their lines of fire were blocked by high buildings, making it a simple task for the enemy to come ashore in small boats undetected. Very soon they were being attacked by Japanese infiltrators from the rear; while malarial mosquitoes harassed them from all directions (their position was a malarial hot spot). This was an ill prepared and poorly chosen defensive line; the orders being received were confused and often contradictory.

With the danger of being surrounded and cut off, the two friends, along with other defenders, left their positions and headed in the direction of the town. Such was the commercial drive in the Crown Colony that Tam and Willie found a Chinese noodle bar still open; it would be their last decent meal for several years. They then came across a group of soldiers who had found a liquor store. Helping themselves to booze and cigarettes, they took refuge in some tall buildings and began sniping at the enemy below. Because of the amount of indiscriminate small arms fire, their actions went unnoticed. Many of the Japanese troops by now were also drunk.

Tam and Willie took pleasure in emptying as many bottles as they could. Years later when visiting dad, they happily reminisced about all the types of expensive alcohol sampled, alcohol they had never tasted before; they found all to their liking with only one exception: Crème de Menthe.

The orgy of violence over, the victorious soldiers began plundering the rich European homes. Their superiors concentrated on the many bank vaults and gold reserves therein. Amazingly, some of the bars were still open and customers were being served by drunken soldiers from different regiments. The battle was lost; drinks were on the house. Only the Japanese bars and businesses were shuttered and closed, their owners had discreetly left the island. This evacuation it seems went unnoticed by the British Intelligence.

Back on Mainland China, Sergeant Devereux and other Royal Scots soldiers, continued to conceal themselves in a ruined block of flats for several days on the outskirts of town. Many of these soldiers were still armed.

☙

"Jack told me that from their vantage point on the higher floors that they could see the victorious Japanese troops committing atrocities on military personnel and civilians who had surrendered in the streets below. The hiding soldiers began to take revenge on any drunken

Japanese troops that entered the building on their own looking for loot. Some of these Japs were clubbed to death, shot or bayoneted. There was no sense of fair play in these killings. The final number of enemy killed was over a dozen. The men decided to move to another deserted building further back from the main road, in case the dead Japanese were discovered by an enemy patrol.

"By the time of the planned escape, the group of soldiers had accumulated plenty of tinned food, but clean water was still a problem. Two men set out to find more water for their escape. Jack was now on his feet, God knows how and he intended to go with the escape party. The two men who went out to find water did not return.

"The escape party moved out that night. While passing the large garden of a big white house they heard groans and muffled pleas for help. To their horror they had stumbled on a group of British prisoners and civilians who had been tied up and used for bayonet practise, some pleaded for water, others begged to be shot. Once untied, several joined the escape party; two Royal Scots remained with the badly wounded. The escape party heard a few shots; later the two men rejoined the group and carried on in silence.

"Jack's wounds soon began to bleed with the extra exertion. The doctor was worried about his deteriorating condition, it soon became obvious that Jack could not continue as he was becoming dizzy and was having difficulty standing upright. Making their farewells and leaving him some tin food, water, cigarettes and his revolver, his comrades left him. They were sure he was dying."

❧

Sergeant Devereux must have watched his disappearing comrades with deep sadness; he was now on his own again.

❧

"Jack managed to eat some of the food despite the pain of chewing and drank all the water before lapsing into unconsciousness. This was just as well for again his thoughts were focused on his loaded revolver … it would release him from his suffering and his hopeless situation. When he awoke it was around midday. He was lying in the open. The flies began swarming around his wounds again. Jack moved towards cover out of the hot sun. Despite his wounds his memory was not affected and he wondered how far the escape party had travelled during the night. In the shade of the undergrowth he slept.

"When he awoke the next day his revolver was missing, so were the tins of food, cigarettes and empty water bottle. He no longer cared for the loss except for his cigarettes; he desperately craved a last smoke. Jack was sure he would die soon from the loss of blood or infection. The deep sword cut at the back of his neck was freely bleeding again; he could smell and taste the stench of his festering head wound. The cotton stitching had rotted and the bandages had come away. His only wish was for a cigarette before dying. He waited for death: death did not come. He recognized a road nearby and crawled up the bank and staggered along it. A Chinaman suddenly appeared; he was holding Jack's revolver. The Chinaman shouted aggressively and began to threaten him with the revolver. Jack began to stagger towards Kowloon closely followed by the persistent Chinaman. He wished he had a weapon to shoot him. Both Jack and the Chinaman stopped when they heard the approach of a lorry full of Japanese soldiers. The lorry stopped, a Jap Sergeant holding a sword accompanied by two soldiers with fixed bayonets, surrounded Jack. Even though he was no longer afraid of dying he did not wish to be bayoneted to death or beheaded. The Japs were drunk.

"The Chinaman began speaking rapidly to the Jap Sergeant and kept pointing at Jack. The Sergeant took the revolver from the Chinaman and shot him in the stomach, the two soldiers then bayoneted the squirming and screaming man as he lay on the road. Jack thought his turn was next but the Japanese are a strange race; when you expect cruelty they can be almost kind or vice versa. Jack did not even bother putting his hands up in surrender.

"The Japanese Sergeant still holding his sword began walking around Jack studying his terrible head and neck wounds with much sucking of teeth and hissing. It must have been obvious to the Japanese Sergeant that the deep wound on the back of Jack's neck was made by a Japanese sword during an attempted beheading. Not knowing the true circumstances of the event, they must have marvelled at Jack's survival. The Japanese

NCO then motioned Jack to kneel, which Jack just about managed to do. He expected the worst. The Jap then with his naked sword began to give his men a demonstration of how he would have struck a clean blow. At that moment, the Jap Sergeant noticed through Jacks blood stained uniform that he too was a Sergeant. He was helped to his feet and gently patted on the back and grinned at; this earned him a packet of twenty players and a box of matches which he gratefully accepted.

"The Jap Sergeant then gave him a drink of water from his own canteen and cheerfully explained in sign language that Jack would soon be dead. He was then carefully helped onto the lorry by the enemy soldiers and the truck continued its journey. In the lorry Jack was asked to turn his head so that they could all have a better look at his wounds, then he was given more cigarettes by the rest of the troops. They were very amused when they observed living maggots falling from the hole in his head. These were front line veterans and many were wounded themselves. All the soldiers were heavily loaded down with loot. Jack was surprised they had not relieved him of all his valuables; his watch and wedding ring were in plain sight, but at the time he did not care, he had finally got his smoke.

"Due to long periods of unconsciousness, Jack was never sure how or when he was re-united with many of his Army pals; his wounds were re-cleaned of maggots and dressed by Army surgeons as best as circumstances would allow. The Japanese Sergeant's name was Yoshida. Jack would find this out later when the Jap Sergeant showed up at Sham Shui Po POW camp."

❧

Later when slaving in the mines of Japan, the sword and bullet wounds on the back of his neck created much interest and gave the Sergeant and his men a few precious minutes' respite from the back breaking work. It also earned him a cigarette or a small rice ball while the Japanese in charge inspected and mulled over his scars. A few minutes of rest could save a man's life, especially a man who often exchanged his midday bowl of rice for cigarettes.

Back in Hong Kong, on Christmas day 1941, General Maltby saw no other option but to surrender. Brigadier Wallis refused. The Japanese used this as an excuse for committing more atrocities. Some people are still unsure of Brigadier Wallis' motives for refusing to surrender: perhaps self promotion?

Initially the captured soldiers were not guarded adequately. This gave the prisoners time to slip away and wander around the ruins salvaging what they could. Some men went to visit their Chinese girlfriends. Very few soldiers escaped. In due course the front line enemy soldiers would be posted to the Pacific Islands and replaced by rear echelon troops and circumstances for the prisoners would change for the worst.

The Japanese turned their attention to the Chinese population in Hong Kong. It was not long before streets were running with blood from the beheadings. Many captured Royal Scots in working parties nearby were forced to watch; Tam and Willie included. Initially the soldiers were physically sick as they watched the spray of blood when the carotid artery was severed cleanly; the executioners took pride in avoiding the spray by positioning themselves correctly. Every time the sword fell, a soft audible sigh of admiration from the many watching Japanese soldiers could be heard. After witnessing a dozen or so beheadings, the act became almost surreal to the prisoners; many men were surprised how heavy a human head was by the sound it made as it hit the road.

Tightly bound Chinese victims waited with typical oriental fatalism, they knew by now that no amount of pleading and wailing would save them. The only consolation for them was that they would soon be meeting their ancestors; suffering and hunger would be a thing of the past. A short distance away the First- and Second-class Nipponese Privates practiced using their bayonets on kneeling live Chinese peasants, the objective was not to kill quickly but to explore the human anatomy; these victims did not die quietly. After the executions, the prisoners were forced to remove the headless bodies and bury them. While doing this, some prisoners witnessed the Japanese forcing tightly bound Chinese civilians both young and old into deep pits and burying them alive.

All over Hong Kong the killing continued. After the war Brigadier Wallis claimed the Royal Scots had folded too quickly. As a result, the regiment were denied the battle honour "Hong Kong" to add to their long list of battle honours. From then on the "First of Foot" gained another nick-name: "The First to Foot it." Even though the RSM and his comrades smiled about this new nick-name when relating the story after the war in Singapore, the soldiers of the Royal Scots inwardly resented the implication. This slur on the regiment's reputation is considered unjust by many.

Hong Kong was unusually quiet after the surrender. Normally all the church bells would be ringing and the sound of Christmas carols would be drifting on the pleasant warm South China Sea breeze. In certain areas of the island, the smashing of alcohol bottles became the next popular pastime; it was the last gesture of defiance, a requiem mourning the lost halcyon days on the island of lotus eaters.

CHAPTER 3

The Telegram

BURMA

❧

"In 1941 nobody in Burma believed that the Japanese could defeat the British Empire. Then suddenly news came to us that Hong Kong had fallen, the Japanese were attacking Malaya and were now moving towards Burma through Thailand. From that day on, I watched the postman every morning as he made his way down our street. One morning he stopped at our gate. My heart raced. I recognized the envelope as army mail: a telegram. I once worked in the Post Office in Mandalay, where I first met Jack. The note was short and to the point: 'I regret to inform you that your husband Sergeant John Devereux 2nd Battalion Royal Scots is feared dead or missing during the battle of Hong Kong.'

"The word 'missing' was to give me hope and comfort during the dark, terrible years that were to follow. Thoughts of my first meeting with Jack in Mandalay, where my family had a house, flooded in. Jack used to arrive at the post office in a snub-nosed *[Bedford]* lorry to collect the small bags of army mail. Every time he came to the counter he always asked to borrow my pencil and would wait until all the other customers had left before returning it. Jack was tall, dark and handsome and always looked so dashing in his Glengarry and tartan trews of the Royal Scots *[1st Battalion]*. One day after I had finished work I found Jack outside the post office waiting for me. He asked if he could walk me home. I said no. Jack persisted on several more occasions and finally I agreed.

"After several weeks my mother asked me to invite Jack to our house so she and all my brothers and sisters could have a good look at him. Jack sat rather uncomfortably in the parlour surrounded by my mother, three brothers and four sisters. My youngest sister Lucy offered Jack a trick chocolate *[chocolate on the outside with an Indian rubber centre]*. We all giggled, watching him try to chew it.

"Jack had to propose to me five times before I accepted. You see, I did not like his surname 'Devereux.' I always wanted to marry a man with a British name; Devereux was not a British name – it was French my mother said, a Norman name. Being half Portuguese, she did not like the French much."

❧

The French and Napoleon Bonaparte were about as popular to the Portuguese and the Spanish, as the English and Oliver Cromwell were to the southern Irish.

❧

"Thank God Jack was a practising Catholic and went to church every Sunday (so he said) or my mother would not have agreed to our wedding. About a year later we married in Taunggyi with all my large family present along with a few of Jack's army pals including Tam and Willie. The wedding reception was held in a marquee erected in our beautiful garden. We had so many different types of food. A dance floor was laid out; we danced to tangos, waltzes, quick-steps and the Charleston. All my sisters loved dancing.

"There was so much food that we invited people passing outside to join us, including the tall Pathan night watchman *[the Pathan would remember this kindness]*. The wedding and house were paid for with rubies, equal to the amount of Burmese rupees. In the evening colourful Chinese lanterns were lit and hung on all the trees. A beautiful full moon gazed down as we drove away to our honeymoon. Not long after, Jack found out that the 1st Battalion was being posted to Palestine. He told me not to worry as he would get a transfer to the 2nd Battalion who were being posted to India; instead the 2nd Battalion were posted to Hong Kong to counter the threat from the Japanese.

"While he was in Hong Kong he managed to get three weeks leave to come back to Taunggyi, where we had set up our lovely new home. This area is one of the beauty spots of Burma. Our bungalow nestled at the foot of the tall purple crags. Jack fell in love with Taunggyi and intended to buy himself out of the army within a few months. After just two weeks leave he was recalled to Hong Kong; we were both bitterly disappointed. I did not know at the time what those four long years had in store for us."

☙

This is another story Mum loved telling me or anyone else who would listen, much to my embarrassment.

☙

"My God – Brian was such a difficult birth – I did not want him, you know – he was deformed! I was screaming my head off, yelling at the surgeon – 'get rid of it – I don't want it!' You were such a big baby – eight and a half pounds! You looked like a suckling pig. I screamed 'take it away!' My mother was shouting: 'Shut your mouth Kate. You are a disgrace to the family – howling like a lunatic – do you think you are the first woman to give birth? It's not good to bring a baby into the world with the sound of screaming.'

"The British surgeon was pulling your head. It's a wonder your neck did not break. He had to use such force that your head became out of shape. When I first saw you I thought my God I have given birth to a deformed child who would end up in a circus; your head looked like a boodi [butternut-squash, gourd]. The surgeon had to re-shape it with his hands."

☙

Mum would smile at me with motherly glee after the telling of this story. I have always put this re-shaping of my head as a possible reason for me suffering terrible migraine headaches every week for the rest of my life. The shape of my head is now normal.

✿

"My mother and I slept together while you were in a cot at the side of the bed. I used to dislike getting up when you started yelling; sometimes I felt like murdering you. My mother used to get angry and shout 'you are the most useless and lazy daughter I have – the child will grow up to hate you.' Later, we used to leave you in the garden by the kitchen window sitting in a tub of water and listening to you cooing, talking to yourself and laughing.

"The surgeon was the best English surgeon in the Shan States and lived just down the road from our house. I knew his daughter, she became a nursing Sister. She survived the war but her poor parents were killed in Taunggyi. The maternity ward was at the foot of the high crags; all the windows had iron bars to stop cheetahs sneaking into the ward and running off with babies."

✿

Mother always believed there were cheetahs in Taunggyi; in actual fact there were no cheetahs left in Burma or India but leopards abounded. Leopards are opportunist and were a danger to children and dogs. These big cats often went to extraordinary lengths to procure canines. Dogs, regardless of size, were taken silently while their owners sat drinking their sundowners on cool verandas in the evening. The remains of their pet would be found wedged high in a tree the following day. Most of the homes in Taunggyi had barred windows to keep out these shadowy and silent predators at night. In Burma, at that time, it was said that there were too many tigers and leopards. Humans were regular victims. Wolves (red dholes), bears and hyenas also took a high toll on domestic livestock. Records from the time show that around six thousand animals were lost every year. Burma also has one of the highest concentrations of venomous snakes in the world, second only to Tanzania. It is estimated in modern Myanmar that the annual death rate from snake bite is currently around 11,000 a year. Pre-war, the number was as high as 18,000 per year, second only to India.

❦

"Taunggyi remained cool in the hot season. The climate of the Shan States is perfect, comparable to a warm English summer. Our house was built on an acre of land and was surrounded by exotic fruit trees. Bougainvillea, gardenias, hibiscus and wild poppies added colour. We also had geese, ducks and chickens kept just for their eggs. If my mother or brothers wanted to kill a chicken or duck, I would follow them around like a shadow crying and screaming at them until they got fed up with all my noise. Dozens of brightly coloured wild jungle fowl also used to visit the garden. I never saw a single snake whilst living in Taunggyi. It was the little tuc-toos *[small house lizards]* that terrified me. I could not stand the way they sometimes fell from the ceiling and shed their tails which kept on wiggling."

❦

Mum was terrified of these small harmless lizards; yet she had no fear of large spiders, some of which were aggressive and possessed extremely painful bites.

The wild poppies Mum refers to were "Moon-flowers" or "Yunnan poppies" (Taunggyi is part of the opium Golden Triangle). These pale innocent looking flowers appeared in most gardens, whether wanted or not. The Hill Tribes had been using opium for centuries and yet there has never been a serious drug problem, for there are strict rules. A user has to be over thirty (retirement age) and he or she must not take the drug until after 6pm, after their evening meal.

My grandmother always kept raw opium as a medical treatment. She knew the secret of scoring the poppy heads at exactly the right time for the best quality resin.

༄༅

"The thought of leaving my house was unthinkable; the news on the radio was always optimistic. We were told the Japanese would be stopped at the Sittang River. When we heard the battleships Prince of Wales and the Repulse had been sunk, everyone was too shocked to speak. We all believed the Royal Navy was invincible. I was so glad my mother and two of my brothers, Cyril and Victor, and my youngest sister Lucy were staying with me in Taunggyi at the time before we fled. It was so reassuring to have my two strong and capable brothers with us when we first set off. Victor was six foot two, blonde, blue eyed and weighed well over two hundred and twenty pounds. Cyril used to stay with the Shan tribesmen while out hunting. After the war, Cyril married the headman's daughter, had many children and became a schoolteacher. We had lost all contact with my oldest brother Harry. He was an officer in the Burmese Army, made up of Ghurkhas, Kachins and other hill tribes. The last we heard of, it was retreating towards the Irrawaddy River. My sister Grace was in Rangoon with her family. Grace had married and was now Mrs Lobo ['Mrs Wolf' in Portuguese] with several sons, Kenny, Cyril, Carl, Oswald and daughters Gloria and Patricia. My other sister Annette married an English Major Wallace in the artillery who became a Colonel after the war. They came to visit us in England with their two children, a girl called Gwen and a son William; they moved to Eritrea and disappeared. We never heard from Annette again despite our attempts to contact her. I hope and pray they are alright.

"During the occupation, my mother worried about my brothers and sisters, they were scattered all over Burma. Every town had its Kempeitai spies and trying to contact family members would be dangerous."

༄༅

Many of the refugees trapped in Burma criticized those responsible for the empty promises and assurances which delayed their departure from Burma to India. The confidence of those in charge shaded the many non-endemic people living there with a flimsy bamboo umbrella of hope; useless against the ever increasing heat of the rising sun. Evacuating Burma just two weeks earlier would have allowed a great many fleeing refugees to reach safety, saving thousands of lives.

General Stilwell who commanded the Chinese armies, it is said, disliked the Limeys; especially the officer class. Stilwell detested General Wavell who lectured him on tactics for defeating the Japanese, just after losing Hong Kong, Malaya, Singapore and Burma. It has been said that president Franklin D. Roosevelt (who was of Dutch and French ancestry) was not a great fan of the British despite helping us win the war. He did not want Britain to regain her empire.

"Do you think your father Herman Unger was a German spy, Mum?" I once asked. She laughed.

⚜

"My father was such a drunkard, he could not keep a secret and made it known that he did not like the British having an Empire. He also disliked the way the British allowed the Indians to dominate the markets and become the biggest landowners. When drunk he boasted, if Germany went to war, he would join their army. His views were well known in Rangoon and Mandalay. He was not popular with our British friends, but he got on well with everybody else, especially the Japanese.

"My mother's first husband was James Talbot, a redheaded Irishman from Galway. He was thirty-five; she had just turned fifteen. He was the inspector of railways in Burma. There was always a railway inspector in the family, for my mother and grandmother never paid train fares as they travelled all over Burma visiting relatives.

"My face is my ticket, Grandmother used to say indignantly, when asked for her fare by a new ticket collector.

"Both my fathers were jolly men, both were alcoholics. Herman Unger was very cruel to animals. When he came back from a snipe shooting trip, dozens of birds would be threaded through the eyes with bamboo: some were still alive. I used to scream at him. He used to laugh and put me on his knee and call me his little dark diamond, his alcoholic breath used to make me feel dizzy. I would never eat snipe at dinner but soon developed a taste for whisky. I used to take sips from the decanter."

⚜

Mother referred to both men as "father." My eldest daughter Kim is sure James Talbot was my mother's biological dad.

⚜

"In Taunggyi the problem was which escape route to take? Just across the border was Yunnan Province, China; this was the shortest route of escape. But Yunnan was a lawless country dominated by war lords and bandits. Plus the route into the mountains would require pack horses.

"My mother and I had a more immediate worry – the copies of my marriage certificate and your birth certificate. Both could still be at the town hall. These documents could be our death warrants. We may have been classed as spies. Anyone in Taunggyi who knew us could denounce us under torture. Mother was also well known in Rangoon and Mandalay, therefore these towns had to be avoided at all costs during our escape. That is why my mother led us into the wilds of Burma.

"The day before we left Taunggyi my mother quickly rushed into town; she found the Town Hall closed and shuttered; all the civil servants had fled to India. There were files and papers lying everywhere, some had been only half burnt. We prayed they had taken all the important documents with them, as Burma was governed from India. But we could never be sure. This made my mother's mind up, we had to leave Taunggyi. The bank was shut. We had little money in the house, just over five thousand rupees and some valuable rubies."

⚜

The question of the whereabouts of the copies of our documents was always a constant concern to my guardians. But I know for a fact that the originals were kept or hidden somewhere by Grandmother, for I still have my original birth certificate, battered, worn and yellow.

"All the Indian shop owners had left Taunggyi earlier; they wanted to reach India before the monsoon. A Chinese ruby merchant my mother knew advised her to leave Taunggyi and trek into Yunnan Province; he would give her letters of introduction. This was most important concerning personal safety and lodgings etc.

"The Chinese traders and shopkeepers seemed to have had better intelligence regarding the war situation than the Europeans. They told my mother the Japanese had crossed the Sittang and were heading for the Shan States. We left on the 17th April. The Japanese entered Taunggyi on the 20th April 1942."

To add to the collapse of morale, the retreating British troops waiting to cross the Sittang were bombed by the RAF who believed them to be the enemy. The static British vehicles, equipment and men made a perfect target; so much so that the bombers returned after rearming to attack again.

The bridge was then blown prematurely. This left many men trapped on the wrong bank and at the mercy of the Japanese. Many Ghurkhas who were non-swimmers drowned attempting the crossing. The men left on the wrong side of the Sittang were extremely bitter, feeling they had been sacrificed.

"The worst news of all to reach us was that the British Army was heading for the Irrawaddy River, towards India. Our hopes that the approaching Chinese Army would defend the Shan States were dashed when we were informed by the Chins and Kachins tribesmen that the Chinese army were not fighting the Japanese but were looting and burning their villages, conducting a scorched earth policy.

"When my mother returned from the town hall, she said we should go to the market and buy as much food as possible for our escape. On our way there we saw British soldiers standing by a convoy of stationary vehicles, chatting and smoking. Their relaxed attitude gave us confidence. They said they were waiting for fuel and that the Koylies *[The King's Own Yorkshire Light Infantry]* were coming to defend Taunggyi and the dump of stores. They seemed unconcerned.

"The market was crowded; we bought as much as we could carry. On our homeward journey a single Japanese plane swept in low; we could see the pilot waving at the crowds below, some of the people waved back. Many of the tribespeople had never seen planes before. Then the bombers arrived. I pleaded with my mother to drop all we were carrying and run home. But my mother began to pray aloud, she even began picking up all the food items that I had dropped. We then stood rooted to the spot and watched the planes release their deadly cargo.

"The bombs looked so small and harmless – like toys, they seemed to hang suspended in the sky. None of us had ever experienced bombing before; we just stood still and watched them fall to earth. The raid was soon over and the causalities were light. Another small plane then circled and dropped leaflets that said: 'Prepare to meet the victorious warrior Gods of Dai Nippon. We will not harm the people of Burma. We are all Asiatic Buddhists. The British have been defeated; the Chinese soldiers are your enemies. If you act honourable, we will give you kindnesses, but if you have anti-Nipponese thoughts, we will give you swords.' There were lots of other promises; each promise was followed by a threat. The leaflets did nothing to calm our fears of the Japanese.

"Reaching home we found that the far end of my beautiful bungalow had been damaged by a bomb, but thankfully nobody was hurt. I was so shocked I could not make up my mind as to what items to take with me.

"Victor, my brother, told us we had six hours to prepare for evacuation to India. We were to take whatever transport available and make our way to the station *[Mother never mentioned which station]* where we were to catch a train to Myitkyina Airport, then board a plane to India. It all sounded so easy. We were restricted to taking only fourteen pounds of personal belongings each. It broke my heart to leave all my lovely things behind – my wedding gifts, my lovely clothes and shoes; nevertheless I filled a pram with baby clothes and food for you.

"My brothers Cyril and Victor went off to find transport as we had none. I was still in shock; events had changed so quickly from a happy and normal life to this nightmare. The thought of leaving all our pets and animals behind broke my heart. Sadly all our pets were killed and eaten by the retreating Chinese army.

"Cyril and Victor returned with an old truck that had red Chinese characters written on the side but it needed more petrol. All communications in the town had broken down and groups of Chinese troops had been seen nearby. Looting of the Indian shops had begun by the local Shans who were now armed. Both my brothers were keen hunters and were determined to bring at least two weapons each; a sporting rifle and a shotgun. They intended to bury them before boarding the plane to India. They buried the rest of their rifles and ammunition in the garden. Cyril was able to retrieve these weapons with the help of the local Shans one night, during the Japanese occupation.

"My mother instructed our servants to look after my home and pets until our return; she also paid them their wages and gave them all the remaining foodstuffs including the meat (venison and other game) in the meat-safe and cool store that were filled with ice blocks delivered daily.

"It broke my heart to watch our dogs being restrained from following the lorry; they seemed to know we would not return. We then drove through the town to the sounds and smells of the alcohol stocks being smashed. To stop the Japanese going wild, we were told."

※

As a man who looks forward to a drink every day, I have sometimes pondered: Would it not make the Japanese even wilder to find all the alcohol had been deliberately destroyed; perhaps not.

※

"We joined the convoy assembling at the edge of town. Here we were given more fuel taken from the nearby army dump. Everyone seemed so calm, confidant and well organized. We waited for any latecomers.

None arrived. Everyone had a good supply of Johnnie Walker. People were walking around with glasses of whisky in their hands, smoking and chatting; in fact it looked more like a group of people about to set out for an afternoon picnic. As we were the last to arrive we were placed at the back of the convoy. We would reach the station the following afternoon. Finally the whole convoy slowly pulled away. The old Chinese lorry sounded as if it was on its last legs. The roads to and from Taunggyi had been cut along the sides of mountains and were very dangerous. Drops of several hundred feet awaited any vehicle that ventured too near the edge; then there were the dozens of hairpin bends to be negotiated. As dusk approached, the whole convoy pulled in under the cover of trees. Cyril and Victor heard peafowl in the jungle and taking their guns went to hunt them. They did not find the peafowl but returned later with small colourful jungle foul which my mother plucked and cooked. Makeshift beds were being prepared and when darkness fell many fires were lit between the vehicles for the evening meal. People began walking around and discussing the following day's journey and deciding where to set up home once they had reached India. Nobody could sleep that night. None of us believed the Japanese would be in Burma for long and were already making plans for our return to our homes. My mother said we should go to Goa; we had Portuguese relatives there who lived by the sea. I knew my mother was worried about her other children. I was always concerned that she would suddenly change her mind at the last minute and stay in Burma, the country of her birth that she knew intimately.

"The early dawn found everyone preparing for the final leg of our journey to the station. Our journey began badly as one of the cars ahead of us would not start. As time was now the vital factor, it was pushed over the precipice and went tumbling into the jungle below causing the monkeys and parrots to scatter noisily. The passengers and loads were transferred to other vehicles and we moved on. It was now imperative that we catch the train and reach Myitkyina airport before the Japanese. I sat in the front of the lorry with my mother as Victor was driving.

"The road we were travelling on was ideal for ambush. The fear was heightened when the convoy passed several dead bodies by the side of the road. The convoy had travelled a few miles further on when another vehicle in the middle broke down blocking the way. Again the people and their baggage were redistributed and the vehicle was pushed over the precipice. We were slowly moving out of the cool of the hills; the weather was becoming hotter and the roads dustier. Soon all the vehicles in front of us were throwing up clouds of dust making it difficult for Victor to see the road ahead and as it was too hot to close the windows, he let the convoy pull away, while keeping it in sight. This was to prove a disaster.

"Suddenly the tyre on the front wheel of our lorry burst and we came to a halt. The convoy continued, leaving us totally alone on the jungle fringed road; the last vehicle disappeared around a bend. We were now in a desperate situation as time was vital. After much searching, my brothers found a spare wheel and some tools but alas, no jack. The train was leaving at one o'clock; it was now ten-thirty and we still had twenty miles to go. Our situation seemed hopeless. Mother calmly began walking ahead to find room at the side of the road to light a fire and make tea; my brother Victor went with her. Cyril went into the jungle to cut a strong branch to act as a fulcrum to change the wheel.

"When Cyril returned he called out to Victor and both my brothers got to work on the lorry. They had barely finished when three armed men in tattered uniforms silently appeared out of the jungle: Chinese soldiers. There was something about their manner that made us feel uneasy; although their rifles were not pointing at us, the weapons were in a ready to use position. The Chinese soldiers looked desperate and were extremely thin. One of them was barefoot and looked about twelve years old. While one watched us the others inspected the lorry and they soon found some of the bread we had brought. The soldiers ate ravenously. Cyril and Victor both spoke a little Chinese and explained our situation; they even offered to give the Chinese soldiers a lift. This had little effect on the soldiers. One soldier asked us if we had any arms and ammunition.

"Both my brothers replied 'no'. Cyril and Victor had hidden their guns under the wooden box seat we had been sitting on in the front cab covered with our blankets. With that, one of the Chinese soldiers climbed back onto the lorry and began going through our possessions.

This made my two brothers angry and it took my sister Lucy and I to restrain Victor. If it was not for their rifles Victor would have flattened both of them, for he was a big and powerful man but with two women hanging onto his arms there was little he could do. The Chinese soldiers then asked for our money and valuables; this time their rifles were pointing directly at us. We were now in despair and knew we would miss our train and the flight to India; we could also be shot.

"It was then that a large party of tattooed Shan tribesmen approached from out of the jungle. All were heavily armed. The Chinese soldiers became afraid and lowered their rifles. There was no love lost between the two races. These wild looking tribesmen seemed to know Cyril. He spoke their language fluently. They demanded the Chinese soldiers' rifles, which were found to be empty; they then took their watches and rings. The Chinese soldiers were then tied up in the cruel way of the Shans and led away. Cyril thanked the headman of the tribe and gave him one of his guns. He said the tribesmen would take the Chinese soldiers out of sight, make them kneel and club them to death which was their traditional and silent method of killing without wasting bullets. My brothers then buried their remaining guns at the jungles edge, at the request of my mother; it was no longer safe to carry them. On two occasions during the war, Cyril joined the hill tribes ambushing Japanese patrols. At the site of the ambush they hid sharpened bamboo stakes covered in poison in the undergrowth to impale the enemy when they took cover.

"We slowly resumed our journey to the station; Cyril thought we might just make it if the roads were not blocked. I could not help thinking of those poor starving Chinese soldiers that would soon be killed.

"Victor began driving the lorry very fast and on several occasions I screamed when it looked as if we were going to fall hundreds of feet into the jungle-clad valley below. All the time I was praying that Jack was alive and we would reach the station in time."

CHAPTER 4

The Perfumed Harbour

PALESTINE & HONG KONG

After his marriage to Kate Talbot, Sergeant Jack Devereux's Regiment, the 1st Battalion Royal Scots, was posted from Mandalay, Burma, to Palestine, where they became a machine gun battalion. To the new recruits just out from Edinburgh, Palestine sounded exotic after the cold and windy confines of Maryhill, Edinburgh Castle and the other frigid, frost bound barracks. Images of romantic desert oasis, sunshine and a scattering of orange trees dripping with fruit came to mind (oranges were as rare in Glasgow as golden oracles). There would be plenty of cheap booze and bints. The new recruits had heard of the pleasures of Cairo with its bars and bordellos. Palestine proved a great disappointment.

There were no whispered invitations to visit their very cheap, very young, very clean and very pretty sister. This damsel or dam would be reclining somewhere in the Arab Quarter, smelling of jasmine and admiring her henna painted hands with sleepy dark almond eyes; eyes that dreamily gazed out between long mascara laden lashes (mascara: an Arabic invention). She waited for the bead curtains to burst open and the grinning inebriated freckled face of a Jock to appear; alas, she would wait in vain. The Arab quarter was out of bounds and a three-mile hike over sand dunes from the Scots barracks.

Palestine soon lost its appeal to the optimistic young soldiers. After studying one groaning, syphilitic camel and marvelling at the novel sight of fruiting orange and lemon trees, many Scots began to yearn for the distant cold windswept hills of Caledonia. Apart from camels and exotic fruit, there was little else of interest except religious relics, melancholy buildings with crumbling masonry and faded artwork of angels. Statues of obscure saints with age worn faces stared down at the passing Scots from bullet pock-marked recesses of empty Christian churches. The Holy Land had been fought over many times during its violent history.

Their brand new heavy hob-nailed ammunition boots (of Boer War design and weight) were not suitable for hot climates or ideal for a stealthy approach and proved too cumbersome on long patrols. Before the coming battle in the New Territories Mainland China, the waiting Japanese could hear the Royal Scots taking up their positions on the Gin Drinkers' Line from over a mile away due to their inappropriate footwear.

The Scots in Palestine blinked in the fierce heat of midday and skulked in the airless shadows, or lay panting in the filtered shade of dry dust coated olive groves and date palms during breaks from patrolling. The regular shrill calls for prayer from a lone white-robed figure high above caused many a Scot to curse and think of home. Even the sheep with their grotesquely deformed fat-tails did not make the Scots feel at home. Both the Jews and Arabs were unfriendly. Even the skirl of the pipes brought hostility; perhaps it reminded the inhabitants of the strutting Turk's past brutal occupation. Only the local flies welcomed them with sanctimonious fervour.

In Palestine the Jews and the Arabs were at war and the British were caught in-between. The Royal Scots were often attacked by the Jewish freedom fighters. The Scots were surprised that Jewish women also fought in the ranks of the insurgents. The Jews wanted their own State to escape the persecution in Europe. This was a recipe for bloodshed. It still is.

According to Tam and Willie, two of dad's friends who often visited us in Uxbridge, the Jews were well organised and planned their raids with military precision. The Jewish fighters specialized in ambush. The only effective way for the Royal Scots to retaliate was with machine guns firing tracers (one every five rounds) while the infantry with fixed bayonets tried to quickly outflank them. The effect of the tracers arcing towards the Jewish fighters and the thought of being impaled on the end of an angry Jock's bayonet, tended to unnerve the attackers. Who could blame them? The Jews quickly melted into the desert night taking their wounded, but sometimes were forced to leave their dead behind.

✥

"In Palestine Jack was soon to be promoted to RSM and hoped to get a transfer to the 2nd Battalion Royal Scots, who were being posted to India. India was next door to Burma and there was much military movement between the two countries. Jack hoped this would allow him to visit Taunggyi more often before he bought himself out of the army. No-one expected a war in the Far East. During his time in Palestine, Jack was sometimes a dispatch rider and he sent me a picture of himself on his motorcycle."

✥

I have a picture of dad on a motorbike in Palestine or India; it was placed on a grand piano in a Country House Hotel I once owned. That hotel was built to look like a castle complete with its own chapel, archway and tower, in 1863. This photograph was often discussed by many ex-servicemen who often stayed. I always took the picture for granted until a number of sharp eyed old veterans pointed out to me several reasons they believed it was a "staged" or "posed" photograph for the benefit of my mother.

✥

"Jack finally got his transfer to the 2nd Battalion along with several other men and NCOs. The news that the 2nd Battalion was being posted to Hong Kong and not to India greatly disappointed both of us. Jack just wanted to get back to Burma and settle down in Taunggyi."

✥

To the other soldiers, Hong Kong was by far the most desirable posting a serviceman could get. The tales that are included in this chapter of what servicemen (including officers) got up to in Hong Kong are based on dad's conversations with his old fellow NCO's and comrades and other ex-servicemen I met in later life who were posted to Hong Kong. My hotel seemed to attract ex-military men both British and German and a few Nipponese. The Germans and Americans cannot resist any building that looks like a castle, even a replica castle.

After the war, Dad and his mates would laugh during their drinking sessions at the mention of certain soldiers' names who were the worst felons at a certain pastime: stealing sexual pleasures without paying. Tam and Willie shared with dad the responsibility of stamping out these unlawful crimes. The lucky offenders, if caught, ended up in the glass house; the unlucky ended up in the VD clinic. The favourite modus operandi of these felons will be explained later in this chapter.

On the voyage east, from Palestine to Hong Kong, the new recruits saw flying fishes for the first time and porpoises that glided and chased in the ship's wake. As soon as they reached the tropics, strange colourful birds rested for short periods on the ship's rigging and eyed the red-faced men below. Even the sea changed colour to a light azure blue. The young soldiers had heard that the beautiful young Chinese ladies were very friendly. And as if to confirm this, on entering Hong Kong Harbour, their ship was greeted by a flotilla of floating French letters which in sheer number dominated the less interesting flotsam. Docking, the men were delighted to see attractive local Chinese women lining the harbour rails. These exotic beauties wore their traditional style *cheug sarm,* tight hip clinging silk dresses, with suggestive slits that reached high on the thighs. These ladies smiled invitingly at the red-faced gawking men from Scotland. To the soldiers aboard ship, it seemed that they had arrived at a serviceman's Shangri-La.

The flies in Hong Kong seemed to be fewer in number, and more particular in their habits. The smell of Hong Kong was a delicate mixture of various odours, both good and bad intermingled, the pleasant aromas overpowering the bad. The air contained a heady combination of spices, a hint of opium and scented joss sticks. Fragrant jasmine and bougainvillea grew in profusion on the white walls of the opulent European pavilions. These were the exotic aromas of the orient.

Hidden in the warrens of the Chinese quarter of Wanchai, sinister vendors peddled short dreams of contentment. Cheap bars lined the waterfront; market stalls sold all the tasty Chinese dishes. You could buy a small cup of fresh cobra blood that cured all ills. The Scots stared shocked as they witnessed old Chinese women painfully tottering by on tiny deformed bound feet.

To the Orientals, the Scots were also a rather exotic race. The number of Scots with flame-hair and even redder skin (always a giggling matter to oriental women) and their strange pale blue eyes amazed the local observers. The only red faces the Chinese were familiar with were on macaque monkeys. The locals found the Lothian accents most difficult to understand and on occasion, intimidating. The sound of pipes and drums caused many a Chinese to place fingers in ears. All the while, the Japanese civilians made mental notes of the numbers of troops and the Regiments arriving.

Across the border in mainland China, within marching distance, veteran Japanese troops continued to train and manoeuvre for the coming attack. They had no intention of using the main roads or the bridges that were guarded by the British, but would manhandle their artillery over the rough terrain. Their light canvas and rubber split-toed boots were ideal for a silent approach at night. The Japanese commanders must have pondered over their meals of prawns, miso and sake, as to why the British seemed totally unconcerned at their close proximity. The answer was simple: arrogance. The Japanese were thought of as coolies.

To the surprise of the British and Commonwealth soldiers in Hong Kong, it was the Japanese bars that sold the cheapest alcohol and the pretty girls working there were certainly the best listeners. The combination of a pretty face and alcohol (worldwide) overwhelms and disengages a man's tongue from his brain. Everything the girls heard of military importance would be passed on to their paymasters.

In the back street shadows, the dimly lit "last-stop" opium dens flourished. Young Chinese men handed over their life savings for this long looked forward to moment. They would never know hunger or pain again. The rest of their short life would be spent in the confines of a small bamboo cubicle gently slipping from one moon-poppy induced dream to another. Their final dream would be a dream of painless death in the soft arms of Morpheus' beautiful daughter. A noisy funeral with gongs and cymbals, plus a loud "wailing and a weeping" (real tears shed) by a crowd of professional Chinese mourners, were all included in the initial price of entry.

Hong Kong was also a haunt of various dissidents. One of the better known was Nguyen Ai Quoc, better known in later life as Ho Chi Minh. We saved Uncle Ho from the French. In the lantern lit shadows of the Chinese quarter, Triads lurked.

The British troops soon realized that they could have made-to-measure cotton shirts and slacks within an hour for a pittance. These items of clothing would be used by those who harboured devious intensions of gaining sexual pleasures without paying. "Jolly Jack Tar a-shore" was the most consistent offender and had all the advantages: a moveable home that had more passageways than a termite hill, bulging pockets that had to be empted in fourteen hours' shore leave and a sailor's desperation and poor taste in judging the qualities and age of the opposite sex when "Oliver Twist".

Servicemen found that all the best places and bars were out of bounds to the common ranks. Snobbery in the British Armed Forces was rampant. Each layer of humanity looked down on those below. A common serviceman could get drunk several times a week, eat well and still have some money over for other pleasurable pursuits that alcohol seems to inflame. Friday and Saturday nights were usually the same for the Royal Scots and the Middlesex Regiment. Primed and ignited by alcohol and the old jokes concerning the Jocks favouring the company of sheep etc. would erupt into fights. Once these matters were settled, there were other attractions of the female variety.

If a soldier had the money, he could afford the price of a higher class female. These beauties resided on Golden Hill (where the officers went). At Golden Hill, a common soldier could nimbly caper in the chambers of a beautiful Chinese girl without the fear of catching the dreaded "French disease" – or, as the French called it, the "English disease". The dispute as to which seafaring nation had introduced this unpopular malady to the innocent natives of the beautiful Pacific Islands had gone on for centuries. In 1941, the treatment for this aliment was akin to the worst kind of torture. It was a case of "five minutes pleasure on Venus; two years of agony on Mercury." The instrument of excruciating pain was the dreaded "umbrella" applied to the one eyed "trouser snake." Old soldiers and sailors of that period loved shocking younger men like me with tales of the umbrella and it was always someone else who had suffered the indignity and screamed their heads off when it was applied to the short arm.

However, for the more tight-fisted, there was the other end of the market: the dark harbour. Indeed, sometimes it was so dark it was difficult to see the faces of the ladies (often with good reason) plying their ancient trade. It was the case of Hobson's choice. However the delights of the dark harbour were not to the taste of the modest, the particular or the faint hearted.

A punter had to stand in line on the quay and wait; similar to standing in a taxi queue. When a taxi did arrive you couldn't say: "I don't fancy the look of mine" and offer it to the next man. The sampans containing the ladies would be queuing up in cab rank just out of the glow of the dim harbour lights. As the sampan hove-to out of the gloom, to the horror of a first time punter, the presence of the Chinese male rower was observed. He would be facing them during the act. The presence of this potential voyeur would be rather off putting to the self-conscious first timer. The indignant and protesting new punter would be vigorously assured by the female concerned, that the rower was as blind as a bat, deaf and dumb and to back this up at no time did the man in question ever speak or make a sound.

There was no time for hesitation, with curses from the impatient men behind: "make your bloody mind up Chum, who did you expect, Marlene Dietrich?" Many a faint-hearted punter would exclaim "bugger this for a lark" and leave. A willing client then had to carefully negotiate his way onto the rising and falling sampan. Money had to be handed over first as these ladies had been caught out before in the past, usually by a skint "Jolly Jack". The rat-arsed sailor concerned had no problems boarding the bobbing sampan. Taking his hurried pleasures, the sailor would then smartly hoist up the Blue Peter along with his bell bottoms and promptly abandon ship, briskly striking out to a conveniently lowered Jacob's ladder. Once aboard his vessel and swinging snug in his hammock, the guilty sailor would be as difficult for the Military Police to locate as the ship's cat at midnight.

Once the money had changed hands the "blind boat-man" would leisurely cast off into the shadows. Needless to say, many a serviceman found it impossible to perform under these conditions. There were no refunds. Business completed, the new punter would soon find himself sitting in a rickshaw heading for the barracks. He would no doubt be pondering the oriental skill of the inscrutable boatman who despite being blind, deaf and dumb, found his way perfectly around the busy harbour and never once collided with the dozens of other milling sampans and their copulating occupants, floating restaurants and the numerous other harbour craft. He would also be hoping and praying he had not caught the dreaded "French disease"!

The more enterprising, health conscious and particular ne'er-do-wells went to Golden Hill to meet a better class of lady, harbouring fraudulent intensions. They would be wearing cheap white cotton slacks, shirt and plimsolls. They would take their pleasures; being a high class establishment you paid after the event. These fraudulent punters would then politely excuse themselves wearing only their underwear and plimsolls and head for the toilets outside. Once outside, they would leg it leaving behind their cheap clothes with the lady, who by then was going through their empty pockets. Then after a few minutes the lady in question would become suspicious and realize she had been well and truly had. She would then rush out and shout down to the crowd below the Chinese equivalent of *"Stop that dirty, thieving, long-nosed white bastard!"*

All the pimps, street vendors and any lurking redcaps or NCOs would give chase. Stealing sexual pleasures was taken very seriously in Hong Kong, the island of fair trade. This practice continued, I am told, simply because the officer clients considered payment before the event was an insult to their honour.

I once asked Tam and Willie (tongue in cheek after a few pints) if the above had anything to do with one of dad's nicknames, "Spring-heeled Jack"? They both smiled and explained that he acquired the name when he won the Indian Army hurdle championship. Dads other nickname was the "Bolshevik." I never did find out the reason why.

CHAPTER 5

The Train Station

BURMA

❧

"Against all the odds we reached the station to catch the train to Myitkyina Airport before the train was due to depart, only to see the train slowly pulling away. We were desolate. Mother urged my two brothers to chase after the slow moving train and jump on and save themselves. This they would not do. If it was not for us, both my brothers would have already escaped into the hills and stayed with the hill tribespeople.

"While my brothers went looking for a more suitable and smaller vehicle to get us to Myitkyina Airport, Japanese planes appeared and began to bomb the departing train. In the distance we could see the train stop and watched as all the passengers began running from the compartments and hiding in the surrounding jungle. My brothers returned. All the motor vehicles abandoned outside the station were without petrol.

"When the bombing raid was over, passengers began to re-board the train. This gave us our chance. We quickly ran towards the train; on reaching it, we found all the carriages crammed full of people and baggage. Luckily Victor, who worked on the railway, knew one of the guards well and we shared his end carriage with his wife and family. And so began our journey to the airport.

"The only damage to the train was a few broken windows and as far as the guard knew, no passengers were injured. In fact, it made us wonder what the Japs had been bombing. All the cooking had to be carried out on a makeshift stove and it was not long before my mother had a hot meal comprising of jungle fowl, vegetables and rice which we shared with the guard and his family. He told us that the train would only stop when necessary to take on water and fuel, so passengers would have to use this time as best they could as all the toilets on the train were not working.

"Large groups of armed Burmese dacoits were also rampaging through the countryside taking advantage of the chaos and the breakdown of law and order. They were seeking out the Indians and any Europeans who were now considered enemies of Burma. The train travelled through the night. Both my sister Lucy and I were hoping to use the toilets at Mogauwg, the last big station. We did not like the idea of using the jungle. The train began to slow down just before we reached Mogauwg. There were hundreds of people waiting on the platform and a few British soldiers sitting on their kit bags looking lost. I was disappointed; Mogauwg was just a big Burmese village; only the station buildings were built of bricks. As the train was already overcrowded the driver continued past the station and stopped some way out of town to take on water for the engine.

"I looked out of the window to see if any of the other passengers were getting off, then I looked down. My God! Our carriage was on a bridge and there was a river below. If we were bombed and the bridge gave way, our carriage would fall into the river. With this in mind, Lucy and I decided not to get off. Thank God the train stopped again soon after to load wood just as it was getting dark, giving us the opportunity to find a quiet spot in the jungle; we had no choice.

"At about one o'clock in the morning, the train pulled into a small jungle station and stopped. We were all surprised and delighted to find Burmese and Indian food vendors selling their wares as normal: cooked snacks, meals wrapped in banana leaves, fresh fruit and soft drinks. My mother was skilled at bargaining with native tradesmen and the amount of food and tasty snacks she bought for ten rupees was amazing. Here, we were able to stretch our legs and use the jungle for our convenience.

"We all knew the stationmaster; he often went hunting with my brothers Harry, Cyril and Victor. On seeing the cramped conditions on the train, the station master added another three carriages that were standing on a siding. We moved into the last carriage with a young English woman called Anne (I can't remember her surname) who came from Brighton. She had two small children, both daughters, one was about two years old and the other was about four. The whistle blew for all the passengers to get back on the train. Everyone was sad to leave that little jungle station, as it still seemed to be operating as if in peacetime.

"Suddenly the English woman began screaming hysterically that her older daughter was missing. She left the youngest with us and suddenly jumped off the train. She then began rushing through the station looking for her child and screaming her name desperately, accusing the food vendors and tradesmen of kidnapping her little girl. The woman was now in a state of extreme agitation not knowing what to do. Returning to the carriage, she stood hesitantly by the doorway. She looked such a tragic sight as the train slowly began to build up steam. Lucy and I were now also crying. My mother told my brothers to do something. Cyril and Victor jumped off the train; the station master was still standing on the platform. Victor asked him to hold up the train while Cyril looked for the little girl. The station master held up the train despite the complaints of some of the other passengers. Although Cyril searched the whole platform area he could not find the little lost child. He then went into the jungle and called out, still no little girl. Cyril was about to turn back when he heard a small voice whispering. A little further on he found her. She had fallen into a steep ravine and could not get out. She was exhausted.

"Meanwhile a terrible row had broken out on the platform between the stationmaster and some of the European passengers who threatened him with violence, until he was backed up by my brother Victor. Everyone re-boarded the train and after five minutes the train slowly began to pull away. The English woman was exhausted, her face badly sunburnt. She had only been in Burma for a short while and seemed to have no possessions to speak of, save one small case. I gave her some clothes and other bits and pieces; her surname was Mrs Taylor, I remember now.

"Now we had all the room we needed to stretch out. I lay down and listened to the sounds of the train and could smell the wood burning engine as it wafted in through the open windows. My thoughts then turned to my husband Jack, was he still alive? I prayed my mother was wrong about her dream the night before I got the telegram."

☙

Both my Guardians were superstitious. My grandmother, I have often been told, was born covered with a veil (afterbirth). This, according to her Anglo-Burmese mother, gave Grandmother certain insights into the future.

☙

"The night before I got the telegram telling me that Jack was dead or missing in Hong Kong my mother woke up with a start and saw Jack standing at the foot of the bed, in uniform. Blood was dripping on his shoulders: his head was missing!"

☙

Perhaps my grandmother was preparing her daughter for the worst? Or perhaps it was just a dream; Grandmother took her dreams seriously.

☙

"I must have fallen asleep. My mother woke me with some food and tea. It was now daylight. The train had stopped again for wood and water. My two brothers and my sister had wandered off along the carriages looking for people they knew, hoping for news of other members of our large family. Suddenly there was an explosion and the train nearly jumped off the tracks then stopped. My mother and I grabbed you and as many possessions as possible and jumped off the train and ran into the jungle. In the jungle we waited for more bombs to fall; none came. The next thing we heard was the train pulling away and could see the engine smoke rising above the trees as it disappeared into the distance. We were heartbroken; the train had gone without us!

"We found out later that my two brothers and sister had also got off the train but as soon as they saw the Japanese plane leave, re-boarded the train and found us missing. Because many of our belongings were still in the carriage they presumed we were somewhere onboard. They then began going through all the carriages looking for us. Not finding us they realised we had been left behind. By then it was too late, as they were miles from where we had got off. They knew my mother would not carry on to India without them.

"Cyril, Victor and Lucy then left the train when it stopped again for wood. They believed Mother and I would make for Indaw, so that is where they headed. If they had carried on to the next station or the airport, we could have all been reunited again. Cyril, Victor and Lucy stayed together and headed for Indaw which had already fallen to the enemy but it was not as yet garrisoned. Finding we were not there, they split up. Cyril and Lucy made their way back to the Shan States somehow, while Victor made his way to Mandalay."

⚜

I believe Victor returned to his old job on the railway at Mandalay. Being Herman Unger's son, a German citizen may have made this possible. Perhaps my grandmother was also using the name Unger, for two years later she travelled from our internment camp at Tada u to bring back her dying son from a village somewhere near Mandalay. She used rubies as bribes. Victor died of cholera soon after. There were so many more questions I could have asked Mother but did not. I believed she would be around for ever.

⚜

"Under a full moon, mother and I walked most of the night along the railway track to the next station. I was exhausted. When we finally arrived, it was crowded, everyone was shouting. It was impossible to search for Cyril, Victor or Lucy in the chaos of the milling crowd, so we sat down and rested. Many people at the station had also lost members of their families and went looking for them. This of course gave other people a chance to climb into their vacated space. My mother took this opportunity to squeeze into a goods carriage with you and made room for me. Then the worst thing happened, every time I think about it I always want to cry. I had forgotten a valise that I was sitting on which contained your clothes and some of my valuables. When I rushed back I could not find it. Mother was shouting at me to leave it. Suddenly the train began to pull away; there were so many people in the way that I could not get back on the train. I was left behind. I ran as fast as I could but I just could not catch up. I watched the train pulling further and further away. Mother was shouting instructions at me, but I could not hear a word. As young as you were, you realized what had happened and were crying. I was so desperate, even now I don't like thinking about it. I will never forget the feeling of utter despair. I had ruined everything. I just stood there balling my eyes out. I had probably lost my husband, my home and now my nearest family. In anguish I began to chase the train again, which by now had disappeared.

"I was now alone surrounded by scrub jungle and away from the safety of the station. I was drained of energy and just sat on the tracks crying my eyes out. I did not know what to do. Without hope, but urged on by an instinct I followed the tracks and prayed for a miracle."

※

This was one story Mother seldom related. Burma is three times the size of Britain. She would never have found us.

※

"It was now getting dark and the jackals began calling in the distance. I felt vulnerable as I walked on the sleepers to make less noise. Jackals will lead a tiger to any helpless human in the jungle, just to scavenge their remains. I was convinced a tiger would appear at any moment out of the jungle and crouch on the railway track.

"There is little twilight in Burma; soon it would be pitch-black before the moon and stars appeared. This hour of total darkness according to my brothers was known as 'the dangerous hour'. It is the time of the nocturnal predators. I felt like screaming. Then to my astonishment and total relief I saw a dim figure walking towards me in the fading light – my mother! She was carrying you; it seemed to me that all our remaining possessions had been lost, left on the train. But I did not care, my prayers had been answered. 'Don't get separated from us again Kate' was my mother's only greeting. But I knew she was so relieved to see me.

"'Quick our belongings are with the Pathan night watchman from Taunggyi, he is looking after them until I return.' said my mother. I was so happy. The train had slowed down for some reason and my mother and the Pathan got off. Handing you over to me, my mother set off at a quick pace. I could not stop crying for joy. I vowed that under no circumstances would I ever be separated or disobey my mother again. Soon our little group were reunited with our possessions.

"This Pathan, who used to patrol our street in Taunggyi, was often given tea and food when he passed at night; he was also at our wedding. The tall proud Pathans came from Afghanistan in the north of India. Pathans were the most feared night watchmen in Burma. They always carried a thick heavy metalled bound stick and a dagger under their robes. The Pathan refused all our efforts to reward him and quickly set off for his home and family nearby. He had no intention of remaining in Burma. He wished to make the journey to India with his family on foot before the coming monsoon. That night we slept in an old railway carriage at the side of the track. It had no door."

The noble Pathan had a good chance of guiding his family through the Hakawng Valley ahead of the retreating Chinese and the advancing monsoon. The steep tracks would be dry, the leach and tick population would still be aestivating. The gravid female malaria mosquitoes would be patiently waiting, sheltering under leaves from the sun, waiting to drop their eggs in the first puddles of the approaching mango showers. I hope this good man made it back to his far off village somewhere in the barren, dry hills of Afghanistan.

"That was the first of many nights spent in the Burmese jungle without a door for protection. The following morning our small family group walked along the railway line to the next station. There was a train at the platform. This was the same train to Myitkyina Airport that my mother and the Pathan watchman had got off the day before; it had been bombed and machine gunned by enemy planes. The dead were quickly being buried next to the railway lines. It had taken the crew all that time to get the train moving again. There was no news of Cyril, Victor or Lucy at the station. My mother prayed that somehow they had managed to reach the airport and had been flown to India. The guard and his wife were no longer in the last carriage; it was now filled with strangers.

"The following day the train reached the station on the outskirts of Myitkyina Airport without incident. We carried you in a sling and were soon walking along a road when night began to fall, but I was not afraid. There were so many other people walking with us, talking about reaching India and safety. Everyone was happy to be escaping the war and leaving Burma. It was dark when we arrived at the airport; the planes had stopped flying until the next day. To our disappointment the Airport was crowded.

"We lit a small fire, made tea and people shared their food. We slept on the grass with the rest of the refugees. I felt safe for once. We would be in the queue for the flight to India tomorrow. That night the edge of the airfield twinkled with small fires as people cooked their evening meals. The following day we were pleased to see that everything was being conducted in an orderly manner. There were both British Army and Air Force personnel present, moving among the crowds of refugees keeping order. They told everyone not to panic as there were plenty of planes scheduled to arrive. Soon we would all be safe in India; the Japanese were still a long way away.

"Those not in the queues waited patiently to join them at the edge of the airfield; today or tomorrow we would all be on a plane to India and freedom. Some of the children played together while they waited, but we kept you in-between us in case you got lost.

"The transport planes began arriving at regular intervals and the people in the front of the queues climbed aboard. My God, so many people got on. 1 watched the planes slowly take off and head towards India and safety. I was scared; I had never been in a plane before.

"I could see my mother was worried about leaving her other children and members of her family behind in Burma. I was determined not to let her suddenly change her mind once I was on the plane. I told my mother: If you suddenly change your mind and don't get on the plane, I won't go to India on my own.

"We met some families we knew that had escaped from Rangoon. They told us Rangoon was a madhouse. The Gloucester Regiment were patrolling the city in jeeps and were forced to shoot looters and arsonists. Every shop window had been smashed; even the military were seen taking what they needed from the shops. Armed dacoits were operating in the suburbs. Brand new American vehicles were being burnt at the docks by British soldiers. Everyone seemed to be panicking, there was no organisation and hundreds of people including soldiers were escaping along the main road.

"All the dangerous animals in Rangoon zoo had escaped when it was bombed. The same happened with the lunatic asylum and Rangoon jail. Mad people and criminals were looting the shops and roaming the streets laughing and shouting and setting fire to everything. It was total bedlam. Fortunately the Japs had not entered the city as yet. The refugees also said that Mandalay was being heavily bombed. Thank God our family were no longer living there.

"I prayed my eldest sister Grace's house in Rangoon had not been bombed or looted. The refugees told us the trains were still running but the station gates had been shut as most of the carriages had been reserved for the Civil Service and the Colonial department. Desperate civilians were climbing on the roofs of the carriages and were being beaten off by Indian police with long canes.

"The following morning the transport planes began arriving again; by midday we were standing in the middle of the queue in the full heat of the sun but there were hold ups as the organizers were giving priority to large groups of new Indian arrivals. We heard later that these people were paying for their passage. The planes loaded up quickly and then took off.

"Due to the loud noise of the planes on the runway, we did not hear the approaching enemy bombers. We all fell to the ground terrified. It was our worst bombing experience up until now. You and all the other children were screaming with fear, even grown ups were crying in despair as they lost members of their family. When the enemy planes left we stood up to find mutilated bodies all around us and hot shards of shrapnel burning the grass. I can still hear the cries for help. Queues reformed again and a few planes began to arrive but now there was no order; it became a free for all. My mother and I prayed for a miracle. Some men fought their way onto the planes that had recently landed; once there, they found their wives and children were missing and strangers were behind them. Many families were separated from their loved ones. They would never see each other again. Some of the arriving planes circled and left without landing. I began to cry. We would not be going to India. Mother decided to leave the airport.

"Walking away from the airfield, many of the greatly disappointed people decided to make the trek to India on foot via the Hakawng Valley. It was rumoured by the refugees from Rangoon that a mass exodus to India on foot was expected by the British Administration in India; food and shelter had been organized along the way for the refugees. This may have been true initially, but we found out later all assistance had ended after a few weeks. People who still believed help was available left with few of the necessities of life and perished. Thank God for my mother's good judgement. She refused to go.

"Many other refugees were convinced that if they stayed together in one large group, the strong helping the weak, it would be possible to reach India. People said it would only take two to three weeks to cover a distance of a hundred miles. But there was one immense problem: the pending monsoon. Not many people had taken this important fact into account. After the war we heard that hundreds of families had disappeared along the trail to India. Some of these poor people were friends of our family.

"Without a doubt my mother's total refusal to be persuaded by me to join the vast throng of fleeing refugees, saved our lives. The Hakawng Valley became known as the Valley of Death."

The Trek to India: The Empire's 1812

This retreat was the British Empire's 1812. Instead of marauding Cossacks there were the voracious retreating Chinese soldiers; instead of snow there was rain; instead of biting frosts there were biting malarial mosquitoes and typhus-carrying ticks. Instead of slippery ice-bound dirt roads there were slippery muddy paths and steep hills; instead of black crows overhead, there were circling vultures.

Both retreats left their trail of human detritus for many years afterwards. It was not difficult to retrace the route taken by the refugees, their jungle vine entwined skeletons marked the way. These late trekkers had been coaxed by the administrators to linger till the eleventh hour. British soldiers escaping to India had to harden their hearts at the sights of misery along the way. Whole families sat helplessly under the dripping leaves, their sunken eyes blazing with typhus fever. Healthy and strong members of a family waited for the weak, until they themselves succumbed.

A fortunate few, anticipating the danger, left early. These people did not believe the picture of false hope placed on a crumbling wall of a dying empire. At the beginning there was some organization. These lucky ones had a pleasant journey to safety. They were taken over the rivers by boat, sometimes even riding on elephants.

The brave soldiers who fought as a rearguard were coldly received in India by the pen-pushers and armchair warriors. These officers found this a convenient opportunity to look down with contempt on these fighting men from Burma. Their reason it is said: "they no longer looked like soldiers."

It was first claimed that the Japanese (who walked into Burma) would soon run out of supplies. The Japanese were in fact short of everything. Perhaps the British Generals in charge of the fighting had a secret weapon to delay the enemy; they left behind vast amounts of supplies. The enemy however were not always happy with their booty of tinned dairy products. Like the Chinese, the Japanese did not eat such food, as it upset their rice-loving stomachs. Milk they considered was only fit for calves. However, we also left behind cases of Andrews liver salts, which the Japs used to clean their teeth and add to soft drinks for the fizz. There were also mountains of bully beef, rice, white flour, sugar and even vitamins; everything to balance the diet of the protein-starved warrior of Nippon. We even left them millions of French letters which they put to good use, not for the purpose intended but in a practice recommended in the Japanese soldier's handbook (masturbation). It was claimed to be cheaper, healthier, and, I suppose, one met a better class of female. This did not go down well with the sexually modest Burmese villagers when performed indiscreetly. These rubbers were also used to make wonderful fighting kites, to protect the ears of their pack animals from biting flies and, as we witnessed in Tada u, as bath caps to protect head wounds when bathing at the well.

So reliant were the Japs on "Churchill's rations" that it proved their downfall in the battle for Imphal and Kohima. So, I suppose you could justifiably say this clever strategy finally worked in the end.

CHAPTER 6

The Lotus Eaters

HONG KONG

The life of officers in Hong Kong pre-war was wonderful, according to one of my hotel guests who was a young officer there at the time. It would be fair to say that many of these young officers were observers and not participants in every pursuit mentioned. There were twenty-two-course Chinese dinners to be had on the floating restaurants in the harbour; that is presumably if an officer could eat while ignoring what his men were doing in the milling and bobbing sampans a few feet below his table.

Banquets and Galas at the famous Grippes were commonplace. Dinner jackets were mandatory. Cocktail parties, dinners at the various clubs and a great deal of promiscuity had to be attended to at that high and privileged level. Life in Hong Kong for the higher-ups was one continuous great dressing-and-undressing rehearsal.

First the young officers were gently roused by their personal servant (batman and wardrobe manager) with a cup of tea. After a bath, they were dressed for parade. Returning from parade, they undressed, bathed and dressed again for a game of golf. Following their game of golf they returned, undressed, bathed, then dressed to visit their mistresses; or better still someone else's mistress or wife, whom they quickly undressed (without help from said batman). Even the CO's wife was not immune if attractive: they seldom were. All females were fair game for these young bloods and dashing blades. In the evening they would dress for the club or even dress up for a fancy dress party to finish the day. This wonderful merry-go-round of dressing and undressing continued to the very end.

Three days before the Japanese attack, General Maltby received a report from a trusted spy on the mainland which stated that the enemy had landed a large number of troops just twenty miles from Hong Kong. Maltby did not believe it.

On the evening of the 7th December, Lieutenant General Takashi Sakai gave the order for his troops to move closer to the British defences on the Gin Drinkers' Line and take up camouflaged positions in preparation for the coming attack. However, Lieutenant General Sakai and his staff were worried. Why was the Gin Drinkers' Line, so lightly defended? Only the 2nd Battalion Royal Scots (below strength) were thinly stretched along this vital position. Was this a trap to lure the Japanese in? He intended to find out and sent out several small reconnaissance units.

Two hundred paces in front of the Royal Scots D Company, a small camouflaged enemy reconnaissance party was in position. The Japanese reconnaissance party squatted in that position westerners find so uncomfortable to maintain. Their orders were to ascertain if the defenders were being secretly reinforced.

The reconnaissance party was led by the young Japanese 2nd Lieutenant Nakamura; his first important assignment. If he could impress his superiors at headquarters perhaps they would stop slapping his face. They might even allow him to command a platoon in the initial attack. If so he could blood his treasured family sword in battle. He raised his father's Zeiss binoculars to study his opponents. He could hear snatches of their strange language and accents. They all looked big strong men just like the Japanese Imperial Guards Division. His throat suddenly felt dry at the thought of perhaps meeting these big men in hand to hand combat.

On Hong Kong Island, life continued as normal; plans for Christmas were in full progress, the restaurants, dance halls and bars were packed as usual. No one noticed that the Japanese shop owners had quietly boarded up their businesses and were leaving Hong Kong under the cover of darkness.

"Jack had been called back from Taunggyi to Hong Kong urgently after only two weeks of his three weeks leave. The island had been placed on a war footing while he was away. But Jack was sure that if the Japs attacked they would be repulsed. He felt the garrison troops and the arriving reinforcements would be enough to defend the island. He also said that his battalion was being moved from Hong Kong to the New Territories. He said the defensive positions had been improved (*this was not the case*) and that The Gin Drinkers' Line would be supported by artillery firing from Hong Kong."

This was true but soon the Scots would wonder who their artillery was actually supporting. Nothing had changed at the Gin Drinkers' Line. In fact some of the trenches had collapsed, others were barely waist deep and in many places the trenches were not continuous. Most of the barbed wire had rusted or been stolen by the Chinese. The thousands of anti-personnel mines that were needed to be dug-in on the approaches had not materialized. It was soon apparent that there were no anti-personnel mines available in Hong Kong. Deep ravines also broke the defence line; here the enemy could slip through without being observed. It was generally presumed by the commanders that the Japanese would use the roads when attacking.

A report was sent to Colonel White CO of the Royal Scots, pointing out the inadequacies of the Gin Drinkers' Line. He was then informed by Brigadier Wallis that defences would be improved by his Rajputs who were resident on the mainland and occupying the Shingmun Redoubt. The improvements did not happen.

"In his letters, Jack told me not to worry, Hong Kong was well defended. He was confident the British Army could hold the island. But mostly our letters were concerned with our future plans of settling down in the Shan States.

"Jack said the availability of cheap alcohol resulted in a great deal of trouble among the soldiers with fighting and insubordination. Discipline among the men was not at its best, many were in prison or awaiting court marshal *[including officers]*. He said that many of the soldiers believed that large amounts of alcohol in the bloodstream killed the malaria parasite. Many Royal Scots were succumbing to malaria *[Dad neglected to mention venereal disease]*. As there were inadequate military police to deal with all the trouble, Jack and the other NCOs were kept busy at the weekends. In breaking up these fights, the NCOs and the Military Police became involved themselves and received their share of injuries.

"Jack was confident that the British Army was better equipped and trained compared to the Japanese. He and Lt Ford once observed some Jap soldiers at a river crossing on the Mainland. They seemed undisciplined and unorganized. He was confident they would not dare attack Hong Kong, until they had defeated the Chinese Army. The new Canadian reinforcements and the Scots got on well together as many of the Canadians were of Scottish decent. New officers had also arrived and he found out he was soon to be promoted to Regimental Sergeant Major."

❧

Some officers and NCOs wanted to take their men out on training exercises and night manoeuvres, in preparation for a Japanese attack. They were overruled. Those in charge did not want to aggravate the Japanese by preparing for war. It was generally believed that the Royal Navy, as a last resort, could always rescue them. The belief that Britannia ruled the waves was still widely held. It is strange that the mighty super battleship Yamato and her sister ship the Musashi, the two biggest and most powerful warships ever built, had gone unnoticed by British Intelligence, hidden behind sprigs of delicately arranged cherry blossom. Apart from walks of inspection, very little else was done to prepare the island's defences. Maltby's initial eagerness gradually waned. Perhaps his hands were tied by those above.

✿

"Jack said the new officers were eager to learn how to command men on the parade ground instead of the battlefield and left too much work for the NCOs. The new officers seemed uncomfortable in close contact with the lower ranks and gave unnecessary orders to distance themselves from the soldiers. It was obvious they could not wait to get back to their own kind. This was due to the social class divide, which for some officers was difficult to breach."

✿

After parades it was the right type of officer who had a smoke and chatted to his men; he had to gain the trust of the Scots before being accepted into their Kirk. The shortcomings of these new officers were obvious to a plain speaking Yorkshireman who worked for Jardine Matheson and described the new officers as "toffee-nosed twats." He was one of the brave Hong Kong Volunteers. These men often in their fifties and sixties were regularly stopped from carrying out training manoeuvres at the weekends by the "toffee-nosed twats" for the most trivial of reasons like being too near the golf course or disturbing the peace on a Sunday afternoon. The Hong Kong Volunteers gave a good account of themselves. Not many survived the war or their imprisonment. In the Japanese Army there were no privileged classes and a rich businessman's son upon being conscripted began as the lowest of the low: a Second Class Private. Promotion came from merit in the field not through family connections or wealth. In Britain it was considered that all public schools produced natural leaders of the common man, both in the government and on the battlefield.

✿

"Jack's letters seldom contained his military duties but he occasionally wrote of amusing events. One Sunday afternoon he was ordered to round-up soldiers to accompany a group of new officers to inspect an island.

They were told to bring wooden pegs and mallets. Most of the soldiers were drunk. They boarded the launch and were surprised to see picnic hampers. Soon they were joined by the officer's girlfriends. The sailor driving the launch was also drunk and pulled away too quickly causing two officers to fall into the filthy harbour to the amusement of the men.

"The officers insisted on returning to their quarters to change. They were driven back by a Royal Scot, who while waiting for the officers, helped himself to more alcohol. On the way back he crashed the transport and punched one of the officers. On reaching the island, the officers did not care to linger among the rocks, as the island's only occupants were poisonous snakes."

⚜

The troops settled into this wonderful life. Some had their own servants, others found Chinese girlfriends and this arrangement was certainly safer than the Dark Harbour. However, the queue at the VD clinic and the cases of malaria grew. It is fair to say that the Royal Scots were well represented in both these queues.

Brigadier Cedric Wallis, Commander of the Rajputs; was to conduct the defences on the mainland but paid little attention to the Gin Drinkers' Line. Brigadier Wallis did not have a high opinion of the Royal Scots. He made it clear that he had little confidence in their CO Colonel White, an Irishman, who was liked and trusted by the Royal Scots.

Brigadier Wallis thought the Scots were lacking in discipline and held the monopoly on venereal disease and malaria. Yet despite his low opinion of the Scots fighting qualities, he had them moved from the island defences and placed them (seriously under strength) in the most strategic and vital position on The Gin Drinkers' Line, a position they were unfamiliar with and which required substantial improvements.

General Maltby received another intelligence report that a Japanese regiment was only a few miles from the mainland border. This he believed and he placed Hong Kong on a war footing.

After the war it was Brigadier Wallis' opinion that the Royal Scots should not receive the Battle Honour "Hong Kong". This seemed unfair and unjust to many. They were the sole target for the initial Japanese attack, while also being heavily shelled by their own guns. Brigadier Wallis himself did not witness the fighting on the Gin Drinkers' Line.

Dad, Tam and Willie often joked about their new nickname "The First to Foot It" after the war and the many fights it caused in the bars of Singapore. General Wavell, the worst offender in underestimating the Japanese Army, was finally replaced by General Slim, a well-respected commander from a working class background. Slim also changed the British tactics. The subsequent battles of Kohima and Imphal were great victories for the British Army. A Japanese soldier who survived described the British soldiers at Kohima as formidable.

The Japanese Army did have weaknesses; the Russians proved this in 1939. The Japanese lost two major border battles fought in the vicinity of Khal-khin-Gol (Halha River) and were totally beaten by the Russian Eastern Divisions led by General Zhukov. The Japanese suffered heavy casualties. The Russians exposed the fact that the Japanese were an outdated Army, employed repetitive and primitive tactics, had weak logistics and lacked large scale mobility. The arid plains of Burma were suitable for tank warfare and our tanks were far superior to that of the Japanese and yet we were constantly out-manoeuvred by soldiers on foot.

The Three British Blunders

Perhaps these blunders were mistakes, deliberate or just down to plain laziness. I have heard that two of these blunders were committed by members of the Royal Scots, one an officer and the other a private soldier.

Firstly, Captain Jones sent out a patrol to the north to check Needle Hill and Shing Mun Valley. Colonel White felt that both areas were prone to enemy infiltration. Captain Jones asked a newly arrived officer,

Lieutenant Thompson, (known as "Bunty" to his fellow officers) to carry out this vital patrol. The Lieutenant was accompanied by twelve armed men. For reasons of his own Lieutenant Thompson neglected to carry out the full patrol as ordered and instead, decided to do some socializing. Had he continued to Shing Mun Valley as ordered, he would have seen below him hundreds of crouching enemy soldiers hiding in the ravine, alerting all the British commanders that an attack was imminent.

The second blunder was to take place an hour later. Sitting in his bunker, Captain Jones wished to communicate with a fellow officer above ground. Surprisingly he did not have a direct telephone line connection so he ordered his runner, a Private Gillie, a somewhat insubordinate native of Glasgow, to take a message.

Although the ground was rocky and uneven, Captain Jones knew the nimble, rock-hopping soldier would make easy and quick work of the task. However Gillie did not seem keen to leave the warmth and the company of Captain Jones' headquarters. Perhaps he was also hungry. He, like all the others, had not eaten that day and was afraid he would miss his rations.

On leaving the underground bunker, Gillie did a rather strange and unexplained thing. Taking the big key hanging near the solid iron doors, the only entrance to the bunker, he locked the iron door from the outside and took the only key with him as he skipped away into the evening mists and oblivion. This action in effect trapped all the men below, some twenty in number, and prevented them from helping their comrades who were greatly outnumbered when the attack came. It also deprived Captain Jones of his command which was vital to the defence of the position. When the Japanese had over run this position many of the frustrated and helpless men trapped underground were killed or wounded by hand grenades dropped through the ventilation shafts.

The last and most significant blunder was made by an intelligence officer during that night. He received a report from one of his trusted agents on the mainland: "Japanese amassing for an attack the following morning." The intelligence officer drove to the mainland to check for himself. He surveyed the ground below for signs of the enemy. What had he expected to see? Perhaps dozens of blazing camp fires or hundreds of Japanese troops' glowing cigarettes as they waited to receive the orders to attack? Instead he saw and heard nothing, just the high pitched chirping chorus made by thousands of auspicious Chinese crickets. Satisfied no attack was imminent, the intelligence officer returned to Hong Kong Island. He reported: "no attack expected the following day." General Maltby issued orders for the troops to stand down.

For some reason this order did not reach the Royal Scots on the mainland. The inhabitants of Hong Kong slept peacefully that night under their blankets of complacency.

The Evening before the Japanese Attack: Mainland China

That afternoon, a thousand yards to the front of The Gin Drinkers' Line, under camouflage, the same young Japanese 2nd Lieutenant Nakamura had resumed his duties of observing D company of the Royal Scots. The young 2nd Lieutenant was to report any new developments back to Lt General Takashi Sakai's headquarters. The attack was due to take place the following morning at 08:00 on the 8th December. Many of the Japanese were apprehensive; this was a battle against an enemy that possessed a massive empire. It was also a battle between two cultures that were poles apart.

Earlier, the young Japanese officer asked permission to join the attack to blood his sword – his face was slapped. "Stop complaining, get on with your duties" ordered a senior officer.

Undercover, Lieutenant Nakamura looked down at his other prized possession; a pair of made-to-measure black leather riding boots, always kept at their shiny best. He then lifted his binoculars and studied the tall enemy sergeant standing on the Gin Drinkers' Line. Why were the British so tall? He studied the handsome face of the Sergeant. Little did he know they were destined to meet the following day.

Unaware they were being closely watched, Lieutenant Ford and Sergeant Devereux chatted in a relaxed manner. The two men discussed the intelligence officer's last talk. Both men were not admirers of these strutting roosters and their many privileges. They always seemed to be holding parties at their spacious apartments and seemed too friendly with the Japanese. The ordinary soldiers' opinion differed slightly. They believed intelligence officers spent their time sitting in warm offices, drinking pink gin, wearing lipstick and kissing each other. That evening to the left and right of the young Japanese 2nd Lieutenant, Japanese infantry units of 23rd Regiment 38th Division took up their positions.

Lieutenant Nakamura took a sip of water; he was looking forward to his evening meal of octopus and rice. He then lifted his field glasses skywards and studied a wing of swallows performing arching aerial acrobatics in the darkening sky. These lively birds reminded him of his childhood. As soon as night fell, he would slip away and make his last report. He hoped it would be acceptable; his senior officers had taken a liking to slapping his face. Inconspicuously melting away as soon as the shades of night descended, he reported back to Lt General Takashi Sakai's Headquarters.

Just in front of the British position, the waiting Japanese troops remained still and as silent as a terracotta army. They had been forewarned. "Any soldier who gave their presence away would be dealt with immediately with the naked sword": decapitation.

CHAPTER 7

An Evil Spirit

BURMA

"We walked sadly away from the airfield at Myitkyina. Some people just seemed to drift off aimlessly, each with their own plan of escape. Two large Indian families called Patel and Gundamoney that we knew from Rangoon, decided to trek to India. This large group that included many strong healthy males began the long trek, vowing to keep close together. Only three reached India.

"Many of the more optimistic groups lingered around Myitkyina airport just in case more planes arrived. The only planes that came from then on belonged to the enemy. We went our own way keeping to the many footpaths that criss-crossed the countryside. When the paths were smooth and crossed open ground, we let you walk in-between us where you would be protected from any danger. Sometime in the afternoon we reached a small row of shabby and abandoned bungalows. Tired, hot and thirsty, all we wanted was to sit in the shade. Rested, we began searching for a well, which we soon found. The deserted houses were devoid of anything useful except for one where we found rice and lentils mixed with rat droppings all over the floor. Your grandmother carefully gathered and cleaned it. There would be enough for a few small meals. Here in one of the gardens my mother found a few ladies' fingers (okra) and a couple of small brinjals (aubergines), but the best find was a large dah: a big Burmese knife, like a machete. This knife was to prove very useful to us and became our only defensive weapon, a weapon my mother would soon need when a dangerous visitor unexpectedly entered a house we were sheltering in.

"We were grateful for the water well, even though the water was a long way down. These bungalows were the homes of Indian workers; it was always easy to tell by the pictures of various gaudy Hindu gods that adorned the walls. I was just so relieved to have a roof over our heads that night even though all the windows had been broken. Any animal or human could enter at will. Anything was preferable to sleeping in the open.

Gradually we were joined by other refugees who had also left Myitkyina Airport. We began to cook the rice and settle down for the night too tired to socialize.

"It was here that a sad and very strange thing happened. While my mother was cooking, I was holding you when I noticed a tiny hunch-backed figure of a very old women coming towards the bungalows. The old woman stopped briefly at each group cooking outside in the open; they paid her little attention so she carried on. I felt so sorry for this helpless old lady.

"On reaching us she no longer bothered to stop; it was as if she had been ignored enough and it had hurt her pride. We both took pity on the old bent woman as she walked past. She looked desperately tired and thirsty despite the fact we could not see her face or neck properly. My mother spoke to her in Burmese and offered her a drink of water. We helped her sit on the porch and gave her the water and a little rice. The old woman lapped the water with her tongue (this is how an evil spirit drinks my mother said later). Her body had a strong burnt smell. Her clothes were also rather strange and the long fingernails of her gnarled hands looked like claws. She clutched a small Shan bag in one hand and did not speak or look directly at us.

"While we were discussing what to do next, the old woman began walking away despite our invitation to stop longer and rest. She had not eaten the rice. For a brief moment we took our eyes off her. The next time we looked the old woman had disappeared leaving only her

Shan bag neatly placed at the side of the track. Thinking she had fallen I ran after her but she had completely vanished. There was no trace of her in the scrub that bordered the wide track.

"It was getting dark and suddenly I felt scared and ran back. What had happened to her? I asked my mother to come with me and look for the old woman just in case she had fallen. I was also curious to see what was in her bag. My mother said 'that would not be safe' as she believed the old woman was an Outoasan, a spirit that takes on many disguises [like the Banshee of Irish folklore]. A human should never take anything left by an Outoasan because one day it will come back and ask for something in return.

"My mother believed she lost her first male child to an Outoasan who appeared every night at her hospital bedside and asked for her baby son in return for a precious gift: Mother refused. Soon the baby boy died of anaemia; my mother believed the Outoasan had drunk her son's blood during the night. On the night my youngest brother Victor died of cholera, an Outoasan called throughout the night. Despite our prayers, Victor died in my mother's arms in the early hours."

❧

These stories were told to me by my mother and may seem incredible for a religious and intelligent woman to relate, or perhaps even believe. But one must remember Mother was born in the Far East. If superstition is female and whispers discreetly in soft cautious tones in the western world, she runs naked and screaming in the Far East. British and Europeans born or living for long periods of time in the tropics sometimes absorbed local superstitions and beliefs; perhaps my grandmother and mother were no exception. One thing I am certain of, both Grandmother and Mother enjoyed the telling.

❧

"Some time in the late afternoon, large groups of people began passing the row of bungalows we were staying in, heading for Myitkyina Airport. These people insisted they had been informed while in Rangoon that the airlift was still in operation and they would definitely get a flight if they had the fare. They had caught the last train from Rangoon which had been attacked on several occasions by enemy bombers. The driver decided to wait for darkness to fall before setting off on the return journey to Mandalay where the train would terminate. My mother told me to hurry and get ready to leave; we had to catch that train. On the way to Mandalay we could get off and be nearer to Maymyo, a place we knew well. My mother felt Cyril, Victor and Lucy may have gone to Maymyo to find us.

"We packed up our few belongings and began walking along a wide path bordered by scrub jungle. None of the refugees staying at the bungalows wished to join us. We were worried in case the train left before we reached it. It would soon be dark. All along the way people had discarded their possessions before the flight to India. There were so many useful things like shoes, hats and clothes. But my mother would not stop. 'There is no time, we could miss the train' she said. The only objects she picked up were a deep Indian frying pan, several boxes of matches and a large lightweight waterproof ground sheet; we now had two.

"It was almost dark when we reached the train. The driver and his crew were sleeping underneath it behind the wheels for protection from bombs. They intended to move off shortly. Some Indian passengers had remained on the train as they had no money for the airfare having been robbed by Burmese dacoits before leaving Rangoon.

"By now we were starving again; you were the only one who had eaten properly that day. In our compartment, which was almost empty, I found some abandoned tin cups, a large metal water container and an aluminium Tiffin-carrier that had been made in Birmingham. It contained a half-eaten mild Burmese curry, rice, vegetables and perajos at the bottom. There was so much we shared it with a young Indian couple who moved down to our carriage for company. We had to leave this Tiffin-carrier behind as it was too big and made a great deal of noise when carried. The train finally moved off and began travelling towards Mandalay; I quickly fell asleep."

Mother bought another Tiffin carrier after the war (for picnics). Dad hated it; at the slightest touch it fell over and made a racket. When Mum was not around and it fell over he would kick it. Of course I used to tell Mother when she returned. This did not endear me to the RSM.

🪷

"The train travelled slowly through the night. In the morning planes were spotted and the train stopped again. The drivers and the few other passengers took shelter in the jungle by the track in case the train was attacked. Fortunately we were overlooked. However my mother had been informed by the Indians that the Japanese were now in Maymyo and decided to leave the train. How far we were from Maymyo I do not know. We were now terrified of Japanese planes and kept to the jungle fringed footpaths.

"After many hours of walking we came to a long row of nice European bungalows at the end of a tree lined drive. Each house appeared undamaged; gardens were filled with flowers and roses, enclosed by white picket fences. The owners seemed to have been in a great hurry to vacate their homes as possessions were scattered everywhere. We needed shoes; there were none to be found that fitted us but we found a wide brimmed straw hat with a long blue scarf tied around the crown. I was hoping we could sleep in a bed for a change. The doors and windows of the bungalows were left open and swung eerily to and fro in the late afternoon breeze. The first south-westerly winds were warning of the imminent 'mango showers' that would herald the monsoon.

"My mother chose a bungalow in the middle of the row for safety; we would stay here and think of our next move. There were no beds; all the furniture had been looted. But there was some food left in the properties, mostly tinned. Also, I found a bottle of gripe water for you and a carton of Tate and Lyle sugar and loose tea. These items were a godsend. To our joy there was still running water fed by a large tank situated high on a metal tower behind the row of bungalows."

🪷

The black and white picture on the bottle of gripe water depicting a baby holding a snake always fascinated me; it was the first picture that I can remember seeing and I used to gaze at it wondering why the snake did not bite the baby.

꧁

"Soon my mother had gathered enough tinned food for several days. The weight of this would pose a problem as my mother and I had also to carry you when you grew tired. So we decided to stay for a few days as the windows and doors could still be shut. Our best find was a tin of Lambert's finest cooking oil and a bar of Wrights cold tar soap.

"After the first night of being alone, many other families fleeing Mandalay began to arrive in their own transport, hoping to cross the Ava Bridge the following day. Soon most of the accommodation was full of refugees.

"Such was the prestige of the British Army that many of the Europeans still believed there would soon be a British counter attack. They did not believe the rumour that the British Army had crossed the Chindwin River. This gave me new hope. However the majority (mainly Indian shop owners) were determined to escape to their homeland. These people carried all their wealth with them, mostly gold, to start anew again in India.

"A group of British people arrived at the bungalows in a lorry. They seemed confident that they could overtake the retreat but they had one problem, they were short of petrol. Some of the men, who were armed, decided to go on ahead and find, buy or steal fuel. They never returned. A very large group of rich Brahmin merchants and their families arrived in their own motorised transport. Staying in Burma was not an option for the Brahmin Indians: the Burmese were robbing and killing them at every opportunity. These Indians had no intention of stopping the night and once their numbers had swelled, set out for India in one large convoy. Before they left, the Brahmins told us that the Japs were on the outskirts of Rangoon and had set up road blocks on the main roads to stop everyone leaving the city.

"Again there was still much talk of trekking overland on foot to India. It all sounded so easy. Again my mother would not be persuaded despite my entreaties to attempt this escape route while there was still time. Thank God my mother could not be persuaded to take the trek to India. This was not due to some premonition of impending disaster but a practical decision based on some knowledge of this valley and the imminent coming of the rains.

"'Do you know how far India is, Kate?' My mother would say. 'That valley is crisscrossed with ravines and hills and will soon be full of disease. Your brother Harry knows that valley, it's full of ticks that carry typhus fever.'"

⚜

What my grandmother was not aware of at the time was that another great danger existed: the Chinese Army. These defeated soldiers would also choose that same line of retreat. They robbed and killed many European and Indian civilians alike. Chinese soldiers were also sick, hungry and desperate to escape.

⚜

"That evening people sat outside discussing their plans for the following day when we were suddenly caught in the headlight glare of vehicles. It was too late to run.

"'Japs!' someone whispered, 'My God!' There was nothing we could do. Then what seemed like our doom turned out to be our possible salvation. A large armed convoy of British military trucks with snub bonnets pulled up. The trucks had come from the dry belt further inland. A British voice called out: 'Any water around here?' It was an Indian regiment led by British officers. They had stayed behind to destroy vital installations and were eager to rejoin their regiment.

"'There are no Japs directly behind us' the officer said. 'Tomorrow we will be happy to take as many of you as possible to the British lines. We should be able to get across the Ava Bridge.'

"'Our Regiment can't be that far ahead' said another officer. Everyone was overjoyed. The soldiers gave the British civilians, who were short of fuel, petrol and advised them to wait until dawn and join their military convoy before heading off. The advice was not heeded. Later that night, an officer sent out a group of Indian soldiers to the main road to reconnoitre the way ahead. They came back with bad news. 'Large parties of Japs are heading for Rangoon on foot along the main road, a long line of burnt vehicles are blocking the highway.'

"This was not the only bad news. They found the three missing British men. They had been tied to trees and bayoneted. There was no sign of their families who had followed looking for them. I hoped they had escaped.

"'A change of plan' said the English officer, 'we will head cross country, bypassing all towns and villages then join the main road again just before the Ava Bridge, then carry on to Monywa.'

"I begged my mother to go along with this new line of escape. We will not have to walk, I argued. Our shoes were wearing out. You did not have any clothes; they had all been left behind at the station. All you had to wear was one of my chemises and a bonnet.

My mother thought about it for a long time and said. 'Do you know what will happen if the Japs capture us in a British Army convoy?'

"But in the end she was persuaded, even though we would be heading towards the fighting; she knew Monywa and its river ferry, which regularly crossed the Chindwin. Everyone believed the British would hold on to the west bank of the river and stop the enemy crossing. The Chindwin was not as wide or as deep as the Irrawaddy. If we could just get there and cross the river on the ferry, we would be safe.

"Early next morning we set off; the blood red rising sun in the east looked like the Japanese flag. My mother said this was a bad omen. The Indian drivers were in a hurry and drove very fast. This frightened us civilians; the trucks would easily be seen from the air by the clouds of dust that followed us, giving our position away to enemy planes. Every time we drove over a bump we were thrown into the air. We were soon bypassing many Burmese villages in an area that seemed untouched by the war. All the same these villages displayed the Japanese 'poached egg' flags. They watched us pass by with silent indifference. The Burmese at this point were pro-Japanese. They did not realize they were jumping from the frying pan into the fire.

"You were frightened and crying because of the speed we were travelling at and the choking dust from the trucks ahead. Water was in short supply and we had to ration ourselves. After travelling many miles that day the British trucks stopped in scrub jungle where we would spend the night. Soldiers went out on patrol to find water. We were so tired and dusty that after a quick meal we all sheltered in or under the trucks and spent a peaceful night feeling safe in the presence of the armed soldiers.

"At first light the following morning we set off again. A few hours later the convoy turned onto the main road [Rangoon to Mandalay]. This was awash with refugees who tried to wave the column of trucks down, but the drivers did not stop. There was just no room; it was so sad to see their desperate faces as they watched us disappear. Shortly after we came to a standstill behind a long line of stationary vehicles; we could hear the battle ahead and see and smell the dark clouds of burning rubber. Many of the vehicles ahead were on fire. Other empty trucks still had their engines running.

"We were approached by several dusty British soldiers; they had bad news. There was fighting further down the road; the Ava Bridge was still open but Monywa was being heavily shelled and attacked. The ferry across the Chindwin River was under fire. It was also reported that the Japanese were now on the West bank of the Chindwin. Our attempt to escape again had come to nothing; here the vehicles had to be abandoned.

"Reaching and getting behind the British lines was now impossible. Many of the other escapees decided to continue and stick with the soldiers for as long as possible. Other refugees in the convoy just wandered away in a daze. We were now in the open and exposed to attack from the air. My mother had had enough. She decided we should head towards Pagan, as this was an area only lightly populated. Your grandmother wanted to keep away from the main road, to escape the Jap bombers and Burmese National Army who were ambushing soldiers and refugees on the highway. Looking for a track that led off the main road and into the wilds, we had to continue as we needed to get away from the sight of dead bodies, bodies that lined the edge of the road. The milestones now looked like communal headstones, except the dead lay unburied. The smell of the dead turned my stomach. The pleas of the wounded broke my heart, we had no water to give. My mother warned me to keep away and out of reach from the outstretched grasping hands of dying people who lay by the roadside.

"After some time, we came to a well-used bullock track that led back into the dry country of central Burma. It was so hot. Normally in peacetime we slept in the afternoon, only going out in the cooler hours. I began to feel dizzy. Sunstroke comes on suddenly and without treatment and water you can die quickly. We were now very thirsty and needed to find water and shade.

"It was on this bullock track that we bumped straight into the column of marching Japanese soldiers. My god, I believed that they would kill us all; instead to our amazement, they paid us little attention but headed towards the main road and in the general direction of Pagan. My mother decided to change direction again.

"Our odyssey in Burma had now begun in earnest as we headed into the wilds. My mother's plan was to remain free as long as possible and await events as they unfolded. The best and safest place to be was the wilds of Burma, providing we could find enough water and food to sustain us and find shelter from the coming monsoon.

"Within a few days we had run out of the tinned food. It was then that my mother's knowledge and foraging skills came to the fore. It was lucky we had cooking oil and the facilities to cook what we found. Dry firewood was plentiful. However we could not stop worrying about our documents falling into Japanese hands. Mother kept telling me what to say if we were ever interrogated. This thought constantly haunted my mother and me throughout the entire occupation.

"Later we found out that the Kempeitai were paranoid about spies. Being found with a radio whether it was working or not was evidence enough of being a spy. The result was always torture and death. Mother decided later to adopt traditional Burmese dress and claim we were Mons Burmese escaping the Chinese Army. This pretence was only possible because of my mother's perfect knowledge of Burmese, their customs and some of the various dialects of its people. To survive we would soon need shelter.

"We headed for the thick dry scrub belt. Once on the other side of the tall cactus plants, we could not be seen from the main bullock track. The scrub jungle and the prickly pear [cactus plants] were difficult and painful to enter and move through, but at least we were out of sight.

"The ripe sweet prickly pear fruit on the cactus plants were protected by sharp thorns and out of our reach. This was a shame, as our throats were parched and the fruit at this time of year contained sweet juice. In a patch of open ground ahead of us, personal items and clothing where scattered in the dust and my mother went to see if anything useful could be found lying abandoned. She quickly came back empty-handed and red-faced.

"'My God Kate – quick!' Mother exclaimed, 'we must get away from here – that nulla *[small ravine]* is full of civilians who have been cut up by dacoits. Some are still alive – there is nothing we can do – they are beyond help!' Above us vultures circled cautiously afraid to land.

"'If vultures are afraid to land, they can see danger nearby. We must leave now!' said my mother. We moved away as quickly as possible. As we walked, we came to higher ground and could see to our joy in the far distance, through gaps in the jungle, the glimmer of a river below us. This was no mirage. The river promised our salvation."

❧

The river Mum refers to could have been any tributary of the Irrawaddy or the Sittang River; we were certainly somewhere between both. From what I can tell Grandmother often changed direction by instinct without consulting my mother.

❧

"We headed towards the thick riverine jungle, so thirsty and tired we could hardly speak. I was afraid to enter the jungle as I had heard so many stories of wild animals attacking people. But the thought of drinking water made me desperate and dulled my fears. Entering the jungle, we rested in the shade. I was terrified of venomous snakes. A terrible thought occurred to me. If one of us was bitten, there would be nothing we could do except wait for death. My mother said that after a bite from a Russell's viper, internal organs would haemorrhage. Painful death would take days. A bite from a cobra would be much quicker and relatively painless; however, this was little comfort to me."

❧

Being bitten by a venomous snake in rural Burma where there was no anti-venom available became a case of "wait and see". Chances of survival were slim, however, sometimes venomous snakes (for reasons of their own or to conserve precious venom) did not inject their protein poisons. This was known as "a dry bite" or "a warning bite".

⚜

"'When we reach the river and quench our thirst, we will follow the path along the bank'" said my mother 'It will lead us deeper into the wilderness. We will always have water to drink, water to wash and cook with. There are sure to be some edible water plants, vegetables and fruit trees growing on the riverbank. This is also the time when fresh water turtles lay their eggs, just before the rains; if we are lucky we will find turtle eggs in the sand banks.'

"I hoped we might find some sweet water melons full of juice. Burma has so many different types of delicious fruiting trees and plants, too numerous to mention. My mother said that due to the annual flooding caused by the South-west monsoons, all kinds of seeds are washed into the river; a few seeds take hold and germinate at the high water mark, providing the young seedlings are not eaten by grazing animals. Burmese river turtles lay many soft rubbery-skinned eggs deep in the sand. The young quickly disperse during the monsoon. All turtle eggs are white and round just like snake eggs. I would never buy or eat them before the war, but turtle meat and their eggs were widely enjoyed throughout Burma. All the same I was determined to frighten away any turtles we saw to stop my mother killing them. Saving small animals from my mother during the war made her so angry and she often threatened to murder me.

"It took us a long time to reach the river through the jungle as the light was dim under the canopy of the trees and trailing vines. We had to look first before placing each foot down because of Russell's vipers. These large beautiful, aggressive snakes did not move or give any warning before striking.

"As we got nearer to the riverbank, we recognized papaya and banana trees by the shape of their large distinctive leaves. We were desperately disappointed when we reached the riverbank to find the water out of our reach, so we sat in the shade of the broad-leaved fruit trees to rest. Only a few wild bananas could be found but we had to be careful of eating wild bananas. We were too thirsty to eat. My mother cut down a young banana tree to get at the heart which was full of insipid liquid that we could drink. Still desperately thirsty, we carried on along a narrow footpath right on the edge of the high and steep riverbank. I was afraid a crocodile might knock one of us into the river with its tail."

⚘

This is a common myth believed by many throughout Burma. Although a large crocodile can launch itself two thirds of its length out of the water (head first) to grab prey on the riverbank, it cannot use its tail as Mother believed.

⚘

"Finally we reached the water. We were so desperately thirsty that we could not wait to boil the water first before drinking. Then we lit a fire with dry sticks and boiled some water and added powdered milk for you. You were a big heavy child – not a big eater, but you would drink anything [I still do, Mother]. Thank God you could walk most of the time in the baby shoes I had brought for you.

"There were many sandbanks in the middle of the river. The water was quite shallow, but flowing and clear. My mother began to search for turtle eggs, looking first for signs of where monitor lizards had been digging. I kept begging my mother to find a Burmese village so we could spend a night off the ground, and have a roof over our heads and the protection of a door. But my mother would always say: 'Humans are far more dangerous to us than wild animals.' We washed ourselves under the shade of trees where it was cooler and we could not be seen from the opposite bank, and then rested. It was so nice to feel clean."

⚘

Most Burmese villagers were now anti-British; they had lost all respect for their former masters. The Japanese after all, were Asiatic Buddhists and rice eaters like themselves. The Japanese promised the Burmese independence and both races held a deep dislike for the Chinese.

"We would wash ourselves morning, afternoon and early evening. Washing always revived us. But I was always afraid of things that lived in the river and the jungle that surrounded it. I always dreaded the coming night. We headed deeper into the rural countryside keeping to the riverbank. The sounds of fighting were now behind us in the far distance but we could still see huge spirals of black smoke high up in the sky."

I wonder if the tall spirals of smoke were from the oilfields of Yenangyaung. It is difficult to gauge where Grandmother was heading.

"Far ahead we could see green hills. Sometimes we could hear dogs barking; this usually meant there was a Burmese village nearby. The thought of sleeping on the ground between the edge of the jungle and the river terrified me; we placed you between us for safety and watched the sun slowly sinking towards the horizon. Thank God you never cried much at night, the noise would have travelled far, attracting not only humans but dangerous wild animals. Despite the fact my mother always cut thorny cactus branches and placed them all around us to deter soft-footed predators, I could only sleep in snatches and kept waking my mother when I heard a strange noise. It was now April. This was the hottest time of the year in Burma, but the early mornings were always cold. We shivered; we needed more blankets."

CHAPTER 8

The Attack

HONG KONG

"The last letter I received from Jack was about a week before his regiment was moved to Kowloon *[Mainland]*. I think this was because their other position was infested with mosquitoes and many of the men were going down with malaria. Jack said he was informed that the Japs would not attack from China but from the sea, so his regiment was in a relatively safe position on the mainland. I was not to worry, he would be returning to the Shan States soon after he had been promoted to Regimental Sergeant Major on the recommendation of his Commanding Officer Colonel White. I began to put the finishing touches to our new home ready for Jack's return. There was so much to do."

New Territories, Mainland China

Two hours before nightfall on the 7th December; the Royal Scots did their best to improve their defensive positions and bring up equipment and ammunition to their open trenches. The men had still not received any food or water that day and would not do so for another twenty-four hours. Water was now in short supply both for drinking and for the thirsty Vickers machine guns.

Early on that day, led by 2nd Lieutenant Ford and Sergeant Devereux, D Company 2nd Battalion took up their positions on the Gin Drinkers' Line. Sergeant Devereux cursed some of the slower men in a language they understood for lagging behind but he knew these men were still suffering the after-effects of malaria, or were just beginning to succumb to the parasites swarming in their bloodstream. Although he had never suffered this strength sapping disease himself, he had seen strong men barely able to walk unaided within a few hours of infection.

Both Officer and Sergeant looked over the vital ground that lay before them without speaking. They could be forgiven for wondering why they had been moved by Brigadier Wallis from Hong Kong to the mainland on such short notice and why General Maltby expected them to hold this position for a vital seven days. A week, Maltby had claimed, was needed to organize Hong Kong's defences, yet months had been squandered.

On the Gin Drinkers' Line the defensive position had changed little since Lieutenant Ford and the Sergeant had first inspected the trenches a few months earlier; perhaps just a few more empty Gordon's Gin bottles had been added by the picnickers. Both men wished that sandbags, barbed wire and anti-personnel mines had been available.

Despite their misgivings, the officer and Sergeant kept their own counsel; it would not be good for the men's moral to air their views. The die was cast. The ground in front of them looked deserted. The hungry soldiers of D Company relaxed after they had settled in and stared into the approaching gloom of twilight. Perhaps the intelligence officer was correct: Japanese soldiers really were afraid of the dark. A mist was slowly beginning to rise from the lower ground ahead; it grew colder. The Sergeant posted sentries and watched the soldiers settle down in the open trenches then gave the men permission to smoke. It would be a long night. The soldiers grumbled at the delay in bringing up their rations. Porridge, cooked in water with a small sprinkle of salt, was all they had eaten for breakfast that day. The soldiers cursed the catering corps and settled down for the night wrapping themselves in their greatcoats.

General Sakai (a Francophile) was confident. He had a low opinion of the British as fighting men, they had won an empire using guns against spears; he often lectured his staff. General Sakai admired Napoleon. His Grande Armée proved unbeatable for eleven years, a record in modern warfare. It was the British Royal Navy that secured the British Empire and it had been defeated by the Imperial Nipponese Navy "The Floating Chrysanthemums." Yet General Sakai was angry; over three hundred of his fighting men were suffering the various stages of "the soldier's plague." General Sakai firmly believed the English had deliberately introduced this malady, along with opium, to China. The Chinese in turn felt it their given duty to pass on this disease to the pristine and pure fighting manhood of Dai Nippon.

To a Japanese soldier, catching this Anglo-Saxon pox was an insult to their Emperor; the punishments were more painful than the treatment. Many infected Japanese soldiers had soon learnt to keep their new acquisition a secret and with good reason. It was not the dreaded umbrella the Nipponese soldier feared, but good old fashioned beating (on the third infection they could be shot). With this in mind the infected soldiers generously shared their affliction among the many unwilling females in their massive empire; they were going to die anyway: Banzai!

Later on in Japan, venereal disease among the Japanese troops presented the POWs, including dad and his group, with a chance to earn money. The idea first germinated in the active mind of an Australian POW. The prisoners made up their own special formulas of "unctions," all guaranteed to cure the clap; these homemade unctions always had three things in common: they tasted terrible, were harmful to man and lastly had no effect on the pox whatsoever. The afflicted Nippon warrior of course, could not complain.

In General Sakai's headquarters the enemy staff officers prayed to their various Buddhas that darkness would fall soon and the usual ground mists would rise and completely mask the soldiers' final approach to their start off positions, ready for the attack the next morning.

The following day at 8am on the 8th December the Japanese attacked the Royal Scots on the Gin Drinkers' Line. First the defenders were saluted with a volley of hand grenades before the enemy engaged. The shock of the unsuspected attack must have been great. To add to the defenders troubles, their own artillery began to shell them from behind. All too quickly the Japanese infantry were in among the Scots; hand to hand fighting began. Individual struggles of life and death took place. The first attack was repulsed by the Scots.

In a short lull in the fighting, the Royal Scots tended their wounded and moved their dead, then cleared the enemy dead from the trenches. Even the experienced defenders were shocked; they had never met an enemy that was not afraid to die. The attacks continued throughout the morning.

During a pause in the fighting, Lieutenant Ford received orders from Captain Pinkerton to attack Golden Hill as Japanese troops were seen establishing themselves there. D Company was ordered to counter attack. Officer and Sergeant roused the weary men. The Sergeant's luck could not continue; he had already received a generous measure of good fortune. Despite being in the thick of the hand-to-hand fighting he was unharmed. He had killed several enemy soldiers and felt the warm turbulence of bullets, the zing of red hot shards of shrapnel and the sharp air slicing sound of a sword stroke.

The bone weary soldiers of D Company moved towards Golden Hill, urged on by their Officer and Sergeant. The men shouldered their weapons and heavy equipment and began the steep slog to the summit of Golden Hill. For many of the exhausted and hungry men this march proved too much; they were forced to crawl on all fours uphill dragging their weapons and equipment behind them. The heavy machine guns of D Company were now low on water. The spare water for these guns had been drunk by the thirsty men. The extra water was supposed to arrive with their food. Lieutenant

Ford and Sergeant Devereux led D Company to the highest point on Golden Hill.

The shelling from Hong Kong had stopped; somehow an officer of the Royal Scots contacted the British artillery and got the gunners to lengthen their range. The Royal Navy (who had ranged their guns correctly) also joined in and began to accurately land their six-inch shells in the middle of the attacking enemy. This gave the Scots a short respite. D Company cleared the enemy infantry from the top of the hill with a bayonet charge. However a counterattack from the Japanese regained their position.

As Lieutenant Ford was wounded, Sergeant Devereux led the next bayonet charge, his eyes fixed on a group of enemy soldiers pulling a mountain gun up the hill with rope. The gun had to be captured to stop it being fired at point blank range at the Scots below. The Sergeant fired his revolver into the straining group of Japanese soldiers and then felt a blow to his head. The strength in his legs vanished. His right eye now only focused on a small clump of grass that was being sprayed red with every beat of his heart. Familiar voices were now replaced by guttural martial tones. From the corner of his eye, he could see sturdy puttied bound legs stop then move on. He expected the bayonet at any moment. It did not come; proof that his severe head wound indicated he was dead or dying. As he watched his blood enrich the poor soil, he felt a deep sadness: he was dying. Afraid to close his one working eye, as it was his only link to the living world, he resisted the dark void that beckoned him to rise up and move towards painless oblivion …

Seeing that D Company was about to be overwhelmed, Captain Pinkerton gave the order for it to withdraw and return to their original positions on the Gin Drinkers' Line. The attacks on the Royal Scots continued. It became clear the enemy could not be held for seven days. The order to withdraw back to Hong Kong Island was given by Bridger Wallis. There was now a danger of the enemy outflanking them. As far as I am aware Bridger Wallis' Rajputs had not come under attack. Colonel White went out to watch the return of his tired and depleted men.

General Sakai now wished to move his headquarters nearer to Hong Kong. The young Japanese 2nd Lieutenant Nakamura was left behind to supervise the loading of the office equipment; his sword still unblooded. Everything loaded, the convoy moved off. The 2nd Lieutenant sat in the first vehicle. While passing near Golden Hill he ordered his driver to stop. "Wait here." These were the last words he spoke.

Reaching the battlefield on Golden Hill he drew his sword and walked among the dead. It was then he recognized the tall Sergeant he had been watching the evening before. He stopped and studied the man that lay at his feet and noticed he was still alive. Time was short, if he arrived late at the new headquarters his face would be slapped by his seniors. The Japanese 2nd Lieutenant lifted his treasured blade. He was nervous ...

By dawn on the 11th December most of the forward troops on the mainland had been withdrawn back to the island. Surprisingly, back on Hong Kong Island that afternoon, life went on more or less as normal. Some cinemas, restaurants etc were still busy; some troops were still drinking in the bars. One civilian couple were being served breakfast by a Chinese servant on their front veranda. Others were already on the golf course.

CHAPTER 9

Wild Dogs in the Moonlight

BURMA

"I was so happy we had a constant supply of water and could keep ourselves clean. I no longer cared it was river water. Later on, this river would produce a few nasty surprises for us. Life in the wilds of Burma was unpredictable even to the wary and watchful. I worried when we were in the water catching freshwater crabs; I always stayed in the shallows while you were happy playing with mud on the bank.

"After quenching our thirst and washing we carried on along the high riverbank; at every opportunity we would drink and wash again in the shade of overhanging trees. Unfortunately the only utensil we had that held water was a big tin-pot with a handle. Early one morning I was sitting down in the shade on the riverbank with you on my lap, when I heard a loud splash on the opposite bank. Although the sun was shining in my eyes, I could just make out that a big darkish animal had jumped into the river and was swimming towards us. My mother was in the Riverine jungle nearby collecting firewood for our morning tea. I became afraid and quickly got up. My mother had also heard the splash and rushed back. We picked up all our possessions and continued as fast as we could walk along the riverbank in case the animal was a tiger. There were no convenient trees to climb for safety. When we looked back we saw the large dark animal standing on a sandbank digging up turtle's eggs. It was a big wild boar.

"The Far East has some beautiful sunsets, yet all I worried about was the coming darkness. To hear an animal at night moving around and not see what it was, terrified me. Burma is a lush and fertile country with abundant natural and cultivated produce. Famine was unknown in this over flowing rice and fruit bowl of Asia. Almost every domesticated edible plant, whether it be fruit or vegetable, had its wild origins in the rural countryside, especially along river banks. The secret was identifying the similarity in the leaves. Yet we had to be careful. There were also many poisonous plants bearing pods and fruit.

"Burma is a gardener's paradise; a small bamboo shoot could grow four inches overnight or a buried seed germinate in a single day in the right conditions. So rich was the natural bounty of this fertile land that a Burmese man could retire at the age of thirty and as a result, large numbers of young men would become Buddhist monks. When the river widened and the banks became less steep we found clumps of Roberts' greens (another name for water spinach) growing close to the water's edge; slowly boiled with crabmeat, it made a lovely soup."

⚜

The first-time visitor to Burma who had travelled via India would quickly notice that the Burmese belonged to a totally different race of humanity than the Indians. Instead of the aquiline bone structure of dark Indo-Aryans, they were now in a country populated by easygoing, smiling Mongolians, who lounged in the shade wearing cool colourful longyis. It was the shrewder, hardworking Indians who dominated the rice and timber trade and the lucrative government jobs.

⚜

"In Burma women conducted their business while smoking thick hand-rolled cigars. Women held an equal position in society and commerce. Any serious confrontations between a man and woman resulted in the woman taking off her slippers with the intention of hitting the man.

Seeing this, the male would quickly retire; to be hit by a female's slipper in public is considered a great insult. A far greater insult was for the female to turn around and lift up her longyi to waist height baring her naked buttocks.

"We continued along the riverbank but often had to go back in the riverine jungle as the path disappeared. When in the river, I was always on the lookout for leeches. The big buffalo leeches were six inches long and as thick as a finger. Unlike the smaller leeches, their bites were very painful. Sometimes when several of these big leeches entered the throats of cattle and became swollen with blood, the animal suffocated. The strange way in which these big leeches swam towards us in the water used to frighten me. With the monsoon, thousands of smaller leeches would also appear. I was told never place my mouth directly into a river or stream or drink from my hands for a species of very small leech could enter the mouth and live and develop in the nasal passages."

🪷

Leeches have no eyes but home in on a victim's exhaled carbon dioxide like blind and legless aliens. A lifeless looking dry belt, after heavy rain, suddenly becomes alive with leeches. Young Japanese soldiers in Tada u loved to torture leeches, scorpions and large spiders in their leisure time; placing them in a fire ants nest after antagonising the ants. Forcing spider to fight spider or scorpion v spider was another favourite. They encouraged us young children and the older boys to catch and bring them more victims. Ironically these leeches were to get their revenge on these young teenage Japanese soldiers who had cheerfully marched up from Thailand pulling their guns. They would soon be taking part in the battles of Imphal and Kohima. On their retreat from India during the monsoon they lay weak and starving on the slippery rain lashed jungle tracks, covered in leeches, begging their passing comrades to shoot them.

🪷

"After our thirst was quenched our hunger returned. As the sun was slowly sinking in the west, I could only think of one thing. Where were we going to sleep that night? I was terrified of walking in the dark.

Fortunately, just as the sun was setting in the darkening skyline, we saw the silhouette of a flimsily, dilapidated fisherman's hut made from bamboo and palm leaves. Even from a distance the hut looked unstable. We climbed up into it on a rickety bamboo ladder. The structure could just about take our weight but only if we kept to the back of the hut. Every time we moved the hut lurched to one side and creaked but I was so grateful to be off the ground.

"These huts are used during the fishing season *[monsoon]* when the rivers are in flood and big fish enter the deep water. While the men fished with long poles and nets, the women cleaned and salted the fish drying them on bamboo racks. In the hot Burmese sun, salted fish dries in a matter of hours. We all loved a species of river fish known as 'butter-fish' because the flesh was white and it carried few bones; butter in Burma is white in colour. This fish made excellent Burmese curry.

"The following morning, we were up early as the hut seemed about to collapse. We continued travelling along the riverbank collecting edible plants and digging for tubers which we kept for our main evening meal. Every now and then your grandmother checked the shallows for tiny fish fry; she was an expert at catching these small fish using the hem of her dress. In a pan coated in oil, these small fry would cook themselves if left in the hot sun. When my mother wanted to light a fire in the evening, she poured some river water on the hard ground and dug a small pit in the earth with the big Burmese dah. Then she would build the sides up with the damp earth she had dug out; this would hide most of the flames at night from anyone passing and increase the heat. We used the deep Indian metal pot that my mother had picked up for all our cooking. My mother was a wonderful cook.

"Evening came but we were not so lucky in finding a place to sleep and had to spend the night on a ledge created by the collapse of the riverbank – but at least we were hidden from view. Mother cut some cactus fronds and placed them in front of our sleeping place for protection. After cooking our meal we settled down on the hard ground wrapped in blankets. With our backs to the riverbank we listened to the jackals calling and watched the last of the sun's rays slowly sinking behind the trees. Soon it was totally dark. We could hear loud splashes in the river; Mother said it was probably large catfish.

"That night I didn't sleep a wink, in the far distant hills we could hear wild elephants trumpeting. We spoke in whispers. I spent most of the night looking up at the starry constellations. You were wrapped in my woollen shawl. We always waited for the sun to warm us before getting up. After walking several miles we came across another fisherman's hut which was strongly built and stable. We could move around in it without fear of it collapsing and decided to stay for a few days to rest. We were so tired having gone without a good night's sleep since we left Taunggyi.

"Here the river was very shallow and full of small fish; my mother began catching them immediately. She used to kneel very still in the shallows with her back to the sun and a few grains of cooked rice in the hem of her dress. The little fish were attracted by the food and sheltered in her shadow. Slowly she would lift the hem of her dress and catch them.

"In the cool of the morning and late afternoon we foraged for food along the river bank. My mother recognised the leaves of a tuber called per-sin-zar-ou; we knew them as sweet water potatoes. The shrivelled leaves indicated that the fat sweet tubers were hidden underground. The only river turtle's nests we came across were out of reach to us in the middle of the river on a sandbank. They had already been found and dug up by monitor lizards or wild pigs. I was terrified of big monitor lizards, which hissed aggressively if you approached them.

"The next morning we were woken up by the sound of dogs fighting. Looking through the gaps in the fisherman's hut, we saw a large pack of dogs drinking from the river. They looked feral. As hungry as we were we waited for the dogs to move on before leaving the hut to forage. That afternoon my mother lit a fire and cooked a meal of small fish and gram [chickpeas]. We were about to eat when the pack of dogs suddenly reappeared and watched us – they would not go away despite us swearing at them in Burmese. Instead the dogs became bolder and growled when we threw sticks at them. We had no choice but to take our food up the ladder and into the hut where you were fast asleep. Some of the dogs tried to follow unsuccessfully. The dogs left just before darkness fell. My Mother said dogs did not like to be in the jungle at night because of leopards. From then on we were always watchful in case the dogs returned; although we could hear them barking in the distance, they did not come back to the hut again. We had not seen the last of this pack of feral dogs.

"Dogs had a symbiotic relationship with the villagers; they were the sanitary inspectors and gave good warning of strangers, predators or snakes entering or approaching the village. In return they were allowed shelter under the huts. Only occasionally were they fed scraps of offal. Venomous snakes killed in the village were also given to them. The Burmese, a very superstitious race, believed that village dogs also gave warning of evil spirits. In most cases when the village dogs barked at night hysterically, it was probably a leopard or a snake and not an evil spirit. It is said that Indian cat-burglars often covered their bodies with leopard fat to frighten off dogs. Like the Japanese, the Burmese never touched dogs and considered them unhygienic. Dog meat however was greatly prized by the Chinese, Vietnamese and Koreans. They preferred it to beef. This was another reason the Japanese and the Burmese looked down on the conscripted Korean soldiers in the Japanese army.

"When the retreating Chinese Army appeared and began shooting the village dogs for food; a few of them escaped into the jungle. The starving Chinese soldiers were quickly followed by the Japanese (not dog lovers) who always took great pleasure in shooting or bayoneting the village pi-dogs. Quick to learn, these dogs left the villages and formed large packs that hunted the escaped livestock also roaming the countryside at this time. These dogs like the water buffalo, were a potential danger to Europeans.

"This was the dry season and the river was shallow, but to be near any running water was a blessing. We now looked like down-and-outs – raga-muffins, our clothes were tattered and worn and our footwear would soon be useless. The money we had was to buy food, not clothes.

"Your grandmother and I used to wade out to about one or two feet of clear water to bathe, but only where we could see the sandy bottom. I was always afraid of crocodiles and pythons that lurked in the shallows of rivers and jungle pools."

"Have you ever seen a crocodile or a python in the wild, Mum?" I would sometimes ask out of interest.

۞

"'No, only at Rangoon zoo, but my brothers used to shoot pythons on the Irrawaddy. Large pythons were a danger to their retrieving dogs. My brothers always carried their rifles with them, even on picnics.'

"One morning while walking along the riverbank searching for drift wood, I saw ahead of me on a sandbank what looked like a long piece of coloured material flapping in the breeze. As I got nearer, I found it was the skin of a very large python. Pythons, it is said, are especially dangerous after shedding their skin. I quickly ran back to the hut in case the snake was still in the vicinity."

۞

Strangely Mother was not fazed by big E-type spiders (mygalomorph). These large arachnids would suddenly blossom aggressively out of their burrows if a foot accidentally touched an invisible trip line at the entrance. They would then raise their thick forelegs and present their long fangs in threat. Mother would pin the large arachnid down from behind with a stick, folding one leg from either side of its thorax and holding them in her fingers, then quickly throw it into the bushes. In Johore Baru after the war, when one found its way into the house, Mum would throw it out of the window, sometimes she had hardly turned her back when the determined arachnid would climb back up again, and glare at her from the window sill.

"Kill it, Mum – kill it, Mum!" I would scream – jumping up and down – like a demented goblin. I still don't do large spiders.

"No, son," she would say softly with a smile, "poor thing." She would then repeat the processes despite the fact that these spiders, after being molested, are very willing to bite. These large spiders are a favourite food source of the Khmer people.

۞

"We were fortunate to find different edible plants and crops on the riverbank during our foraging trips including peanuts which we had to dig up. Despite the variety of vegetables that we foraged, I still craved meat and used to dream of all the different meat dishes we used to have every night at home. Savoy grill for breakfast, lunch at one, Tiffin at four and dinner at nine. Most of these mealtimes include meat in the form of pork, lamb cutlets, chicken, partridge, wild duck, snipe and beef. How I now regretted leaving some of that delicious food on my plate.

"There were some large crabs in the river but they were too quick for us and scuttled into deep murky water where we were afraid to follow. We stopped at this fisherman's hut for several days bathing in the morning and in the afternoon before eating what we had found. As food was now getting difficult to find in this area we were forced to move on. We continued our journey along the riverbank and came to a very large area of tall elephant grass. My mother said it would be too dangerous to follow the path through it. We were forced to make a detour around the edge and after a while found ourselves back in scrub jungle near a village that had been destroyed by the Chinese Army. There was a strange smell that hung over this village and several burnt bodies lay by the water well. We moved on quickly fearing that the well may have been contaminated by the Chinese.

"Continuing, we ended up in old paddy fields and walked along the bunds that divided them. The earth was cracked and dry and difficult to walk over in our worn out shoes. After walking about an hour, we could see in the far distance a cattle-patti *[cattle station]* and hoped to reach it before nightfall. Unfortunately night fell quickly and we had no option but to stop and wait for the dark hour to pass. My mother and I sat back to back on the waterproof ground sheet while covering ourselves with the two blankets. You were always tired after a long day and soon went to sleep in my lap.

"When the moon came up we could see just as clearly as daylight, you could read a book in strong moonlight. The river below us looked like a silver ribbon. When the moon rose higher we began to walk to the cattle-patti, it was now lovely and cool. For some reason something made me turn around; silently following us was the large pack of dogs.

We tried to frighten them away but they would not leave; when we stopped they stopped. Suddenly we heard guttural voices. Without realizing it, we were now near the bullock track again, which must have run parallel to the river. We stood still and waited. The pack of dogs suddenly disappeared.

"Thank God you were fast asleep in the sling I had made for you on my back. We could see lights flashing. The only people who would move at night were Japanese soldiers. For a moment we stood frozen till the voices faded in the distance. Turning, we began heading back towards the river. After some time we came to a high bund; climbing over it we sat down and fell asleep listening to the 'did you do it' birds [plovers]."

🪷

Mum used to tell me these birds slept on their backs with their legs in the air – to stop the sky falling on them.

🪷

"The following morning, we left early as we were still near the bullock track. We reached the riverbank beyond the elephant grass and waded into the river for a quick wash but moved on as there was no tree cover on our side of the bank.

"Occasionally we saw people in the distance on the far bank of the river and one day came across fresh cloven hoof footprints in the sand made by Japanese soldiers. They had forded the river some time earlier that morning. Thank God they didn't follow the riverbank!

"We travelled along the river without incident for several days, sleeping in places that offered cover and shade. Then one day while washing and collecting water to drink, several indistinguishable shapes floated passed in the water. After closer scrutiny my mother exclaimed 'My God, Kate – they are human bodies! Covered in tiger prawns – they're eating them!' These bodies had limbs missing. It was impossible to know their nationality. I felt sick to my stomach to think that we had been drinking and washing in water that had flowed over dead bodies. I never ate tiger prawns again.

"Continuing cautiously along the bank, we came upon several more bodies in the river. Then we saw smoke on the horizon. Mother said we should not follow the river anymore.

"That night we slept under lantana bushes away from the river, but were forced back to the river to get water the following morning. The dead bodies had disappeared. We boiled the water. It still tasted terrible.

"My mother wanted to bypass what looked like a village ahead, but the thought of finding pure clean water made me beg her to seek out a well. Cautiously approaching through the scrub, to our surprise we came across large Godowns (warehouses) and a row of bungalows. We later found out this small town was called Yu. It was a hive of activity: looting! Burmese villagers, mostly women and children, were looting the warehouses near the river. My mother greeted them politely in rural Burmese but apart from some quick looks in our direction they did not trouble us. Our priority was to find a well, which we soon located behind the row of small brick bungalows. It was so nice to drink clean fresh water again. As usual all the bungalows had been picked bare, all doors and windows had been taken away. We entered one of the bungalows and watched as many loaded bullock carts left Yu while empty bullock carts were arriving. My mother called out in Burmese to an old woman walking behind a bullock cart. 'What is happening, wise grandmother?'

"'The Chinese merchants have run away,' the old woman answered, 'they set fire to the buildings – we put the fires out. We are now helping ourselves.' After a quick rest we began looking behind the dwellings that once belonged to the Chinese workers. Inside each of these bungalows we found a traditional mud and brick fireplace. A heavy smell of Chinese incense and aniseed hung in the air. Every back garden contained neat lines of vegetables. My mother insisted we thoroughly wash these vegetables as they would be infected with human liver fluke eggs. Most Chinese of that time were infected with liver flukes because they used human manure. The Chinese are a clean race, but their habit of eating partially cooked vegetables put them at risk of infection. My mother picked one of the better small bungalows and we settled in, we were so tired. The Burmese villagers were far too busy helping themselves from the Chinese Godowns to worry about us.

"After resting I went poking around and found the best find of all, an old pram. For some reason the pram was full of earth. I quickly cleaned it out, hoping there was nothing nasty buried in it. This wonderful find could carry you and our few possessions. The pram was old, deep and had hard tyres that squeaked. Your grandmother was delighted and put cooking oil on the wheels to stop them squeaking, then headed towards the warehouses. I stayed behind and looked after you.

"After a while I became concerned at my mother's long absence, we could not survive without her! My mother soon reappeared, red-faced and sweating. The pram was full to the brim with small bags of rice that had red Chinese characters written on them.

"'I am going back' said my mother 'we have to get all we can – there is so much left – we will have to hide everything.'

"'I want to come – I am afraid waiting here,' I told my mother. We all set off to join the other freeloaders; I felt so guilty that we were stealing. On reaching the warehouses I saw Burmese of all ages enjoying this family day out of looting from an old enemy."

๕๒

It was here where one of my first distant memories kicks in. There was a large pile of white sugar in the open. I joined all the other young Burmese children trying to run up this pile of shifting sweetness. We naked children stopped occasionally to bend down and lick the sugar.

๕๒

"Tins of Lyle's golden syrup were scattered everywhere. The picture of the dead lion surrounded by bees always fascinated you: 'Out of the strong came forth sweetness' was the legend around the picture. I always had to convince you that the dead lion was surrounded by bees and not flies. That picture, which looks exactly the same today, and the picture on the gripe water bottle depicting a baby holding a snake were your only storybooks. This syrup is one of the secret weapons of Chinese cookery even now. For some reason the Burmese looters were ignoring this product as a food stuff or sweetener; they all preferred the many sacks of jaggery (lumps of brown sugar) stored in the warehouses. They had found another practical use for Golden Syrup; it was great for lubricating the wheels on their bullock carts, as grease was in short supply. We took at least half a dozen tins. My mother could not resist loading up another three small sacks of good quality rice.

"On several occasions some of the women looters asked my mother what some of the labels said in English, or why she was taking them. She pretended not to know saying only that she liked the colourful labels.

"Free running salt was a valuable commodity in rural Burma at that time and my mother took several small bags. Salt usually came in big lumps or blocks and you had to break it with mortar and pestle. We also took a big tin of cooking oil and several small bags of dried shrimp. Dried shrimp can be used in many ways, is a good sauce of protein and lasts for months. Balachaung (a relish) and henjo (vegetable stew) were a favourite of the Japanese front line troops. The Japanese army issued dried shrimp and dried eels (I did not like dried eels – they were slimy) as hard rations, together with a 24lb bag of rice which they had to carry themselves."

🪷

Before the invasion of Burma, Japanese agents made a precise study of wild food in the country with the help of Burmese villagers as their soldiers were expected to live off the land.

🪷

"We hid most of our loot in a large empty warehouse nearby under piles of empty gunny sacks and only kept enough food for our daily needs. We did not wish to be caught stealing especially by the Japanese who had written in their leaflets that looting was forbidden. When I think about it we were in such a dangerous position staying there.

"Though exhausted, Mother cooked a large evening meal. The only baby food left was a tin of powdered milk and gripe water. Most of the other baby food was left behind at the train station. My mother and I had to resort to the Burmese way of feeding you; chewing the food before giving it to you. You got used to this type of feeding and would stand in line waiting to be fed when other mothers were feeding their own children. The Burmese thought this most amusing and used to feed you.

"Even though we now had food and a roof over our heads we could hardly consider ourselves safe even in the loosest terms. We were constantly looking over shoulders. The following day all the warehouses were deserted as people had gone back to their villages. We began to feel uneasy so kept a low profile talking in whispers. We expected the Japanese or the Chinese soldiers to arrive at any moment. Even without these physical dangers, any deserted town will always have its own ghosts. The bungalow only offered protection from the elements.

"As night approached my mother and I slept uneasily; we always felt vulnerable. We decided if we had to leave quickly, we would escape into the thick surrounding scrub jungle behind the bungalows with just our basic possessions."

CHAPTER 10

Sham Shui Po POW Camp

HONG KONG

By Christmas day isolated groups of soldiers, including Tam and Willie, were still holding out or hiding in the more remote parts of the island. Hong Kong was unusually quiet. Normally all the church bells would be ringing and the sound of Christmas carols would be drifting on the pleasant South China Sea breeze. Now the sounds of breaking glass replaced the sound of carols as bottles of alcohol were being smashed; this was the Lotus eaters' last gesture of defiance, mourning the lost halcyon days. Alcohol was the second most common spirit on the island after petrol.

The sounds of smashing bottles was often punctuated by the drunken singing of Cockney voices from the Middlesex Regiment or the just as distinctive Glaswegian or Edinburgh accents of the Royal Scots. Champagne bottles were being rolled down slopes in the streets and exploded like grenades when the gas inside the bottle expanded. The smell of gin and whisky and cordite dominated. Not all parts of Hong Kong had been touched by the fighting. Even before the fighting had ended several of the bars were still open, their Chinese owners long departed; free drinks were now being served by soldiers who were drunk themselves.

Some of the long term British inhabitants of the island were surprised to notice that many Japanese professionals who where once resident came back in uniform as officers and grinned happily at their former clients.

It may be appropriate to mention at this time, that many of the Indian defenders who fought bravely throughout the Hong Kong, Malayan, Singapore and Burma retreats, after capture were given the opportunity to join the Japanese cause. The alternative was to be used for live bayonet practice. Many did join the Japanese and were shipped to Singapore and Burma. Others refused to betray their salt and paid the price with a painful and traumatic death.

British prisoners, including many Royal Scots who were out collecting Japanese dead, observed a line of Sikh prisoners, hands tied behind their backs, enter a depression behind St Stevens College where they were about to be used for live bayonet practice. Japanese soldiers with fixed bayonets stood in front of each prisoner. An order was shouted and each Japanese soldier slashed at the prisoners' thighs to cause them to fall over. The British prisoners watched horrified as a deadly game of cat and mouse began as the bound prisoner by instinct desperately tried to protect his vital organs from the bayonet thrusts. This atrocity haunted them for the rest of their lives.

On the mainland, Sham Shui Po Prisoner of War Camp awaited the British troops. This camp was a POW Camp in name only. The barbed wire fences would be erected by the prisoners later. Amazingly, it seems that the Japanese found supplies of barbed wire stored on the mainland; barbed wire that was once desperately needed by the defenders of the Gin Drinkers' Line.

By now Sergeant Devereux was in Sham Shui Po POW Camp although he was not aware of his precise movements due to long periods of unconsciousness. There were only a few iron beds in the medical area of the camp; the Sergeant was lucky to be on one of these. Most of the badly wounded were placed on the concrete floor. Food in the camp was adequate for the first few days. Some prisoners had time to collect tinned food before entering camp. There were also still many warehouses in Kowloon, albeit damaged; the more able prisoners helped themselves while the guards were still celebrating their victory. At the beginning the Medical Staff were not overwhelmed by the number of wounded patients. This would soon change.

Back on the island hundreds of disarmed Allied and British soldiers were being marched into captivity back to the mainland. Many prisoners had not eaten or slept for days and were physically spent. Friends helped each other and the wounded. Many prisoners still had their hands tied with telegraph wire; those who fell on the march were quickly bayoneted by the guards. Their screams spurred the other exhausted prisoners onwards.

☙

"I am almost sure that Jack was in the POW camp on the mainland after his capture. The wounded were being treated by military doctors and orderlies who were mostly volunteers. The wounded here were lucky; small amounts of drugs were still available. However there was no cat-gut to stitch Jack's wounds and so cotton thread was used again instead. Many of these men with stomach wounds died as complicated operations could not be carried out. The poor men who had been bayoneted in the stomachs soon had another serious problem: ants. Tiny ants were crawling under the soldiers' bandages and biting them."

☙

I wonder if these tiny ants were "Pharaohs Ants" brought to Hong Kong from the holy land by the Royal Scots. These miniature carnivorous ants caused problems in UK hospitals during the 1970s. Now overcrowded, Sham Shui Po camp was rife with disease; diphtheria and dysentery began spreading throughout the prisoners. Within days strong healthy men looked like walking corpses. Some prisoners quickly gave up hope when they found out that the Japanese Navy now ruled the Pacific. Perhaps they had heard of the sinking of the *Prince of Wales* and the *Repulse*, and the attack on Pearl Harbour.

Without hope of immediate rescue by the navy, the mind and the body of the weaker men withered.

There was also the cultural shock of being under the complete control of a brutal Asiatic Army they could not identify with. Many died. Others waited in vain for rescue by the American equipped Army of Chiang Kai-shek or the communists' army.

That night Tam and Willie (still in Hong Kong) decided to escape, and made their way to the harbour leaving their weapons behind. Tam, the non swimmer, had second thoughts about entering the water in the dark. Both men were so drunk they could barely walk. An argument ensued and they came to blows just as a Japanese patrol spotted them. After having their faces slapped, they were ordered to continue fighting each other, which they did willingly to the delight of the Japanese soldiers. Japanese soldiers found inebriation amusing. They were then given lessons on how to bow to their captors correctly and had their faces slapped again for good measure. The two friends ended up in Sham Shui Po POW camp and soon found themselves looking after soldiers who had suffered minor wounds caused by the small Japanese fragmentation grenades. By the time they met up with Sergeant Devereux he was able to walk around the barracks. Food was now becoming scarce. Tam and Willie were able to join the burial parties that left the camp under guard. The Japanese cremated their dead first with much ceremony. These outings for the fit prisoners were a chance to steal food and other useful items. As the perimeter fence was not completed around the camp, many prisoners began to sneak out and visit their Chinese girlfriends who lived nearby in Kowloon.

❧

"To Jack's surprise, the Jap Sergeant who had first captured him occasionally came into the camp and would inspect his wounds, showing great surprise that he was still alive. At the end of each visit he received a packet of Players cigarettes. With much sign language and a few words of English, the Japanese Sergeant gave his name as Yoshida and conveyed that his Regiment was being posted to Australia, which had already fallen.

"Jack told me that he dreaded the re-dressing of his wounds because it was extremely painful, especially the removal of the old dressings that had been pushed deep into his head and neck. Although he was hungry, the act of chewing was agony; he constantly heard and felt the torn muscles and sinews in his head making strange noises. After eating he could taste blood in his mouth. The entrance wound of the bullet in his temple had almost healed but the exit wound was still weeping."

⚜

By August 1942 nearly 200 prisoners had died of disease or of their wounds; others had just given up the struggle when no salvation was in sight. Then came another shock; over 600 prisoners were to be shipped to Japan. These men were handpicked by the Japanese and classed as "trouble makers." The *Shi Maru* left Hong Kong in early September and reached Japan safely, loaded with a full cargo of troublemakers. It seemed that these prisoners had more than enough room below decks to sleep in and were often allowed on deck. The Japs now wanted another 2000 fit men for work in Japan. These prisoners would not be so lucky. Selecting fit men for Japan was a most difficult task for the British Officers, as there were no fit men as such. The officers in command refused to carry this out and the Japanese were forced to make the selections themselves.

The prisoners selected were told by a Japanese interpreter, 2nd Lieutenant Wada "You are going to a wonderful place, the beautiful cherry blossom islands of Dai Nippon where you will be treated well." Many men were eager to leave.

The Sergeant was one of the prisoners selected. One thing I know, Dad's head wounds were soon to be re-infected by maggots either on the way from Sham Shui Po POW camp to the *Lisbon Maru*, or in the No 2 hold of the ship while waiting in harbour. Perhaps the flies in Hong Kong were also eager to see the beautiful islands of Dai Nippon.

Many miles to the South of Hong Kong, the *Lisbon Maru*'s sleek nemesis, the American submarine *Grouper*, was quietly slipping her moorings at Pearl Harbour for another war patrol. This would be her second war patrol under a new and more aggressive young commander.

CHAPTER 11

A Ghost Town

BURMA

"When the looters left, a shroud of suspense and silence descended on Yu. It made us feel very uneasy and we began to fear the next arrivals; would it be the Chinese Army? If the bodies we had seen in the river were the Chinese merchants and workers, reprisals would be based on an eye for an eye. Then there was the Japanese who had warned against looting. My mother knew that it was a risk to stay but we had all that we needed at Yu, a roof over our heads and clean fresh well water."

The Chinese Army were extremely protective of the lease lend equipment and stores, even denying it to their British and American allies. Chinese soldiers were still filtering through Burma into China and India. The Japanese were by now in most of the towns and the cities, counting the spoils of their victory. The loot and equipment the enemy had acquired greatly helped them extend the war. Much of the stores captured in their conquests helped sustain their troops in the Pacific for a year. They were exhausted; they had constantly marched and fought battles across southeast Asia without respite. The victors got drunk on their own heady hubris of success and our Johnny Walker. They had conquered vast territories across three time zones in a matter of weeks. They had outfought and outmanoeuvred the Americans, British and the Dutch. Dai Nippon now ruled Southeast Asia, the surrounding oceans, seas and the skies above. With the fighting now over, the Japanese would soon introduce their strict laws; punishment would be immediate.

❧

"My mother feared that if we overstayed our welcome at Yu we could also become victims of Dacoits. This situation would continue until the Japanese took full control of Burma. It may come as a surprise to many that when the Japanese Army controlled Burma, criminal activity was almost eradicated. Fear of Japanese physical reprisals and immediate justice made Burmese Dacoits and criminals suspend operations. The reasons for this, Jack told me after the war, was the high regard the Japanese have for conformity, order and respect in their society. Anti-social behaviour of any kind brought dishonour to the whole family; they became pariahs. Immediate justice also applied to the behaviour of their own soldiers. The Japanese have always been a law-abiding race living in such close proximity to each other in their overpopulated islands. Harmony and honesty is paramount in their culture.

"We found out in Tada u, that once a Burmese Dacoit was caught by the Japanese, he was forced under torture by the Kempeitai to name his village and his relatives. The poor man would then be taken back there and hung from a tree by a metal hook inserted under his jaw. Two Japanese guards would be left behind to make sure he was not helped in any way by relatives or other villagers. He took days to die. His desiccated dead body would have to remain hanging in the tree as a lesson to all. How terrible it must have been for families to watch these men slowly die and not be able to help.

"I never knew what was going on in my mother's mind; I just left everything to her. I seldom knew what day of the month it was. Yu became a ghost town; my mother and I flitted from shadow to shadow of the ruined buildings and spoke in whispers. The water wells were still sweet but low. The Burmese would never think of contaminating any well with dead bodies; contaminating one well meant ruining the whole conduit of underground water.

"To cook our meals, my mother lit fires with the driest tinder so as not make smoke. We spent much of the day watching the dusty road that entered and left Yu; we were always ready to escape into the scrub jungle behind the bungalows. My mother had found out from the looters that there was a village about two miles away that held a market. She had decided to change our identity by dressing like Burmese but this would use up all the spare money we had for emergencies. Next day after hiding our personal possessions in the scrub jungle behind the bungalows, we walked in the direction of the village and soon began following a well-worn path.

"After a long walk we reached the village and market. Some kind of celebration was going on. There were musicians and dancers. But the main attraction was the beautiful young female snake charmer; a member of a religious sect that worshipped the giant hamadryad [king cobra].

"Every year certain young virgin females were chosen to go out into the jungle alone to capture a large hamadryad. They had to do this without harming the reptile. When they had finished a display with the snake and earned their sect money, they then had to release the snake back into the jungle, in the exact place they had found it. If the snake was harmed in any way they would lose their sacred protection and be bitten. There was no anti-venom for the bite of the hamadryad at that time."

⚜

I do not remember this particular event, but I have seen these beautiful snake charmers at work when they were invited to Tada u, where we were finally interned. This act was a favourite with the Japanese officers and their young soldiers, many of whom had never seen a dangerous snake. First the sounds of cymbals, lutes and drums. Two men then carry out the tall basket; knocking the lid off with a stick, they quickly retire. Immediately the large head of the hamadryad would appear.

Sixteen feet of graceful snake spills out of the basket like quicksilver; its first instinct is to attack the audience only to find its path blocked by the beautiful snake charmer. She dances gracefully and soon captures the snake's sole attention while avoiding its powerful strikes. Every miss causes the hamadryad to hit the ground with its nose; the snake soon tires and becomes reluctant to strike. Picking her moment perfectly, the girl kisses the king cobra on its head.

❧

"The village was full of small Japanese flags. My mother told me to keep my mouth shut as my Burmese was poor. She said she would tell anyone who asked that I was a little simple and didn't know the father of my child. I did not like this one bit, especially when they all stared at me. I told my mother that I had no intension of acting like a mad woman and chewing grass. 'Just keep your mouth shut' was all she said.

"We bought two cheap Burmese longyis and white cotton blouses and a greased paper Burmese parasol. We did not have enough money for slippers. With the little money left over we bought snacks from the stall holders. You loved the sweet orange fungus that grew inside old coconuts. We were now destitute. The villagers told my mother that the Burmese National Army was responsible for this area until the Japanese took over. This area would come under the Japanese administration at Meiktila. The local BNA was still busy following up the British retreat. On the way back to Yu, we changed into Burmese dress and threw our old ragged clothes away.

"Arriving back at Yu we were both surprised and frightened to find a pack of dogs sheltering underneath one of the warehouses in front of our bungalow. As if intimidated by the emptiness, they remained silent. These canines may have been the same pack that had followed us some days before. The following day we noticed the dogs leaving silently at midday only to return a few hours later with distended stomachs. My mother was convinced these dogs were feeding on dead humans somewhere. At night they completely disappeared into the deep recesses of their shelters. Sometimes they barked at night, which terrified us. Your grandmother said they had probably smelt a leopard. Her wisdom was soon confirmed when we wandered further afield to collect sweet tamarind pods. We noticed the half eaten carcass of a dog wedged high up in the fork of a tree. I began to feel nervous at nights; we had no doors or windows to protect us.

"One night my mother and I heard angry voices in the distance. We were terrified and could not go back to sleep. We waited until sunrise and collected all our possessions ready to escape into the scrub jungle behind the bungalows. My mother went out to investigate. She saw various types of expensive clothing scattered on the ground outside between the houses. She came in and said that there were people in one of the bungalows further down the road. 'We must leave as soon as we can' she said in whispered tones. We all remained silent; by now you seemed to sense our fear.

"Then we heard voices again – European female voices! Peeping out of the window I saw two girls arguing and immediately recognized them as two of the De Souza girls from Rangoon. They had moved to Rangoon from Moulmein but their home was in Portuguese Marco. I used to play tennis with Maria De Souza in Maymyo (a place people went in the hot months). The De Souzas were a rich Portuguese family. I was so happy to see them but at first they did not recognize me.

"The De Souzas had left Rangoon in good time, just before the bombing began. Their father had stayed behind to wait for his brother who was up country trading. The family set off in a large convoy of vehicles. Like most rich people with plenty of servants to cater for their needs they took with them few vital necessities but concentrated instead on their valuable possessions. A few mile stones out of Rangoon they were attacked by Burmese. Their Chinese servants vanished or were killed. But these robbers were in a hurry; Rangoon was there for the taking and the Japanese had not yet arrived. Leaving the main road, the De Souzas were fired on by the BNA, one of their relatives was killed and their youngest brother wounded. He soon died and had to be buried in the jungle later; his shallow grave was unmarked and would remain unknown despite much searching after the war. The remaining family of six comprised their mother, her sister and two other female relatives had walked to Yu. Their father and uncle would catch up later they said, with everything they would need. With Portuguese passports the De Souzas did not have reason to fear the Japanese. Portugal was neutral. It was the Burmese they feared.

"By the time the De Souzas reached Yu on foot they were exhausted and starving. They were expecting to be met by their Chinese employees at a crossroads. The Chinese were not there. Worn out, they fell asleep in the jungle. They finally stumbled into Yu to find shelter in the empty houses. That afternoon the De Souzas moved into the next bungalow and began cleaning it up; my mother did all the cooking, they collected the wood. The neat Chinese vegetable gardens were now almost bare due to the attention of the wild boars. Within days the vegetable gardens would be reduced to piles of disturbed earth. My mother felt that the De Souza family had some business connections at Yu and the goods in the warehouses. We did not tell them about the bodies in the river.

"I was breastfeeding you one morning sitting on the floor while the De Souzas slept next door. My mother was in the back garden digging for ginger, when suddenly I saw movement at the open doorstep and the head of a big lizard appeared. I banged the floor to frighten the reptile away; the lizard promptly rose up and spread a hood: it was a cobra! I screamed to frighten the cobra away, my scream alerted my mother who quickly approached the snake from behind and killed it with her dah. It was a very big snake. I said that I was not spending another night here, as the mate of the snake she had just killed would come looking for revenge. My mother told me not to be so stupid and that this was a myth. You were fascinated by the still wriggling reptile and danced around it like an excited imp."

Mother would often emphasize:

"It was only feet away – if I had not screamed the cobra would have attacked us."

John "Jack" Devereux as a young man. The message written on the
photograph reads "All Love Ever, Jack x".

LEFT: Brian with his grandmother, Harriet, in Taunggyi in 1940.

BELOW: Cyril Talbot who was sheltered by a Shan tribe during the war. He married the headman's daughter and became a schoolmaster after the war. Sitting with him are his wife and many children.

ABOVE: Riding in the
Welsh mountains.

RIGHT: Brian's mother,
Kathleen – "Kate" –
aged 18.

ABOVE: The Japanese Army crossing the border between mainland China and the British colony of Hong Kong, 1941.

OPPOSITE: Japanese artillery firing at Hong Kong, 1941.

BELOW: Japanese troops assault Tsim Sha Tsui Station, 1941.

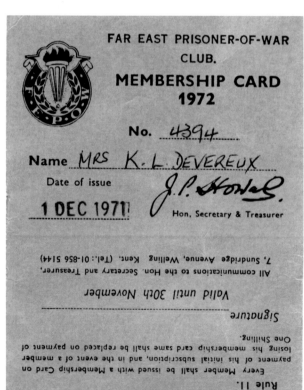

FAR EAST PRISONER-OF-WAR CLUB.

MEMBERSHIP CARD 1972

No. 4394

Name MRS K. L. DEVEREUX

Date of issue

1 DEC 1971

J. P. Howell.

Hon, Secretary & Treasurer

This card must be produced at all
Club functions upon request

Rule 11.
Every Member shall be issued with a Membership Card on payment of his initial subscription, and in the event of a member losing his membership card same shall be replaced on payment of One Shilling.

Signature

Valid until 30th November

All communications to the Hon. Secretary and Treasurer,
7, Sundridge Avenue, Welling, Kent, (Tel.: 01-856 5144)

Public Health 20 S   FORM C.

RETURN OF BIRTH.

No.62

Name of circle..............................Taungbaing

Name of village tract or town ....Maternity Home

Date of birth..............................7th April 1940.

Name of child.............................. Brian John Devereux

Sex of child......... ,....................Male

Whether born alive or dead.................Alive

Name of father.............................Mr. Deverettex

Name of mother.............................Mrs. K. Deverenex

Race or nationality of father.............. European.

Religion of parents........................Roman Catholic

Occupation or status of parents............Soldier

Ward or village at which birth occured......Maternity Home
   (enter street and house No. also)
Ordinary place of residence of parents.....Taungbaing circle,
                                                    Taunggyi.
Serial No. as entered in Birth Register (16S)- 113

Date... 7th April 1940.

Name of informant.........................

Sd/- Mg Lwe

Signature of Registrar.

....
"True Copy"

Secretary.
Town Committee
Taunggyi.

Kate and Jack with their first grandchild and Glenis in Uxbridge, London.

Hong Kong in the 1950s, after the Japanese occupation had ended and the territory returned to the British Royal Navy.

Harriet. Without her fortitude and determination, the family's fate would have been very different.

Mother would never believe that all snakes were deaf to airborne sounds and only felt ground vibrations; perhaps it would have spoilt her story. Venomous snakes should always be decapitated; many people have lost their lives by closely inspecting a supposedly dead snake. I am sure I remember this event, or perhaps it was placed in my mind by the constant repetition over a fifty-year period by my dear mother.

☙

"We gave the De Souzas bags of rice and other items of food. They were so grateful. In return they gave us a very large amount of Burmese rupees in paper money. They also gave my mother some pure silver Maria Teresa dollars which are accepted worldwide. The Burmese rupee (printed by the British) remained the most popular currency throughout the occupation, despite the worthless Japanese paper money (known as 'banana money') that was later in circulation. Most of the money carried by the De Souzas was new and of high denominations; my mother advised them not to flaunt new notes and to age the money by rubbing it in dirty water, then change it as soon as possible for lower denomination notes. Whether they took this advice later on is hard to say, but more tragedy awaited this rich and naïve family. Only three out of the remaining eight members of their family were to survive the war. We were to meet up with them at Tada u but only Maria would ever leave their single room to visit us.

"The De Souzas had so much silk clothing in their possession that they decided to leave much of it behind on their next leg of their journey. I think they hoped to go to Moulmein and catch a boat to Macao which was a Portuguese colony accepted and respected by the Japanese. But first they intended to wait for their father and uncle who would soon catch them up with more transport and servants. No trace of their father or uncle was ever found after the war."

☙

CHAPTER 12

The *Lisbon Maru*

SOUTH CHINA SEA

The Japanese as a race never liked idle hands, or feeding men who were not working for their keep. In Japan, prisoners who had committed serious crimes (stealing was one) were beheaded at the beginning of autumn. The reason for this practise was brutal, frugal and practical in the eyes of the Nipponese: why feed useless criminals during the hard winter?

As most of the manhood of Japan were in the services, prisoners of war would be used as slave labour. In late September 1942 over 1,800 British POW's were ordered out onto the Sham Shui Po parade ground with all their belongings.

The reaction of the prisoners to the move to Japan was mixed. Some believed conditions would improve. The POW camps in Hong Kong and the New Territories were now overcrowded; serious diseases were rampant and the food consisted of a starvation diet. Chinese civilians were dying of hunger, anywhere else had to be better, even Nippon. All the chosen men were then given a medical examination (Japanese style: a glass rod up the Khyber as described by a soldier from the Middlesex Regiment) and about two thousand men were pronounced fit for travel to Japan. Sergeant Devereux was among the fit men as was Tam and Willie. They were lucky; despite being in the thick of the fighting they had not sustained any injuries.

The selected prisoners were taken by boat to Hong Kong Island and then slowly made their way to the harbour on foot. The hot sun smiled down on this ragged column of humanity who staggered and shuffled to the docks. These men had once been proud soldiers who swaggered behind the pipes and drums. Japanese guards flanked the prisoners, urging them on with the butt of a rifle or a jab with a bayonet. All the while the local Chinese looked on impassively, their inner feelings a mystery. It is certain by now that Sergeant Devereux was able to walk unaided. In the camp he had acquired another set of kit. As with all soldiers the men of the Royal Scots stuck together; the remaining soldiers of D Company were no exception. The doctors and medics at Sham Shui Po had saved Sergeant Devereux from serious infection. He would soon need all his strength.

🪷

"The five months at the prison camp in Hong Kong allowed Jack to grow stronger; thank God he didn't know what lay ahead. He had only praise for the dedicated medical staff that looked after the seriously wounded and the men who risked their lives stealing medical supplies and drugs from outside. Brave local Chinese citizens also risked their lives passing drugs and throwing food over the camp fence to the prisoners."

🪷

By now all the front line Japanese troops who had been guarding them had been posted to the Pacific Islands. Their replacements were Class B, all under five foot rear echelon soldiers, who were always more brutal to the prisoners, especially those who towered over them. The tall Sergeant would soon learn a practical lesson.

The *Lisbon Maru* was an old rusting 7000-ton merchant ship. Her Captain was forty-three-year-old Kyoda Shigeru; he would turn out to be (or so he said at his trial), more humanitarian than Lieutenant Wada (the army interpreter in charge of the prisoners). Captain Shigeru would be tried after the war and given a long sentence; the notorious

Lieutenant Wada was sentenced to death in his absence; like many of the other war criminals he vanished off the face of the earth.

All British Navy personnel had been ordered into No 1 hold, the most forward and uncomfortable hold in the bow of the ship. It was reasoned by the Japanese, that being Navy personnel, they would be used to the rising and falling of the bow as the ship cut through the seas. Soon No 1 hold was full to bursting in the suffocating heat.

The Middlesex Regiment and the Royal Scots and a few smaller units were packed into No 2 hold, the biggest hold of the *Lisbon Maru*. This hold was divided into two levels with rough planking. The Middlesex, Royal Engineers and the Royal Corps of Signals were on the first floor level. The Royal Scots were placed in the lower level. Only two crude wooden ladders led from the lower level to the second level, from which four wooden ladders led up to the upper deck. The first level was by far the safest and healthiest level to be in.

Little fresh air reached the Scots in the lower level. This hold must have been stiflingly hot and claustrophobic while the ship was still at anchor. Within a few hours several men died of suffocation. In No 2 hold, others went mad and had to be knocked out before they harmed anyone. No 2 hold was originally intended for 1,000 prisoners with no room to spare; this number soon swelled. This sudden rise in numbers was due to the fact that some astute prisoners from No 1 hold and No 3 hold decided to change accommodation at the very last minute. They did this despite the beatings from the Japanese guards as they ran the gauntlet to No 2 hold and jumped in. There was little the angry guards could do; one white man looked much like another. The guards had no intention of going down into No 2 hold to find the culprits. These gauntlet runners had improved their chances of survival.

The men of the Royal Artillery were in No 3 hold at the stern of the ship. No 3 hold was the smallest and was to prove the most dangerous; it had portholes. The men of the Royal Artillery got to work straight away on the portholes. Unfortunately these portholes would prove to be death traps.

On the 26th the Japanese soldiers arrived on board. These were seasoned veterans from the war in China and the battle of Hong

Kong. These soldiers had played their part in the well known "Rape of Nanking." They were all in a good mood and laden with their items of personal loot. Usually Japanese soldiers were granted leave every two years and were looking forward to seeing their mothers, wives and children. On the 27th the *Lisbon Maru* sailed.

While the prisoners were waiting for the Japanese troops in the sweltering holds many who had arrived relatively healthy and had walked to the harbour unaided soon became ill in the hot foul smelling depths below where there was no ventilation. It was estimated at that point over 75% of the prisoners were ill. Many kinds of different skin diseases now flared up.

⚜

"At first Jack and other prisoners were allowed to walk on deck and socialize. The naval prisoners on deck were the first to notice there were no escort ships in attendance to discourage submarine attack. They told the other prisoners that the *Lisbon Maru* was a sitting duck for any submarines lurking in the area. Jack was just glad to be out of the sweltering hold in the cool sea breeze with his friends. But he was not happy about leaving Hong Kong; he was now going further away from the Shan States and Burma."

⚜

The doomed *Lisbon Maru* steamed out of harbour. The weather was hot. The entire group of prisoners watched Hong Kong slowly slip by, each with his own thoughts of halcyon days long past. Many men had left their wives and family behind in the tender care of the Japanese; for these men this was a traumatic event. Soon the old merchant ship slipped past Stanley Point. The *Lisbon Maru* kept close to the shore for much of the way. They only saw one other ship during the whole voyage. The following morning the prisoners were served tea and rice; in the evening they got rice, bully beef and tea. This addition of bully beef was thanks to the foresight of Colonel Stewart, a very brave and caring officer of the Middlesex Regiment; the bully beef was to last for two days. This officer's quick thinking and organisational skills saved many men in No 2 hold from suffocation and drowning as the sinking ship went down. Unfortunately Colonel Stewart did not survive his imprisonment in Japan.

The men below took turns to go up on deck, this continued for several days as the ship followed the coast line of China. Other officers unfortunately did not follow Colonel Stewart and his junior officers' good example and formed their own small groups, divorcing themselves from the welfare and suffering of the men in their care and often pulling rank for their own benefit. The behaviour of these officers bred resentment among the men.

✿

"Jack and the other prisoners were roused at 6am for roll call held at 7am on deck, followed by breakfast consisting of a small ladle of rice and onion soup. To while away the time, soldiers played card games and indulged in sing-songs. Jack never liked talking about what went on in No 2 hold especially during the sinking and the scramble to reach the ladders."

✿

The beginning of this journey was not pleasant for all prisoners who were immobile. The sufferers of beri-beri did not sleep at night. They moaned and cried with pain and were forced to walk around all night (just one light bulb lit the lower level of No 2 hold) despite the lack of space and curses from their comrades; in the morning they fell into exhausted sleep, often missing their rations. By now all holds of the *Lisbon Maru* were awash with filth that sloshed around with the ship's movement. Many of the dysentery sufferers could not make it to the heads in time. The toilet facilities were makeshift, unstable bamboo structures slung over the side of the ship and lashed with rope that loosened with the ships movement. When the lucky few did reach these toilets, their ordeal was not as yet over; first they had to keep their balance on a pitching and rolling ship.

To add to their humiliation they were intently watched by the front line Japanese troops who crowded the rails above the deck; this was their kind of humour. They leaned on the handrail and waited expectantly, their crude interest quickly turning to laughter at the monkey-like antics of the skeletal prisoners as they struggled to keep their balance on the swaying unstable structure, desperately trying not to fall over into the foamy drink. All prisoners knew that if they fell there would be no rescue, only the sounds of fading laughter from the warriors of Nippon high up in the Gods. And to make the show more interesting for the watchers, a long sinister shadow took up post below the squatting men. For the unobservant prisoners, the watching Japanese troops took great pleasure in pointing out the predator's arrival. It does not take much imagination to visualize the horror of a prisoner with failing strength sitting on this swaying toilet seat, looking down between his scrawny legs and seeing a large solitary shark eyeing him expectantly. The watching Japanese soldiers always seemed disappointed when the prisoner made it safely back on to the deck.

Far to the distant south the new American submarine *Grouper* was heading for the seas between Shanghai and Japan. Here the submarine would wait in ambush for any Japanese ship heading back to the homeland or any vessel heading out westward. Although it was the ambition of every submarine crew to sink an enemy aircraft carrier or a battleship, it was America's stranglehold on Japan's merchant shipping that crippled their war production. Unfortunately this situation encouraged the building of the notorious Burma Siam railway, a project believed impossible by western engineers. The building of this railway is a tribute to both Nippon ingenuity and cruelty. Thousands of lives (both civilians and military) were lost in this jungle hell. After all, the Japanese had more than enough live prisoners to spare.

CHAPTER 13

The Toddy Drinkers

BURMA

⚜

"At Yu, the De Souza family had tried to persuade your grandmother to make the journey to Moulmein with them. We also had relatives in Moulmein. But my mother had other plans. Perhaps she realized the De Souzas' menfolk would not arrive or maybe she felt we would be more obvious if our numbers swelled and be a more tempting target to Burmese Dacoits. I tried to convince my mother to travel with the De Souza's, as it would be nice to have company of my own age, but my mother would not listen. She said that if the Japanese arrived at Yu, the De Souzas would not be harmed as they were residents of Portuguese Marco and if the Chinese arrived first, they would not be harmed as they had trading connections with the Chinese. She also observed that the three De Souza sisters often argued and sometimes ended up screaming and pulling each other's hair; this could also be dangerous."

⚜

Grandmother may have also considered that finding accommodation and food for two adults and a child was far easier than for an extra six adults. But this is only a guess on my part. We were to meet the De Souzas again at Tada u.

৺

"One morning after many tearful farewells, our little group left Yu with our pram loaded down with looted stores and as much water as we could carry. I think we stayed there for about nine days. My mother warned the De Souzas not to make their presence obvious. They now had plenty of food and were looking forward to the arrival of their menfolk.

"We headed further into the dry belt. You were walking for longer periods which made the pram easier to push. Dressed as Burmese, we felt less conspicuous. As we continued, we picked up small dry pieces of wood for the fire that night and collected sweet prickly pear fruit that were now fully ripe and falling to the ground. We carried on further inland into the real dry country. Even though the monsoon may not reach the dry belt, flash floods from the distant hills turned the chaungs *[watercourse]* into rivers. In the dry belt, villages are protected by tall cactus hedges which made it difficult to know if they were populated, for at the hottest time of the day there was little activity as everyone rested or slept.

"Some pro-Japanese villages were ordered to deny retreating British soldiers water by removing the pulleys, ropes and buckets. For us to obtain water we would have to enter the village; this could be dangerous. This practice was new to my mother and was against Buddhist principles to deny water to travellers, for Buddha himself was a traveller. We always kept some water for emergencies and to fill your bottle. The water shortage would continue till the coming mango showers. Until then we had to make do. We travelled two or three miles a day. The pram was heavy to push; the land we crossed was full of deep cracks and ruts. Sometimes we were forced to cross dry sandy chaungs. The heavy pram had to be heaved and shoved, it was very hot and we tired quickly. We also had to keep an eye on you. When we were distracted you ran off laughing. Although we saw no dangerous wildlife during the day, the sandy beds of the chaungs were full of animal tracks – mostly snakes, deer, jungle fowl and peacocks.

"As soon as we saw a tree or a big bush providing shade we stopped and rested and cooked our main meal. Now that my mother had all the right ingredients, the food was always lovely. We saved the kungi water *[water the rice was cooked in]* for you. Mother always cooked more than enough lunch, leaving some for the evening, which we ate cold; that way we did not always have to light a fire that could attract unwelcome attention. Villagers usually investigated fires that were nearby. Some of the big trees had large noisy bats in them that we called flying foxes; we never slept under these trees. Crossing a well used bullock track, my mother spotted a stone water trough that was used to water bullocks. The water in the trough was undrinkable but the thin trickle that fed it was clear. We filled our tin cups and drank, but only half-filled our containers as we were so nervous that Japanese soldiers or Burmese dacoits could appear at any moment.

"One hot furnace-like afternoon we stopped in the shade of a tree surrounded by bushes; we hid the pram full of food out of sight. Sitting in the shade, Mother began cooking a Burmese curry. We noticed people walking nearby and realized we were near another bullock track. Then a young pretty Burmese girl came into view; noticing us, she left the track and began walking towards us. My mother told me to keep my mouth shut and let her do all the talking.

"In Burma it is not unusual to be approached by strangers who may politely enquire as to your destination and place of departure; in return they will give you their opinion on the route you have chosen. They may even enquire about your marital status and occupation etc.

"The smiling Burmese girl greeted my mother politely and sat down. She started a conversation about the coming monsoon. She said she was a student from Rangoon, heading to her village a few miles away for the coming water festival. Like all hungry students worldwide, she was anti-this and anti-that, in fact anti-everything, favouring anarchy. Students in Burma were anti-British. They desired self-rule and independence. And like all students she had strong political opinions.

"'The long nose "Meow phue" (white monkeys), have left Burma – Burma is now free. The Japanese are Buddhists and rice eaters like us. Soon Burma will be independent and govern itself' the girl said.

"'Where are the British now?' asked my mother.

"'Running to India' she answered.

"This was terrible news. Even though we knew the war was going badly, we always hoped for a miracle. India was such a long way away.

It was hard to believe there was no British Army left in Burma after all those years. The young female student was obviously hungry and enquired about all the ingredients my mother was using, as if testing her knowledge of Burmese cooking. We invited her to join us and share our food. The young student was impressed with mother's curry.

"'Stay the night at my village' offered the pretty Burmese girl, 'we have plenty of water and empty huts. My uncle is the headman.'

"I hoped my mother would accept this offer but she said we had to cross the dry belt before the rains; her mind was made up. It was such a shame; I was looking forward to sleeping under a roof and drinking fresh well water.

"'You speak excellent Burmese' said the girl to my mother.

"'I am Burmese' said my mother, 'from the south west.'

"'Ahhh … then you are more Mons than Khmer' said the girl knowingly, 'but why are you here in the hot season?'

"'We came here to escape the Chinese Army' answered my mother.

"You were quite taken by this pretty Burmese girl and kept trying to lift up her longyi, she found this quite amusing because of your age. Thank goodness she did not ask any more awkward questions. After eating and thanking my mother, the pretty young Burmese student left. We packed our things and crossed the bullock track immediately after the girl was out of sight, picking up as many mangoes as we could along the way. These mangoes were small and very sweet; they were our favourite and called 'Alfonzo mangoes', first brought to Burma from Goa by the Portuguese. We moved away from the direction of the girl's village. My mother was not taking any chances as we were now carrying a great deal of money.

"We walked as far as possible that afternoon and were thinking of finding a place to sleep when we noticed palm trees in the distance. This was now the real dry belt; water would be extremely scarce. Before we could reach the palms, peacocks informed us of the approaching night with their weird calls. That night we slept in the middle of a cactus thicket; the ground was so hard. We eventually fell asleep to the calls of the roosting peacocks. The following morning we walked towards the tall palms to seek water. There were no wells or springs above ground, but all the tall sugar palm trees were being tapped high up in the canopy by somebody for their juice. It would have been lovely to be able to drink fresh palm juice, but the trees were too high to climb.

"After two or three days travelling we had no water left and were very thirsty again. My mother tried cutting cactus plants; some cacti stored water but all we got was an inedible sticky milky substance that was poisonous. Eating the sweet mangoes now only added to our thirst.

"That afternoon we came to a small village surrounded by palm and coconut trees. Where there's a village, there is always water. While I waited, Mother took out small rice bags from the pram and hid them among the cactus plants to be picked up later. As we got nearer to the village we could see it was by the side of a large dirt road. On the far side of the village there were many guava trees growing around a massive banyan tree that gave plenty of shade. Under the palm trees were women making palm toddy. Further back from the track stood several huts, under which lay many large earthenware containers full of fermenting palm juice. These huts belonged to toddy makers. These people had darker skin and came from the hills; they were gypsies. As usual it was the village dogs that spotted us first and raised the alarm. The women and children stopped their work and came out to watch us. We approached them slowly, looking forward to sitting in the shade. Seeing we were only two females and a child the toddy makers relaxed. They were pleased when my mother asked to buy their toddy and some palm fruit. She then offered to buy water. Water was given freely. To charge strangers for water is considered taboo.

"There were two types of toddy, sweet or dry; you always loved sweet toddy and could not get enough. The native women used to keep giving you sips of sweet toddy when we were not looking. They were also selling blocks of lovely 'guava cheese' also known as 'guava jelly'. The large fruit of the palm trees were also for sale. This fruit called 'nungue' by the Burmese had a soft, firm opaque jelly-like centre that was full of sweet water and was very tasty. Although they spoke Burmese, these native traders looked different and had their own language that my mother did not understand. They were small in build without tribal tattoo markings like most hill tribes and their dress was unfamiliar to us. As they used the word 'paani', Indian for water, perhaps they were of Indian descent. It was never wise to enquire as to where these tribes were from. While their men travelled to the main bullock tracks and the distant main roads to sell toddy to the passing travellers, the women stayed and brewed the alcoholic palm juice, made the guava cheese, and baskets from palm fronds. They seemed totally unaware that a major war was going on.

"There was a boulder strewn spring nearby where these people drew their water. We asked permission to drink. The pool was not very big and these tribespeople had earthenware jars collecting water as it fell from the rocks in a thin trickle so it took us some time to collect water, but the water was cool and clear. Several red-faced working macaque monkeys were chained to the trees and pulled faces at us. We had to keep you away from these vicious monkeys, even the dogs were afraid of them. These big primates were trained to climb the trees and bring down the cup of tapped palm juice without spilling a drop; they would be closely watched by their owners. The monkeys would also be watching their owners; if distracted for one moment, the monkey would take a quick drink. I used to love watching the monkeys and the faces they pulled at their owners, when their backs were turned.

"After drinking the spring water, we settled under the shady palms and bought more sweet toddy and Guava jelly. These tribal women were fascinated by your size and the trusting way you approached them and sat on their laps. Soon you were running around with their tiny dark naked children in the shade of the palms. Many of the hill tribes near the Chinese border considered any newborn baby a year old at birth, thus a two year old child of theirs was in fact considered to be a three year old.

"My mother warned me to be careful as some of these tribes would often kidnap children who took their fancy and take them back to their distant villages. This was a habit of many of the small hill tribes; it introduced new blood and genes to their race.

"We noticed an empty hut on stilts; although tattered, it would be more comfortable and safer than sleeping on the ground. The tribespeople had no objections to us using the hut. These people were not rice growers and were delighted when my mother gave them some rice and salt. When we were alone we emptied the contents of the pram into the hut and used the small bags of rice as pillows hidden under blankets along with our other valuables. And as a safeguard one of us stayed close to the hut at all times.

"It was at this village that I heard the cry of the Outoasan for the first time, even though I had heard many stories relating to this frightening sound from my mother, brothers and other members of our large family. The Outoasan arrived that evening while we were all sitting outside around our fires. Everyone stopped talking, as it was believed that human voices attracted the being. Mothers quickly grabbed their children and valuable monkeys that were now chattering nervously and rushed into the safety of their huts. We did the same but we could see straight through the big hole in our tattered door. We made the sign of the cross and covered ourselves with our blankets with you tucked in-between us. We listened to the screams of the Outoasan as it came nearer. Then silence. We breathed a sigh of relief hoping the creature had moved on. Suddenly a scream, the creature was now sitting in the banyan tree opposite our hut. We could see this tree in the moonlight through the large gaps in our tattered door and expected the creature to appear at any moment. Although we waited, the Outoasan did not scream again."

᭡

To add foundation to this superstition, this creature came to Tada u and screeched the very night my uncle Victor died of cholera. As I grew older I certainly became very afraid of the Outoasan's arrival (Mum always reminded me). I firmly believed these screams were the doings of an evil spirit. It was not until many years later that I found out the truth from a devout Jain who had lived in isolation in the wilds of both India and Burma. These frightening, spine-chilling calls are made by a big creature of flesh and blood, a solitary migrating "brain-fever" bird and not by a Banshee, Sherrill, Outoasan or Djinn. This big speckled bird is the largest member of the cuckoo family and migrates from beyond the Himalayas south, across south East Asia. It seems this bird only calls in April and May just like its close European relative.

I am surprised that the source of this yearly terror was unknown to the endemic people at that time, for they knew the jungle and the wildlife intimately. Perhaps they were all too afraid to go out and investigate at night. Maybe Grandmother knew the truth. Our family always loved a good ghost story.

✿

"We stopped in the toddy-maker's village for quite some time, but one morning we were surprised to find that they had all left. These hill tribes did not trust the lowland Burmese and felt safer back in their jungle-clad hills. Now having the pick of the accommodation we moved into a better, stronger hut with an intact door.

"The mango showers were now beginning to grow heavier and the flow of water in the spring had increased. With the toddy-makers gone, there was enough water for us to bathe every day. By now fuel for cooking was becoming a problem and we had to use coconut husks, which made a great deal of smoke when burnt on a fire. This could attract unwanted attention and with this in mind, we began to burn old dry palm fronds instead that we pulled from the roof of a dilapidated hut. There were many old coconuts lying around which contained a sweet fungus that my mother began to harvest. One night I woke up and heard an animal under the hut. It was moving around making loud sniffing noises. I prayed it was not a tiger or a leopard. I quietly woke your grandmother, who listened and said it sounded like a pig. After a while the animal moved off. The following day Mother decided that because the pig had visited she would go and check to see if the rice we had hidden before entering the village was still there.

✿

CHAPTER 14

The *Grouper's* Second War Patrol

EAST CHINA SEA

The American submarine *Grouper* was attached to the Midway Patrol Group, comprising *Cachalot*, *Cuttlefish*, *Nautilus*, *Trout*, *Flying Fish*, *Grayling*, *Gudgeon* and several other submarines. After the battle of Midway Island, *Grouper* (a new submarine) had not sunk a single enemy ship. On her return to Pearl Harbour *Grouper* received a new, more aggressive commander; Lieutenant Commander Rob Roy McGregor. He was a man proud of his Scottish ancestry; a sprig of wild heather hung by the periscope, his lucky charm. The battle of Midway Island was a turning point, a great success for the American Navy but this good news was unknown to the prisoners of the Japanese (or the Japanese public). The prisoners aboard the *Lisbon Maru* did not know that the Japanese navy were no longer the masters of the Southern and Eastern Oceans. The Imperial Navy had lost some of its finest aircraft carriers, battleships and experienced pilots at the battle of Midway. The "Floating Chrysanthemums" as the Japanese proudly called their Imperial Navy, were now on the defensive.

The *Grouper* was now on her second war patrol. Unknown to the new commander and the many crew aboard, the submarine was soon to become famous or infamous, through no fault of her own. The *Grouper* was one of the new impressive large submarines but like all American submarines she had one drawback: defective torpedoes. These weapons had faulty firing mechanisms, many failed to explode on contact and another problem was that they often ran too deep in the water. Surprisingly the British and German Navy had the same problems. In fact a British destroyer suffered the indignity of sinking itself by one of its own torpedoes while escorting an artic convoy to Russia. It seems the torpedo did a lively U-turn! It was the Japanese who had developed the most deadly and reliable torpedoes, a torpedo known as the "Long Lance." This torpedo had the longest range, ran straight and fast at the correct depth and when it hit an enemy ship it always tended to explode. Fortunately the Japanese Navy did not see fit to share this technology with their German allies. If they had, we may well have lost the Battle of the Atlantic. In one sense we are lucky that the warriors of Nippon did not like sharing anything – apart from the clap.

The above facts remained unknown or made little difference to the half-starved and ill POWs suffocating and dying in the filthy holds of the *Lisbon Maru*, now sailing around the Zhoushan archipelago.

Reaching its patrol area in mid-September, *Grouper* damaged a small merchant vessel but soon lost her in a heavy rain squall. A few days later *Grouper* targeted another merchant vessel and fired three torpedoes; all three torpedoes missed due to faulty and erratic mechanisms. Again *Grouper* moved position and headed along the Chinese coast, hoping her luck would change: it did. On 20th September she spotted a Japanese cargo ship of around six thousand tons. The Submarine fired a single torpedo; it was enough to break the ship's back and she sank in a matter of minutes.

The *Grouper* moved position and soon spotted another target. The ship began to zigzag, having seen the submarine. As it was a clear moonlit night Commander McGregor decided to abort the attack and move again. He knew his intended victim had sent out a signal to an anti-submarine patrol and given them his position. He and his crew were well aware that all American submariners caught by the Japanese Navy were usually tortured then beheaded on deck almost immediately.

The next night *Grouper* sighted a large freighter heading north hugging the coast. This ship seemed unaware of the submarine's presence. Commander McGregor decided to steam ahead on the surface then dived and waited in ambush: the *Grouper* had found the Lisbon Maru. As usual with the Japanese, there was no red cross displayed on POW ships signifying their human cargo.

On board the *Grouper* everyone was tense and concentrated on their given tasks. The torpedo crew went to their stations; all six fish (torpedoes) were loaded into their tubes. They waited for the order to fire from McGregor. Having made his adjustments, the order came to fire three of the torpedoes at short intervals.

"All torpedoes running fast and straight" reported the tracker. A hush fell over the submariners. The crew knew how long the torpedoes would have to run before impact and carefully counted the seconds waiting for the explosions: none came. All three torpedoes missed! Immensely disappointed at the results, the crew silently cursed their faulty torpedoes, the American Navy, the man who designed them and his family. It seems they were risking their lives to no purpose. Disappointed, Commander McGregor ordered the remaining three torpedo tubes to be fired. Incredibly, they also missed.

CHAPTER 15

Caught by Surprise

BURMA

⚜

"It was a stifling hot morning without a breeze, at a time when the extreme heat coaxes the mind into drowsiness and distorts fluid reasoning, paralyzing the brain from instant reaction and quick judgments. I was sitting in the shade under the palm trees alone waiting for Mother to return, my mind idling. It was now so quiet and still. You were playing nearby in the shade of the palms with some stones. Suddenly I heard vehicles approaching from behind a cactus screen about a hundred yards away. I could not believe my ears. But when the sound grew louder, for some reason I thought they were British vehicles and did nothing. I just sat there.

"Out of the dust cloud appeared a convoy of vehicles that came to a halt a short distance from where I was sitting. It was only after the dust had settled that I noticed to my horror, that some of the trucks were flying the Japanese flag. Before I could do anything, you where running towards the trucks. My mother rushed back when she heard the approach of the convoy. Then to our relief, Indian soldiers and their families climbed down from the trucks. The Indian soldiers carried weapons and stayed by the vehicles. One of the well-dressed Indian women walked up to my mother and said they were stopping for a rest in the shade and to cook some food. But first they needed water. My mother told them about the spring in the rocks. The woman spoke to Mother in Hindi and said they were returning to Loikaw, where they had once lived before the war. But first they were going to an Indian village to pick up some respected and important people who feared an imminent attack from Burmese dacoits. She also confirmed that the British had retreated across the Chindwin and the Japanese were now in full control of Burma.

"My mother said the Indian lady asked why we were wearing Burmese clothes and living here. My mother said we were Portuguese and had lost all our possessions in the bombing of Rangoon. We had to buy Burmese clothes as nothing else was available and we were now heading for Moulmein to be with relatives. This was an important answer as it turned out these people were from the Congress party of India that was anti-British. My mother also told the truth that masquerading as Burmese protected us from the attention of dacoits.

"By this time you were playing with their children. The Indian women were quite taken by you and your friendliness. One of the married women said to my mother that if we were finding it difficult looking after you she would include you into her family and pay us in rupees. Mother said you were her last surviving grandson after the bombing. These women must have felt sorry for our pathetic little group and offered us a lift in one of the end trucks carrying their possessions. Mother accepted as they were going further into the dry belt and it would save us all that walking. We collected all our possessions and climbed into a covered truck at the end of the convoy that contained mostly furniture and carpets. The Indian soldier guarding the truck helped us take the pram aboard and we waited until everybody was ready to move off. Unfortunately we had no time to collect the hidden rice. During that time a civilian car appeared from behind us and slowed down as it went past.

"'My God!' said my mother – 'it is full of Japs.' We had no option but to stay where we were and prayed we would not be discovered. When the Indian soldiers and their families had finished eating, the convoy moved off. We passed many Burmese villages displaying small Japanese flags during the journey. In the afternoon after a long dusty drive we stopped at a small red brick built town.

"Several people passed the lorry wearing tall hats. Mother said they are Parsees. The Parsees were a wealthy Indian religious sect; owning most of the land in Burma. They were also the main money lenders.

This of course made them very unpopular with the Burmese who often had to sell their land to the Parsees in order to pay their debts legally through the British courts.

"At the side of the road there were several Indian market stalls selling food and other items. Some Burmese people were also present. The Indian soldiers began walking around the food stalls, leaving the drivers to guard the trucks. We seemed to have been forgotten. After a while my mother climbed down and had a good look around. It was then that she noticed the car of Japanese officers had been leading the convoy. Everyone it seems, including the Japanese, had left the convoy and had walked into the town. My mother came back and said we should leave immediately. We struggled to get the pram down and then made our escape down a small narrow lane. As we walked further down the lane we came upon a larger market.

"'We desperately need aspirin and medical supplies,' said my mother. All the drugs looted from the British were now being sold openly in the market. I begged my mother not to go, but she said this could be our last chance to obtain drugs, drugs that could save our lives in the future. She pointed to some trees in the distance and told me to wait there and not move. I was always afraid when my mother left us but I did as I was told. Putting you in the pram I headed towards the trees on the outskirts of the town and waited in the shade nervously. Thank God we were dressed as Burmese.

"The trees were full of sweet, ripe mulberries, scattered on the ground. I started to pick fruit off the trees and gave some to you, you loved them; the rest I kept for later. It was too messy to sit under the mulberry trees so I went a little further and sat in the shade of a banyan tree waiting for my mother. I was getting worried.

"It was then I became aware of a terrible smell. Soon after a procession of Parsees came out of the town dressed in white and wearing their strange hats; they were carrying something. Suddenly the sky was filled with vultures that quickly descended and settled on the tall trees nearby. The terrible stink was getting worse.

"I was so relieved when my mother returned. She had brought lovely Indian milk sweets, chapattis, some thick string, a tin of Andrews liver salts; antiseptic cream and a carton of aspirin tablets. But the best buy of all was some scented Pears soap. 'Quick, hurry, we must leave,' said my mother. Keeping to the path that led out of the town, we walked towards a line of trees. All the vultures had disappeared but we could still hear them squabbling. Nearing the trees the smell grew worse, yet we needed the trees as cover in case we were spotted leaving the town. Once we reached the line of trees, the path ahead led past a tall white building that had no roof or windows. The smell became overwhelming but we were afraid to leave the path. We hurried past just taking a quick look through the open doorway of the white building. Even my mother was shocked at what we saw. Dead bodies wrapped in white cloth were lying on the floor; vultures were tearing at their faces and the white material that covered them. There were also clean-picked human skeletons everywhere. Some of the new corpses had no eyes or eyelids: the first things eaten by the vultures. Other bodies were only partially eaten and seemed to be moving their arms as the vultures tore at them. The Parsees did not believe in burying their dead.

"We crossed ourselves and your forehead then quickly left. I threw the mulberries away and could not eat for days because of the smell and the taste in my mouth. It was still the hottest time of the year. My mother had filled the tin water container at the Parsee village; even though I was thirsty I only took one small sip. The smell and the taste of the water reminded me of all those dead bodies covered by fighting vultures. I did not drink again that day. Your grandmother said the Parsees were a very hygienic race; not burying their dead was part of their religion. I still could not drink. When I was finally forced to drink the water from the Parsee well (because I was breastfeeding you), I tasted dead bodies.

"Out of the village boundaries and the cultivated areas, we now found ourselves back in the scrub jungle of the dry belt. The calling of peacocks warned us that night was imminent. My mother began to look for a suitable place to spend the night. The following day we awoke to the call of the peacocks and set off early without breakfast. At around midday, the heat was so intense we were forced to find shelter in the shade of a large bush but had to keep moving every hour or so in order to stay in its shadow. While you and my mother dozed I kept watch.

"When my mother woke we noticed dark clouds gathering in the far distance. 'The monsoon will soon be here,' my mother said, 'we must hurry. All the chaungs will be impossible to cross once flooded;

we must continue in the cool of the evening and find safe shelter before the monsoon arrives.'

"We kept you in the pram to avoid any delays, and dressed you in a long silk chemise that once belonged to one of the De Souza girls, and put a bonnet on your head. We both pulled and pushed the pram using the string my mother had bought from the market. Shady trees were now becoming rare; wood for the fire was also scarce so we slept without a fire that night.

"At around noon the following day we could walk no longer, there was no shade to be found. We placed a blanket over the pram and sheltered under it. Before we realized it, a large group of wild looking people were approaching us. Most of the men and the elders were mounted on small Shan Ponies. The women were leading draught animals that were laden with their belongings. All the men were tattooed on their legs, arms and bodies and carried the Burmese dahs in their belts; some carried rifles.

"My mother got up and approached one of the elderly women sitting on a pony and spoke to her in village Burmese; pointing to you in the pram, she asked for water. The old woman said they were short of water themselves. The Burmese are generally fond of children and a long discussion took place. I thought they were discussing whether to kill and rob us. Finally the elderly woman took out a water container and carefully poured half a small coconut shell for each of us. Mother asked where the nearest water was to be found and if the Japanese were near. The tribeswomen pointed and told her that there was a village nearby. The tribespeople then continued their journey.

"This group of rough tribespeople looked like dacoits or opium traders to me. My mother thought they were a Chin tribe who had left their village because of the war and were trying to escape to the Yomas Hills far to the west. We turned and headed for the village in the direction the tribeswomen had pointed, but by nightfall we still hadn't found it. We had to stop for the night in the open again. As usual, we spread a waterproof sheet on the ground and covered ourselves with two blankets. I always made sure the blankets were well tucked under us as snakes and scorpions were known to seek the warmth of sleeping humans.

"If it were not for the mango showers that came the following day we may have died of thirst. Having filled our containers we continued on our journey and came across some tomari bushes *[Chinese gooseberries]*. We spread our blankets over these bushes and rested in the shade. The following day the mango showers began in earnest and we laid out all our vessels to collect as much water as possible. When one filled up we drank it and placed it out again. We also washed ourselves in the rain. These mango showers were not as heavy as they were in Taunggyi. You used to sit naked and play in the puddles like an urchin. These showers continued and deep puddles appeared, sometimes containing the larva of mosquitoes, tadpoles and even tiny fish. I was so happy we could wash ourselves every day with soap. We still could not find the village in question so my mother decided we should just head towards the distant hills and hope to find shelter. Sleeping outside would be out of the question when the rains began. The rain had flooded out many of the venomous creatures that lived in holes in the ground. Scorpions and centipedes were scurrying around, even during the day, which was very dangerous, so I carried you everywhere; a sting or a bite could easily have killed you.

"We were forced to move to higher ground and by the afternoon were all very hungry and stopped to cook food. Dry tinder was a problem. It was while your grandmother was poking around looking for dry twigs underneath the bushes to light a fire, that she saw and killed a large and beautiful Russell's viper. I would never eat snakes knowingly but it was sometimes difficult to ascertain what was in my mother's dishes; snake looked a lot like fish. I thank God none of us were bitten. While we were interned at Tada u, Maureen James, an Anglo-Indian girl who used to be a nurse, worked for the Japanese in the admin building. She told us there were several deaths due to snake bite among the many Japanese troops who went out on patrol. All the anti-venom in Burma was commandeered by the Japanese who ruined it by not storing it at the correct temperature. As a result many Japanese soldiers died despite receiving the anti-venom injection. Believing it to be ineffective the Japanese doctors at Tada u stopped using it."

☙

CHAPTER 16

The *Lisbon Maru* is Attacked

EAST CHINA SEA

On board the *Lisbon Maru* that morning, just before the *Grouper's* attack, those men who managed to sleep for a short while woke up and wondered what the new day would bring. The dysentery suffers who still tenaciously clung on to their dignity, hoped they would be allowed access to the swaying heads to relieve themselves before the stabbing pain in their contorted innards became unbearable. These men did not wish to add to the already soiled water splashing on their comrade's legs in No 2 hold. They waited. Perhaps their captors were not ready for a good laugh yet? Maybe the sea was not rough enough to cause a weak squatting prisoner to lose his balance and fall into the jaws of the waiting shark below. Perhaps the shark was late?

Other prisoners lying in the filth were too weak and remained silent, they did not have the energy to ponder on points of dignity or be angry at their situation; they just accepted their fate. Atropos, who cuts the threads of life, stood silent at their sides, waiting.

Where Sergeant Devereux was in No 2 hold at this time or what his physical condition was, is unknown. Mother always tended to skip past the unpleasant incidents. Perhaps the Sergeant never told her the whole truth regarding the conditions, or the whole story about the sinking. But there must have been a reason why he always bit his nails to the quick after the war. My mother, sister and I never fully appreciated dad's ordeals in full measure: how could we?

If the scenes that were soon to play out on the *Lisbon Maru* were similar to the other POW hell ships like the *Avsan Maru,* the *Byoke Maru* or the *Oryoku Maru* that were also torpedoed on their way to Japan, dad would have good reason to exclude these details from mother. Some POWs on the above ships, when driven by indescribable thirst and the resulting madness that accompanies it, killed the weak and dying to drink their blood. The insane had to be killed with bare hands by the sane. Acts of cannibalism in dark recesses were carried out by small groups of starving prisoners.

The hungry men in their cramped stinking holds swore like only sailors and soldiers can swear. They rubbed their aching sinewy limbs and cursed their living purgatory and then cursed those above them, who enforced it.

The prisoners in No 3 hold (Gunners) suddenly heard a gurgling noise on the other side of the ship's plating. It was believed this new noise came from the ships faulty propeller. In No 2 hold they heard what they described as swishing noises. The men in both these holds continued to discuss what these noises might be; perhaps the ship's engines were playing up? Not one of the prisoners in No 3 or No 2 holds came up with the right answer. This was not the case with the sailors in No 1 hold. These old salts knew exactly what the sound was: torpedoes! If there were a few doubting Thomases present, they were soon convinced as the second torpedo skimmed just below the ship's hull. The sailors listened to its passage, wide-eyed. The third fish (torpedo) removed all doubts when it struck the bow right by No 1 hold; luckily it did not explode. The sailors inside this hold could only pray.

Shortly afterwards above decks, Captain Shigeru gave the alarm: "Torpedo attack!" The enemy crew raced for the guns on deck; the lookouts soon spotted the submarine some 6,000 yards distant. The ship's heavy gun opened fire. According to the Captain of the *Lisbon Maru,* he took evasive action, which caused the second fan of torpedoes to miss his ship, and then began to zigzag his course to confuse the attacker. In actual fact all the following torpedoes fired by *Grouper* were faulty or had run too deep.

On board the *Grouper* another three more torpedoes were fired from the forward tubes.

"Torpedoes running fast and straight sir," the tracker reported. After two minutes and ten seconds total silence, more misses. The periscope was raised, the target was slowly changing course and was hoisting a distress flag. The ship continued firing inaccurately at *Grouper* with its heavy deck gun.

At 8.45am Commander McGregor in desperation fired two more torpedoes set to the depth of only six feet. After a long wait an explosion. The Lisbon Maru received its death blow. While Commander McGregor was watching the ship through binoculars, a lookout spotted a Japanese bomber coming straight at them. The *Grouper* had no option but to crash-dive. The crew of the submarine took evasive action and prepared the boat for depth charge attack, then waited in silence, their hearts pounding as they contemplated their possible fate. Dying slowly of suffocation in darkness on the bottom of the sea bed was not a thought to linger on. This was the *Grouper's* second and largest kill. Slowly the *Lisbon Maru* stopped and began to list.

Shortly after diving, the submarine's electric motors were used to leave the scene of attack: she was now the hunted. Not long after, the crew of the submerged submarine heard three depth charges exploding near her pressurised hull; their excitement turned to fear. Each man aboard the submarine confronted his own personal fears. Some visualized capture and kneeling on the deck of an enemy destroyer, a naked blade descending.

Back on board the *Lisbon Maru* the prisoners heard noises at the hatches. The men below believed that the Japanese sailors were opening the hatches to let them out. In fact the Japanese were reinforcing the hatches with timbers and lashing tarpaulins over the top to keep them in. This action was a deliberate effort to suffocate or drown the helpless men below. Lieutenant Wada the Japanese Army Interpreter did not want any survivors or witnesses.

Once the prisoners below in No 2 hold realized their captor's intensions, plans to break out began. This was organized by Colonel Stewart of the Middlesex and his junior officers. Below the Middlesex Regiment on the next level were the Royal Scots; they could only wait helplessly. The single light bulb on this level that barely illuminated the hold was suddenly switched off from above by the Japanese. The Royal Scots were now in complete darkness. Blind panic ensued. From somewhere candles were produced which provided a weak flickering light in the foul thickening air.

Many men not in close proximity to the life-giving ladders began to panic. Fighting broke out in the far corners of the holds to try and reach the area of the ladders. Men already on the ladders leading to the top level of No 2 hold were pulled off by those below. A free for all began. The weaker and exhausted prisoners were slowly pushed to the bottom of the hold where they were trodden into the polluted mess. In the panic it became the survival of the strongest. Many men had to be restrained or knocked unconscious. If the panic spread it would only quicken their deaths by using up the little oxygen remaining in the polluted air. A sharp eye was kept on the candle flames.

Somehow the free for all was contained by the officers and NCOs and reasonable discipline regained. As the filth of this hold began to rise, men were forced to take to the pumps. In the flickering candle light, the scene at the bottom of No 2 hold (Royal Scots) where many scrawny, demented, half-naked men fought each other, while others frantically worked the pumps, must have resembled a scene from Hades.

In the first level of No 2 hold Colonel Stewart took command and organized his officers. The prisoners began a search for tools to break out of the holds. Using whatever tools were at hand they tried to force the hatches open. But without luck; they were trapped.

Above deck, the Captain of the *Lisbon Maru* argued with Lieutenant Wada (or so he said) that if the ship sank all the prisoners would drown; this was not the way of professional seamen. But after a long heated discussion the Captain was overruled by Lieutenant Wada of the army.

Soon the Japanese destroyer *Kuri* appeared alongside and began to take off the Japanese troops and their wounded; she then left the scene. At least a dozen armed guards remained onboard ship to make sure the prisoners below would not escape suffocation or drowning. It did not take long for the men trapped in the three holds to realize their captors were abandoning ship. As a result efforts to break open the hatches were redoubled. At 10am the air down below in the holds was becoming dangerously toxic, especially for the Royal Scots. Many of the men had passed out and were now drowning in filthy water.

Several miles away the Captain of the *Grouper* felt safe enough to surface; his batteries were low and the oxygen in the submarine was beginning to read at a dangerous level. After waiting a little longer, rechecking that the sounds of pursuit had died, *Grouper* surfaced. The men aboard smiled; the celebrations could wait till they returned to Pearl Harbour. Although a kill would be credited to them, the *Lisbon Maru* was still afloat. In fact it would take another full day for this ship to sink. The Americans were unaware of the life and death struggle that was now taking place out of sight in the bowels of the Japanese ship.

Back in No2 hold aboard the *Lisbon Maru*, the ship gave a sudden lurch and it became apparent that she could not remain afloat much longer.

A British Private produced a long butcher's knife; with this, Col Stewart ordered a Lieutenant Howard and a Lieutenant Potter to try and break through again. They managed to push the long blade between the planks and cut the ropes that lashed the tarpaulins holding down the hatch door. This action allowed the two Lieutenants and some men to force open a gap, through which precious light and oxygen rushed into the holds and revived the gasping prisoners.

On reaching the deck Lieutenant Howard and Lieutenant Potter then noticed some British gunners from No 3 hold (this hold was the first to begin sinking) trying to squeeze through the portholes; these men soon become stuck fast: they would drown. These two brave young officers, helped by others, then began working on all the hatches to free the rest of the prisoners. Only some three or four dozen gunners would manage to escape before the hold was eventually flooded.

Initially the Japanese guards left behind to stop a breakout, strangely took no action and idly watched the men emerging through the hatches. This did not last long before they opened fire. Eventually some sailors in No1 hold managed with help from those on deck to force their hatches open. Below the Middlesex, the Royal Scots began to push and force their way up. Some men climbed over each other, others fell back into the hold. It was impossible to calm the suffocating men. Somehow order was regained again by the officers of the Royal Scots as more fresh air entered the ship. An orderly queue was formed at the base of the ladders allowing men to gain the upper level as most of the Middlesex Regiment were now on the ship's deck. Trying to dodge the bullets coming at them from the Japanese guards above, Royal Scots soon took their place in the top level of No 2 hold. Then two things happened simultaneously: the ship tilted stern down and one of the two ladders leading up from the bottom of No 2 hold snapped. Unfortunately, ninety per cent of the men trapped in No 3 hold, now underwater, drowned. All the portholes were blocked by dead men who had tried to escape earlier. It is said by witnesses that these brave gunners realising there was no escape, began singing "It's a long way to Tipperary" until the water rose above their lips.

The men in No 1 hold helped by those on deck, also began to climb out. By now the firing from the Japanese guards above had ceased. Groups of Gunners and the Royal Scots, who had escaped at the beginning, rampaged through the ship. Some were looking for alcohol, others for revenge. Many of the Japanese guards were grabbed from behind and thrown over onto the main deck where they were killed by the waiting prisoners.

On gaining the freedom of the main deck, the prisoners found that the ship had stabilized momentarily. It was a pleasant sunny October day and they sat around quietly smoking. Others more cautious of going down with the ship, jumped straight into the sea.

Tam and Willie among others, raced through the ship looking for loot. A large container of cold rice was found along with a liberal amount of Japanese beer kept in squat round bottles, individually wrapped in rice straw. Bottles of sake were also found. Soon there were drunken prisoners marauding around the ship looking for any Jap guards still alive. Some of the men who initially jumped into the sea noticed islands in the distance and began swimming towards them. These men were lucky, for the ever shifting currents were in their favour at this moment. This would not last long. Others less confident swam a reasonable distance away from the sinking ship and trod water, so as not to be sucked down when the ship went under.

The accidental sinking of the *Lisbon Maru* was a tragic mistake of war. Most of the heroes (a word used too often in modern times) of the sinking, both men and officers who risked their lives helping to save others, sadly died in Japan during their imprisonment. Fate can sometimes be cruel. The sinking cost the lives of hundreds of Allied prisoners.

The Japanese broadcasters were quick to blame the Americans for sinking a POW ship. The Japanese wireless news was soon picked up by the submariners: crew and captain were stunned. By now they could do little about it, for they were still being hunted from the air. Of course, this was excellent propaganda for the Japanese, who soon informed the world via Tokyo Rose [female English-speaking propaganda broadcasters].

CHAPTER 17

Mango Showers

BURMA

After leaving the Parsee town and its death house, my grandmother and mother wandered aimlessly for many days towards the distant hills. They were hoping to find the village they had been told existed by the tattooed hill tribe. Despite searching, my guardians saw no obvious signs of the presence of a nearby village. Instead the skeletons of domestic animals and sometimes even humans adorned the baked red earth with their bleached white bones. As the "mango showers" increased, an indication of the impending monsoon, the need to find suitable shelter was paramount. They continued to head for higher ground, avoiding the jungle.

"We found ourselves entering a wide cultivated area containing fields of gram *[chickpeas]*, sugarcane and ground-nuts. Some of the crops in the fields had been burnt. Flocks of jungle fowl and kelagee pheasants were feeding in the fields. There was water in all the irrigation channels from the mango showers but it was too dirty to drink."

Grandmother was totally the opposite from my mother when it came to killing small animals for food. When necessary she would kill then pluck or skin any edible wildlife; whether it was covered in fur, feather or scale, within half an hour it would be cooking.

❧

"Finally we came across a small dilapidated village. We approached cautiously as there were no dogs to announce our arrival. Reaching the first huts we were disappointed, it was not a permanent village, only inhabited by a few ill-looking Burmese. The next disappointment was that the water in the well was so low, we could not reach it. This would remain the case until the monsoon filled the underwater conduits. We would have to rely on the mango showers.

"An old toothless Burmese woman living there told my mother that the crops belonged to Parsee money lenders. The old woman also said that some time earlier a large body of Chinese soldiers had passed through and burnt some of the crops to deny them to the Japanese. However, due to the war, the Parsees had not appeared to supervise the harvesting of their crops, leaving the local Burmese workers to help themselves. She and a few others were now the only inhabitants and would soon be returning to their own village called Pybaw [*pronounced Pee-baw by Mother*] some two or three days away on higher ground. My mother believed the few Burmese left in this village were opium addicts and had borrowed money from the Parsees.

"When asked, the old woman said that she had seen no Japanese troops – only the Chinese soldiers. This woman also warned my mother that wild elephants sometimes came out of the jungle at night to feed on the sugarcane fields and that these elephants were unpredictable and dangerous. My mother never let the opportunity of stocking up with food pass so we stopped in this village for several days to harvest chick peas and ground nuts. For the time being we had a flimsy roof over our heads and could sleep off the ground; this was a luxury for us. During every mango shower we would stand under the eves of the huts and wash and collect drinking water from the run off. Although this village had no fruit trees it was dotted with large tamarind trees. Both types of tamarind pods were available (sweet and sour). Tamarind was a much used condiment in eastern cuisine. We threw sticks into the trees to knock the trailing pods down. You would run and pick up the pods and sometimes the large falling pods or the sticks hit you on the head quite hard; you were a sweet natured baby and always laughed; you must have had a thick skull. You loved the sweet tamarind pods, poor boy you were deprived of the correct nourishment to grow strong and healthy.

"One morning my mother told me that all the remaining Burmese had left; we were now alone in this deserted make shift village used only for harvest time. The mango showers grew heavier, the ground was quickly turning into a quagmire, but most worrying was that some of the deep chaungs were filling up with water, they would soon be impassable. Pushing the heavy pram in the mud was becoming extremely difficult. Luckily for us, by midday the mud was baked hard again by the sun. It was time to move on but something happened that made us stop longer. Your laughter woke us up; you were leaning over the pram watching a young piglet that was sheltering underneath it in the shade. As soon as my mother woke up and saw the suckling pig, she picked up her knife and chased it; I soon began running after her trying to save it.

"I can still see my mother's angry red face while holding the big knife in her hand shouting … 'Kate you may be my second youngest daughter – but if you try and save that pig again – I am going to murder you with my own hands!'

"The little pig was finally caught – despite my protests – and that evening my mother cooked it in golden syrup in one of the communal mud ovens situated outside the village. I had not eaten properly since the Parsee death house. The suckling pig smelt so delicious I could not resist. It was good to taste crispy crackling and pork fat again.

"The rains were becoming heavier and finding water was no longer a problem. Before we left the village, we got out all the remaining new notes we had been given by the De Souzas and crumpled them, placing them in puddles of muddy water to make them look old. We then spread them out in the sunshine and waited for them to dry. Now we were ready to leave and make for Pybaw."

❧

My grandmother had a good knowledge of medicinal plants and was always on the lookout. I can still remember the vile taste of these concoctions and used to run like hell when my two guardians began whispering and looking at me. Gran also used raw opium as a medicine and usually had a dark block of raw opium resin handy. Ground down and mixed with water or sweet palm toddy it acted as a kind of laudanum once so popular in the western world for pain relief. Chewed opium can also be rubbed on flesh wounds to ease pain; I would soon need this painkiller, when a parasitic infection that I contracted reached a dangerous stage.

✵

"On the bullock track heading for Pybaw I was afraid of meeting elephants but we saw none, only some footprints in the mud and elephant dung in which you loved searching for beetles. Late that afternoon we stopped under a large cottonwood tree [Kapok] for the night; in the distance we could hear cattle. The next morning we took cotton from the fallen pods and after drying it in the morning sun, filled two empty rice bags; we now had pillows. We rested beneath this tree for another day to get our strength back.

"On the third day after walking for several hours, we could see dozens of paddy-birds [cattle egrets] in the distance and later many cattle with young Burmese children looking after them. We were afraid to walk past the big Zebu bulls that blocked our path. My mother called out to the young Burmese children to drive the bulls away from us. These youngsters, some only about five or six, showed no fear of these massive animals. It would have been nice to buy fresh milk from the cattle herders but their hands were filthy."

✵

My mother was always very hygiene conscious. After the war she had a weakness for the many different types of food that the local hawkers sold. "Have you washed your hands?" she would ask. The hawker would grin and nod his head.

"Show me."

The hawker still grinning would hold out his hands for inspection, probably taking pleasure in the fact that he hadn't washed his hands for a week. My mother would call our Chinese housekeeper and ask for a bowl of water and soap. The hawker would then have to wash his hands under supervision of my mother and the Chinese housekeeper's keen eye. And then, if my Dad was not at home we would all sit around a table including the housekeeper, cook and the Arma (nanny) and eat the vendor's food; it was a wonder my mother did not invite the hawker in as well to join us, for she had a generous and soft nature. The hawkers, both Indian and Chinese, did not take offence at this performance, for they knew Mother was a soft touch and a good customer, and regular custom in the East is valued.

CHAPTER 18

Pongyis

PYBAW BURMA

❧

"We reached Pybaw mid-afternoon. After going through the usual performance with the barking village dogs, villagers appeared and engaged us with the usual questions. It was late afternoon when we found the headman; my mother asked if we could rent a hut in the village until the monsoon season was over; he agreed. I thanked God my prayers had been answered. My mother said the headman would be happy to be paid in money or opium; later my mother found out that the headman's wife was an advanced opium addict along with many other villagers. Obtaining opium was becoming difficult in Pybaw and elsewhere because of the war. According to my mother, the best opium in Burma came from Afghanistan, but it was much more expensive than that of opium produced in the Shan States. The routes from India and China were now closed, so most of the addicts depended on the Shans, Karens and Chins for their supplies. Although the hill tribes were considered enemies by the Japanese, a blind eye was often turned in return for bribes.

My mother took care never to enquire about the presence of Japanese soldiers in Pybaw in case people became suspicious that we were trying to avoid them. The villagers were certainly pro-Japanese, as there were many small Japanese sun flags being displayed.

"I was so grateful to have a roof over our heads; our wandering life had come to an end. We were given a well-built hut on short stilts not far from one of the water wells near the crossroads of the bullock tracks. This was the last water well in a conduit of three wells situated in other parts of the village. The hut we were given had a strong and sturdy door that could be closed from the inside with rope. But best of all, the hut contained a small mud oven on a slab of flat rock set in clay.

"A large Buddhist temple stood at the far end of the village. We could hear the subtle sound of wind blown temple bells in the cool of the evening and smell jasmine that grew wild by the Pagoda. There were many Pongyis and novices in their saffron robes walking about when we arrived. We always had to be careful of these Buddhist priests who were well educated and politically minded; they had a great influence with the villagers. Many Pongyis spoke English.

"We were all so tired after our wanderings; as soon as we entered the hut with the pram we fell asleep straightaway. It was so nice to have privacy and be able to close a door. As Pybaw was not far from the Karen Hills and on the edge of the dry belt, the rain and the accompanying wind was now much stronger.

"The following afternoon we walked around the small market looking for something to eat. The vendors were selling ordinary items and cooked food but out of sight there were goods for sale taken from the warehouses near Yu. We recognised the red Chinese characters, as Burmese script is totally different from that of the Chinese. All villages had been warned in advance by Japanese agents and leaflets dropped from their planes that looting or any damage to property was unlawful. All booty left behind was now Japanese property.

"Mother bought us another set of Burmese clothes and new slippers at this market, as our own had worn out. She also bought more aspirin; this was the only pharmaceutical drug we had to treat everything during the war. Aspirin had many uses but despite this it was not popular with the Burmese villagers or with the Japanese, as it gave them indigestion. I was hoping we would find some toothpowder, but my mother said using toothpowder would give us away as not being Burmese. They would use charcoal and a yellow twig of some tree to clean their teeth.

"Soon all the food stalls had their braziers heated and the smell of various Burmese dishes drifted on the air making us hungry. The stall holders were selling all kinds of Burmese dishes like moingha, garnished with chopped boiled eggs and raw onion. There was another food item on sale called 'par-a-jo', which we all liked. I used to try making them, but they never tasted the same as those bought in the market or the ones your grandmother made. It was a mixture of large lentils, chillies and other ingredients and deep fried in peanut oil. We sat by the stalls and ate while your grandmother spoke with the villagers. They were eager to know all about us but directed their questions to my mother only. I did not like the idea of being thought of as backward but my mother had told me not to speak. My mother answered all their questions and asked questions of her own. You were soon happily playing with the little village children.

"One day soon after we had arrived, your grandmother came into the hut and said all the food looted from the warehouses near Yu had disappeared from the market. This probably meant that the Japanese were arriving soon. My mother began hiding our possessions and food in-between the thatch matting of the walls in our hut. A few days later a large Japanese patrol arrived and their officer was seen talking to the headmen. We knew this would happen sooner or later; the Japs were now tightening their grip on Burma. Even so, it was still a shock to us. We were very fortunate we had arrived and established ourselves in the village before the Japs appeared.

"The Burmese villagers were happy to see the Japanese troops, as they would provide protection against any of the retreating armed Chinese soldiers. At that time we did not realize that the Japanese were intending to stay permanently in the village, for Pybaw was situated at a strategic crossroads. The Japanese troops were greeted as liberators by the villagers. Several huts were made available to them near the crossroads and the well. The soldiers were led by a Sergeant Enoda. The first job the soldiers did after placing their packs in one of the huts, was to shoot and bayonet any dogs in the vicinity attracted by the smell of dried fish and eels that the Japanese had brought with them. The Burmese, despite not being dog lovers, were rather shocked at this action as the py-dogs had their uses.

"Another shock awaited them when the Japanese thought nothing of bathing naked by the well. They would vigorously rub their bodies with clean white towels till they took on a pinkish hue. Although the Burmese were Buddhists like the Japanese, this kind of nakedness in public did not go down well. The villagers complained to the headman who in turn complained to Sergeant Enoda. Naked bathing was stopped. Village dogs suffered in many ways during the occupation in places where Japanese troops were billeted. The Japanese pride themselves on cleanliness and considered the presence of dogs unhygienic. By contrast, for the many Koreans who served in the Japanese Army, dog meat was a national dish.

"Jack says that he and other British POWs also took every opportunity to capture and kill any stray dogs or cats within sight; such was the craving for protein and the strength and wellbeing it brings to a starving body. In fact, most prisoners considered cat a tastier meat than dog."

⚜

The arrival of Japanese troops in Burma generally went smoothly with the locals as the Burmese were considered allies, but in other countries this was not often the case. The inhabitants of a village in Malaya, after watching the British Army retreating in panic, waited expectantly for the Warrior Gods of Dai Nippon to appear. While waiting they proceeded to cook up the waste food for their pigs. Suddenly two scruffy and blinking Japanese scouts appeared out of the jungle gloom and stared at the Malayan villagers with open mouths.

Soon the main body of Japs appeared, led by an officer who promptly slapped the headman's face while soldiers beat up the young men for not bowing to their liberators. Seeing the pig food cooking they mistook it for the villagers' midday meal and quickly polished it off, and then for good measure (public relations) raped two of the village girls before leaving. No doubt the villagers soon wished the return of their former less rapacious old masters, the British.

✿

"Not far from the water well at Pybaw near the crossroads of two bullock tracks, the Japanese set up a roadblock, a check point with a big bamboo pole lowered across the track. All passing traffic was checked including Japanese military vehicles. There were about two dozen Japanese soldiers under the command of Sergeant Enoda (Gunso). Sergeant Enoda was big for a Japanese soldier. He had a bull neck and small piggy eyes. All the Japanese soldiers were terrified of this non-commissioned officer who would often beat them with a bamboo stick when they were on parade outside the guardhouse. We often heard him bellowing at his men from our hut. We also heard from the Burmese trackers that accompanied his patrols that he tortured suspected dacoits and insurgents for information.

"Sergeant Enoda had a pet, a kind of drill monkey. It was chained to a big pole near the guard house and was a vicious brute. It only feared Sergeant Enoda, even the py-dogs were afraid of it. This monkey was a great amusement to the young Japanese soldiers and they would tease it when Sergeant Enoda was out on patrol. They would throw a gunny-sack to the monkey containing a live chicken; the monkey would take the chicken out and would immediately begin turning the squawking bird around inspecting it. Then holding it down with his hind legs would begin to pluck the poor live squawking bird till not a single feather remained. I always felt sorry for the poor bird having all its feathers removed while still alive. Once they gave the monkey a sack with an angry cat in it just to see what would happen. The monkey's surprised reaction and the resulting fight between the two sent the Japs and the watching Burmese into fits of laughter.

"One morning the big monkey was missing, it had been killed by a leopard. When Sergeant Enoda returned two of the soldiers were beaten by him for allowing this to happen. Everybody was pleased to be rid of this vicious drill monkey.

"Most of the Burmese villagers including us kept away from the guardhouse, but you and all the naked village children were always hanging around staring at the Japanese soldiers. Sergeant Enoda and his soldiers seemed to like little children and used to line you all up as if on parade and make you stand to attention. He taught you all to bow to him correctly. He would walk around with a stern face as if inspecting his troops, giving light whacks with his stick to any child that got it wrong. All this would be watched with amusement by his men. Sergeant Enoda sometimes did monkey impressions to make the village children laugh. But he would also bellow at the children if they disturbed him when he was busy, this sent them all running and screaming in every direction, you included.

"Sergeant Enoda would soon become friendly with my mother, often sitting with her outside our hut; all Japanese welcomed those who spoke Nippon Go correctly. My mother and Sergeant Enoda also had a common interest: knitting. My mother was a fast and skilful knitter and often knitted with many needles. Japan is, after all, a cold country in the winter, and perhaps the knitted items were to send back to their families. Most of the Jap soldiers here and at Tada u were keen knitters and were delighted when they found large amounts of knitting wool in Burma. Many of them had served in Manchuko [Manchuria]. All Japanese soldiers had a great fear of catching a chill in their stomachs; for this reason most of them wore a cloth belt of a thousand stitches around their waists. They also believed that this belt had the power to deflect bullets."

🪷

In the west, a man knitting in public would be considered effeminate; to Nipponese manhood there is no such stigma. It was not uncommon for us to see a group of front line soldiers sitting around after bathing, knitting quietly and softly grunting to each other in that way of theirs when at repose.

🪷

"Perhaps my mother's stern face and proud demeanour reminded Sergeant Enoda of his own mother who had died; he was then adopted by his grandparents, as is the custom. I believe all Japanese men have a special place in their hearts for their mothers. Sergeant Enoda's presence would soon save my, Mother when she had a confrontation with an armed Japanese soldier, I was terrified she would be killed. Despite this friendship, Mother told me never to trust him.

"In the damp humid conditions of the monsoon the ingredients we had taken from Yu would soon go mouldy, so my mother decided to make sweet cakes to sell in the market. Sergeant Enoda gave Mother permission to do so and she set up a market stall in the village. We needed small change instead of the high denomination notes and Maria Teresa dollars given to us by the De Souzas. These cakes became a favourite of the Japanese soldiers.

"We had reached Pybaw around mid-May; soon after the monsoon fully broke. The warm rain came down in sheets, thank God there were no high winds with the rain as yet. It usually begins raining early in the afternoon and stops in the evening but it could continue all night and all day sometimes. The rain in the afternoon was so warm and we used to stand outside fully clothed like the locals, washing ourselves under our garments, as was the custom."

A deadly tug-of-war

"It was near the guard house where the Japanese soldiers had set up a check point that an incident happened. I became terrified my mother was going to be shot or bayoneted by a Japanese soldier. She was so brave.

"One day, the usual long convoy of trucks bringing supplies to the Japanese check points was delayed by Sergeant Enoda in the belief he and his men were being short changed by the supply troops. Sergeant Enoda worked himself up into a fury. Very quickly a large crowd of villagers had gathered to watch the confrontation between the two Japanese sergeants. The Japanese troops in the guardhouse turned out with their rifles and fixed bayonets. Sergeant Enoda was a higher ranking Sergeant and wore a small purple tag on his chest that everyone respected. He slapped the supply sergeant's face. The face-slapping incidents always amused the watching Burmese villagers.

"We were selling cakes in the nearby market and heard the commotion. My mother asked me to look after the cakes so she could see what was happening. By the time my mother reached the crossroads Sergeant Enoda was in a blind rage shouting at the other sergeant. He then jumped up onto a truck and began searching for something he felt he and his men should be getting. After a short while I became worried for my mother and left our stall to see if she was alright.

"The sergeant was standing on one of the trucks throwing items of captured tin food off onto the ground, like tinned cheese which the Japs did not like. He then found a case of tinned sardines in tomato sauces, which the Japs loved. His men helped themselves, the rest were gathered up by the villagers. My mother got a couple of tins.

"Still Sergeant Enoda was not happy, there was something else he was looking for, he could smell and hear it. Climbing down, he listened along the line of trucks and then climbed onto another lorry that was covered in British Army blankets and began throwing these onto the ground. Hidden beneath the cover of blankets were bamboo coups full of chickens.

"Sergeant Enoda then went into another rage and began bellowing at the supply sergeant while throwing the coops full of fowls onto the ground. Many of the chicken coops broke and the birds quickly escaped chased by the villagers and the Japs. It was the woollen blankets that your grandmother was interested in. She picked one up and told me to take it back to our hut.

"It was the second blanket that caused the trouble. Mother was spotted picking it up by one of the Jap transport guards. He rushed over and began pulling the blanket from her; she would not let go and a tug-of-war ensued. Transport and supply Japanese soldiers were not the sturdiest of men and my mother was bigger and heavier.

"The tug of war was being closely watched by a smiling Sergeant Enoda and his troops. They made no effort to intervene but their presence must have given my mother more confidence to continue. She finally won the blanket, gave the slightest of bows to her Japanese opponent and quickly left with her prize. Two extra wool blankets were a godsend to us on chilly nights. The Japanese soldier who lost the tug-of-war was furious and, as he was only a Second Class Private, could only slap the faces of the Indian truck drivers, which he did.

"The Jap transport sergeant had also lost face – there was only one thing he could do. First he slapped the guard who had lost the contest, then slapped the Indian drivers' faces again for good measure. As some of the Indian drivers were taller than him, he stood on the step of the cab to do this. Slapping over and honour satisfied the convoy was about to move on when one of the trucks would not start. This would not be the first time we saw a Japanese soldier beat the truck engine with a stick."

🪷

I still remember these blankets: one was dark brown and had a blue stripe down lengthwise; the other was grey with a blue stripe. The two blankets remained with us in Singapore, Malaya and England, perhaps they reminded Mum of her mother's brave tug-of-war in a far distant country. I began to dislike both blankets. The Sergeant Major would wrap me (arms pinned to my side) like an Egyptian mummy when I had a temperature "to sweat out the fever" he used to say. Struggling to free myself was impossible, I could not move my arms and legs as the wrapping was so tight and I became hot and claustrophobic to the point of panic. Mum used to release me at the first opportunity. I would then quickly disappear, calling the RSM all the Burmese swear words I remembered.

🪷

"After the blanket incident, life carried on in the village as normal. As usual my mother and I sold cakes in the market. Her best customers were the Japanese soldiers who loved her cakes, but they always paid in their cheap printed occupation money and she had to take it. At that time everyone was now expected to use Japanese money (known as 'banana money'). The Burmese rupee was no longer encouraged by the new masters. The Burmese rupee was still preferred throughout Burma by the villagers and the vendors. Opium was also a currency.

"By that time the Japanese soldiers got to know my mother quite well, and treated her with respect, calling her Oka-Sama, 'Mother' and often used to bargain with her. The pay of a Japanese soldier was extremely low and they regularly counted their money. My mother speaking Nippon Go, her noble unsmiling manner and her honesty gained their respect."

❁

I can clearly remember a long line of young Japanese soldiers queuing up for Grandmother's cakes. The soldiers may have seemed old to me, but many new recruits were still in their teens. As you can see by her photograph (see plates), Grandmother had high cheekbones; when I was older she reminded me of an Apache, or perhaps (wearing a pointed fur cap), a Mongol Tartar.

❁

"When the Japanese soldiers began to talk to me, my mother always put them in their place, with a sharp word in Nippon Go or a dirty look; she was very good at dirty looks. One day during our stay at Pybaw, we suddenly noticed you were missing. We asked the villagers if they had seen you and were told that you were at the checkpoint with the Japanese soldiers.

"On hearing this news we both became extremely worried, in case you said something about your father, as you could talk by then. We both approached the guard hut, in which a group of Japanese soldiers were lounging. As soon as we got near to the open door we heard laughter from the Japs and then heard your laughter. When we looked through the door there you were standing on the table naked doing a jitter bug, stopping every now and then with your mouth open while the Jap soldiers threw small round biscuits into it. They then laughed at the monkey faces you pulled while trying to bite into the iron hard biscuits with your unstable milk teeth.

"Your grandmother picked you up and gave you a good whacking with her slipper for running away. The Japanese soldiers laughed at the painful faces you pulled. Looking back we were lucky in the sense that the Japanese troops we met were front line soldiers. However, with the wrong officers or NCOs, all Japanese soldiers were dangerous and capable of terrible atrocities.

"The soldiers at the check point were fresh from battle and were enjoying a rest from their forced marches. The Japanese were now surveying their new domain and stationing troops in most big villages. These troops were the new law and order. They were also here to control the hostile Hill tribes *[mostly Karens]* who often ambushed both Japanese and the Burmese troops. Even with the help of the Burmese, the Japanese never fully conquered the tribes that lived in the hills.

"One day a British truck arrived full of dead Japanese bodies. The headman of the village was ordered to collect wood by Sergeant Enoda. While this was taking place, the bodies were left in the truck. The smell was terrible. Any py-dogs attracted to the rotting corpses were shot. The young Japanese soldiers loved killing dogs; it was terrible to hear the yelps.

"The hard-working Japanese could never understand the Burmese lackadaisical attitude to work and lamented the time it took for the wood to arrive for the cremation. In the beginning bodies were burnt separately but as the war continued and casualties mounted, they burnt bodies communally. The smell was so strong that many of the Burmese vacated their huts and cursed the Japs. The burning bodies would sometimes move, sit up or raise an arm in salute to their emperor, as the Japs loved to believe. It was probably the contraction of sinew and muscle. All the ashes were then reverently placed in small wooden boxes with much bowing and scraping. These were to be sent back to the shrine at Yasukuni; on hearing the news their families would then proudly fly a black flag above their house.

"The one thing my mother and I dreaded was the strong winds that sometimes accompanied the heavy rain. Our hut used to sway and the walls used to bulge with the force of the wind. We would rush to the bellowing wall and support it with our bare hands. Even though you were young, you used to help us and think it was great fun."

I can remember these incidents; on many occasions both my guardians would be praying loudly to God and all the saints to save the hut being blown away like Dorothy's house in the Wizard of Oz. The loud praying and beseeching used to scare me more than the high wind. However when the wind stopped, they would sometimes lose their balance and almost go through the flimsy wall; their prayers would turn to curses.

❧

"The monsoon attracted many different species of frogs and toads. They seemed to be everywhere; this was their time to breed. The calling from these amphibians in the evening not only came from the ground but also from the trees. Frogs and toads were never harmed by the Burmese, as they were considered to be auspicious. They also kept down the insect population in the paddy fields.

"Another problem was the rat population *[the black rat]* forced from their burrows they entered the huts. Both amphibians and rodents attracted snakes, mostly rat snakes and sometimes cobras. If cobras were detected during the day by the village dogs, they were dispatched by the villagers and were then quickly devoured by the dogs. It was never safe to walk at night without a lantern and a stick."

❧

In Burma, large quick-moving rat snakes were always left in peace and were sometimes allowed to live in the rafters of some of the huts, from where they would happily watch the goings on below with interest. These rat predators can grow up to nine feet long. At night, when everyone was asleep, these efficient snakes would descend to hunt.

❧

"Second class privates up to the NCOs and junior officers always had a strong desire to learn about the world at large. Many Japanese lower-rank soldiers had no idea where England, America or Portugal was exactly. They were confident the Japanese Army would soon conquer these countries and that they would be garrisoned there: 'Were America and England cold?' 'Could rice be grown there?' 'Did the people there understand Nippon Go?' This thirst to learn covered a wide spectrum.

"When not selling cakes to the Japanese soldiers my mother would sit and knit woollen items. As keen knitters themselves, Jap soldiers would approach and ask what stitch she was using. The bull-necked Sergeant Enoda would sometimes wander over in the evening and sit with my mother and knit, sometimes he would bring her wool and small food items. Many Jap soldiers used converted chopsticks as knitting needles.

"The monsoon was now in full swing and saved us the trip to the well at the Japanese checkpoint. The next water well was some way away in the middle of the village, not far from the Pagoda. We avoided using this well in case we were questioned by the Pongyis. We would soon have a more immediate reason for not using this well; people more dangerous than Buddhist Pongyis also lived there hidden away. Although we did not know it at the time the monks were looking after another type of human that also dwelled in Pybaw: lepers. We had hoped to stay in Pybaw for as long as possible; these people would eventually force us to leave after the monsoon.

"It was a great shock to us when we first saw them. One late evening after the rain had stopped, my mother and I were at the market for our evening meal. Wood was becoming scarce. With most of my mother's time taken with making cakes she had little time to cook for us as well; you see, fuel was not easy to collect in the wet weather. It was not safe to wander far into the jungle to find it. My mother had to buy wood fuel from village men who went into the jungle with their bullock carts. That night as we walked around the market, we noticed a line of lanterns coming from the Buddhist monastery. We thought this was some kind of religious procession, as the Pongyis were in the lead. It was not until the Pongyis had passed that we saw who was behind them. Poor people, some who could barely hobble on their stumps that once were feet, others who crawled on the ground. But it was not until we could see their eaten-away faces that we were really shocked. My mother whispered that we must leave as soon as the monsoon stopped because the lepers were suffering from the most contagious form of the disease. Wet leprosy!

"The leper colony was hidden behind the Buddhist temple which was near the second water well; this was the well we were sometimes forced to draw our water from when the Japs were bathing at the well near out hut. This must also be the well the lepers used. From now on my mother said we would have to walk a long way to the third water well, which was on higher ground, the first well on the underground conduit.

"The villagers believed that leprosy was a spiritual affliction of some kind and lepers would be reincarnated as healthy people in the next life. Many of the Burmese villagers in Pybaw had relatives in the leper colony. As lepers are sensitive to the sun it was now more comfortable to leave their sanctuary as the evenings were cooler. According to my mother many of the lepers in Pybaw were also opium addicts; it alleviated their pain.

"It was here in Pybaw that we believed you picked up a serious external parasite infection by sitting on the damp mud with the other village children. This infection would only manifest itself at the internment camp months later.

"Soon after the chicken incident, many different garrison troops arrived and camped in tents on the cattle pastures just outside the village. These garrison troops would be taking over from the front line soldiers, conducting anti-guerrilla warfare in the hills against the Karens, Chins and Kachins who were pro-British and attacking and killing Japanese troops. The hill tribes were expert jungle fighters. We prayed that my brother Cyril was safe with them. But the worst news of all from Sergeant Enoda was that many Burmese National Army troops and a detachment of Kempeitai would soon be resident in Pybaw to conduct anti-guerrilla and -dacoit operations. My family was well known in Rangoon and Mandalay, and Mother was concerned that some of the Burmese officers in the BNA would recognise us. Soon after, Sergeant Enoda suggested to my mother that we should move to the internment camp at Tada u, which was also a transit camp for Japanese troops. My mother was convinced that Sergeant Enoda had seen through our pretence of posing as Mons Burmese. This was confirmed when we reached Tada u and found it was an internment camp for foreign aliens."

We must have remained in Pybaw for some time after the monsoon waiting for the muddy bullock tracks to harden before travelling. I must admit I don't remember much about this period except for one incident: my first toy, a giant grasshopper with colourful wings. The new grazing had encouraged the sudden emergence of locusts and large grasshoppers.

As the first locusts appeared all the women would go out to collect them. Initially locusts are only capable of crawling on the ground in swarms (until their wings grow) and are easy to scoop up in large bamboo baskets. Locusts are cannibalistic. Each locust, if given the chance will eat the one in front. This and the search for fresh vegetation kept them constantly moving forward. If a locust or cricket was placed on bare skin it would bite. At this time of year their bodies were soft; ideal for frying in ground nut oil. This harvesting of locusts provided an annual food supply and was always eagerly anticipated. The Burmese and Khmer always harvested the locust swarms at this soft stage of their life. Collectively, throughout Asia, this practice seems to suppress the numbers of locusts to below plague proportions. I have often wondered why only a few African tribes collect and eat locusts; they are after all a good source of protein and if cooked correctly, very tasty.

⚜

"Pybaw market was the only place where I ate fried locusts cooked in peanut oil, and only because my mother bought some. They were quite crunchy and tasty if you could forget they were insects. Other strange forms of food in the market were the big bird-eating mygalomorph spiders [wrongly called tarantulas] cooked alive in the flames. These spiders lived in deep burrows in the ground. Curiously, the lowland Burmese did not eat these spiders, only the people from the hill tribes."

⚜

The lower ranks of Japanese soldiers took great pleasure teaching us children to bow to them personally, especially when they were alone.

They seemed to love giving instructions; I suppose it gave them a sense of importance. The young soldiers also enjoyed wrestling each other during their time off from guard duty. They would often pick two young children to wrestle each other while they took on the important role of referee. That is why I have always been a good wrestler and as far as I can remember have never been beaten by any of my peers, regardless of size, except one – A slim small-boned Chinese boy who went to a school for rich Chinese children in Johore Baru after the war. After leaving my school, I would walk home past their school. The rich Chinese boys would be waiting near the gate for their chauffeurs to take them home; I would hang around the gate and challenge each one of them to wrestle me. We would end up rolling around the ground watched by their bemused chauffeurs. This small boned boy was as slippery as an eel and I could never pin him down.

❀

"The monsoon had reached its end and the bullock tracks were drying out. Despite our fear of catching leprosy and meeting the Kempeitai, we had to wait a little longer. The village and its market were now becoming crowded with different Japanese troops. Sergeant Enoda and his troops were ordered to rejoin their regiment based at Tada u, then leave for the front line somewhere. There was still an ongoing war with the American and Chinese troops in the north of Burma."

❀

Unfortunately grandmother did not know everything concerning Tada u. A nasty shock awaited us. If grandmother had been pre-warned, I doubt if she would have wanted to register at this internment camp and transit station for Japanese troops.

❀

"My mother finally decided we should take the advice of Sergeant Enoda and go to Tada u as soon as possible so she went to see him in his command hut for permission to travel, as written permission was vital. His office contained a simple desk, a pencil and two small thin writing brushes to dip into black ink and carefully paint kanji symbols. Despite being busy organizing the move to the front lines, he gave mother a document written on a piece of cheap yellow Japanese paper. My mother said it took him a very long time to complete the document as he took great care to write each character as if it was some intricate form of artistry. Mother could also use the document to ensure our safe passage when we stopped in Burmese villages. Everyone feared the Japanese Imperial Army stamp and understood that Nippon justice was immediate without trial."

CHAPTER 19

The *Lisbon Maru* Sinks

EAST CHINA SEA

Things had now quietened down on the half-submerged *Lisbon Maru*; the sailors still aboard knew it would not remain so. The singing by the brave trapped gunners in No 3 hold had long since stopped, all were now dead. With the possibility that some men were still alive in air pockets, Captain Cuthbertson (Royal Scots) asked two men, one a Corporal Isaacs and another man of the same Regiment, to enlarge the entrance of No 3 hold, now under water.

After several attempts the two men were forced to abandon their search. The entrance of No 3 hold was choked with dead bodies several layers deep, their hair swaying like fine seaweed with the movement of the waves, their eyes and mouths still wide open as if still in song. Every man aboard had listened to the brave gunners singing until the sea water stifled and choked their voices mid-note. The free prisoners roaming the decks above the drowning men stopped and stood silent in respect and admiration for the gunners who accepted their fate with such human dignity. I repeat, the word "hero" is now lightweight, used too often these days by people who have forgotten our real past heroes.

If there were any sharks in the vicinity, attracted by the underwater explosions, they did not make their presence obvious. For sharks are cautious predators. If sharks had been clearly visible to the men on board, I am sure many would have thought twice before jumping over the side. No sharks were initially present when the American troop ship *Indiana* went down: sharks then appeared and claimed 600 victims. It was later said that oceanic white tips were responsible.

All estuaries in warm seas are dangerous especially during war and famine; there would be no shortage of dead bodies in the mouth of these rivers in this part of China. The most dangerous species here are the bull-shark and the tiger shark. In the tropics when standing in open water, never turn your back on the open sea, is good advice. Prisoners, who had jumped off the *Lisbon Maru* as soon as they had broken out of the ship slowly began to regret their decision. Treading water in the strong current was strength-sapping for these already weakened men. Some struggled back on board. Stronger swimmers, with the help of favourable currents, had immediately struck out for the nearby islands and were lucky enough to reach their sandy beaches. Others less fortunate were pummelled on the sharp rocks that surrounded some of the other islands. These islands just off the coast of China were the Zhoushan Archipelago which was made up of around five hundred main islands.

Some distance away, the watching Japanese aboard the destroyer *Kuri*, noticing some of the prisoners were reaching the islands, began to launch boats. At this stage they still wanted no witnesses and began shooting prisoners in the water. Prisoners in the sea who tried to climb aboard the Japanese boats were beaten back. They were clubbed and shot. The prisoners aboard the *Lisbon Maru* and those in the water noticed the Japanese soldiers set up a machine-gun on the deck of the destroyer. Other prisoners, despite their efforts, were slowly being swept out to sea; their watching companions were helpless to give assistance. Many men including some of the sick and wounded were crowded on the decks trying to regain a little strength in the fresh clean sea air. Other prisoners with more vitality began tying anything together that would float.

☙

"Jack said that a bobbing shaven head was spotted keeping close to the keel of the ship, trying not to be noticed. It was one of the Japanese guards who up until then had escaped the attention of the prisoners. As soon as the guard realized he had been seen, he began trying to attract the attention of his comrades. Several Royal Scots began to throw down large pieces of broken hatch to kill the guard. This proved unsuccessful and several prisoners jumped in and swam towards the terrified Jap who then began screaming to his comrades to be rescued, poor man."

※

If his comrades had heard his shouts they made no attempt to save him. As far as they were concerned he was already dead. The prisoners pummelled the guard and held him under. This also happened on other hell ships also sunk by American submarines. I was once told by an American tourist, himself a POW bound for Japan, that when his ship was torpedoed, many of the prisoners in the water took a chance to exact revenge on Japanese guards and civilians also in the sea with them. These killings were witnessed by their countrymen who where also in the sea but out of reach of the vengeful prisoners.

In No 2 hold of the slowly sinking *Lisbon Maru*, prisoners could still be heard below in the darkness. Many of these men were wounded but conscious, just managing to keep their heads above the filthy water but did not have the strength to reach the deck. Again Captain Cuthbertson of the Royal Scots (wounded himself) bravely volunteered with the help of others to be lowered down on a strong rope to rescue many of these men now too weak to save themselves. Captain Cuthbertson like Colonel Stewart (Middlesex) unfortunately did not survive his imprisonment in Japan.

※

"Jack said when he finally climbed up on deck it was wonderful to fill his lungs with fresh air and feel the warm sun on his face. He began to search for men from D Company. Wandering on deck he came across some men sunbathing, some playing cards, while others held conversations with soldiers in the water, as if on holiday. A dead Japanese guard was lying on the deck. The guard's rifle was thrown overboard on the command of the senior British officer in case someone began firing at the Japanese, which would bring immediate retaliation from the destroyer nearby.

"Jack had no intention of jumping into the sea straight away as many Japanese boats with armed men were now in the vicinity and single rifle shots could be heard. He was hungry and began roaming the ship *[probably also looking for cigarettes]*. In the galley there were several men helping themselves to cooked rice from a big tub and fish paste from a stone jar; he quickly joined them. After the war, Jack couldn't tolerate the smell or sight of this pungent fish paste called 'narpe' in Burmese. There was plenty of fresh water available, as much as he and the others could drink. Everything he owned had been left behind or lost in No 2 hold in the rush to get out; he did not even have a water bottle to fill with fresh water. How he would bitterly morn the loss of his water bottle later. Jack was soon given his first cigarette of the day."

⚜

Tam and Willie were sitting with other men on the deck in the warm sunshine, smoking Japanese cigarettes and drinking looted sake. Tam, a non-swimmer, dreaded jumping into the sea. He said later, after the war: "There were nae public swimming pools in the Gorbals – only public baths and public huses."

After resting, prisoners who had reached the safety of the islands moved inland in search of food and shelter. The Chinese fishermen living on the nearby islands in the Chusam Archipelago, Chekiang District, always kept a sharp eye out for Japanese ships approaching their islands, for the enemy had more or less left them alone so far. On seeing the *Lisbon Maru*, then hearing the explosions and observing the bobbing heads in the water, the fishermen believed the men in the sea to be Japanese and turned a blind eye. They had no intention of going out fishing that day.

Some British prisoners belonging to the Hong Kong Volunteer Force, who could speak the Shanghai dialect fluently, were blessed with favourable currents and managed to reach the adjacent Chusam Archipelago. They explained to the villagers that the men in the sea were in fact British prisoners. These brave Chinese fishermen immediately took to their boats and began to pull the exhausted prisoners from the sea, despite the fact that a Japanese warship was present. To make matters worse a storm was beginning to rise and the notorious currents of this estuary were pulling men past the islands and out to sea. Those who made it ashore were looked after by the fishermen's families, feeding and clothing them as best they could.

So great was the poor Chinese fishermen's contribution to saving the lives of so many of the prisoners that after the war they were justly rewarded for the risks they had taken. The villagers were given a monetary reward and a large brand new motorised fishing boat donated by all the men who survived the rescue and imprisonment.

🪷

"The Japanese, on seeing so many prisoners being saved by the Chinese decided to pick up the men in the sea instead of shooting them or waiting for them to drown."

🪷

The three older gentlemen, members of the Hong Kong Volunteer Force who first reached the islands, were Mr Evans, the manager of a British cigarette company in Hong Kong, a Mr Johnston (occupation unknown) and a Mr Wallace, editor of a Hong Kong newspaper. With the help of the fishermen, they escaped to the mainland and reached the Communist guerrillas. These three men were responsible for organizing the gift of the boat and money after the war.

Finally the *Lisbon Maru* lurched again and the seamen still aboard knew the ship was beginning her noisy death throws. The sea rushed in forcing the air out from every opening and causing loud roars that ended in sinister hisses. The ship was going down stern first.

🪷

"As the ship began to sink, Jack and his group planned to jump into the sea and board two rafts that had been roped together. Many of the Scots

184 • Escape to Pagan

were poor swimmers or non-swimmers and had to be persuaded to leave
the ship. In fact many soldiers were determined to stay on board for as
long as possible. What the men did not know was that the ship's bow was
resting on a sand bank in only fifty foot of water but this would not last.
When the ship finally settled the decks were deep under water. The non-
swimmers clung to the high mast, the only part of the ship still visible.

"Jack *[a good diver and swimmer]* ran towards the bow of the ship
and jumped in after the two made-up rafts had been pushed overboard.
But when he surfaced he could not locate the other men or the rafts.

"Jack said he found the sea warm and wonderfully refreshing; it gave
him new reserves of energy. Despite his happiness of being in the open
air and the reviving sea, his head wound began to sting from the salt
water. Unknown to him, the large and deep exit wound on the back of
his neck had become infected again by maggots that were not visible to
the naked eye."

❧

Although the Sergeant did not like reliving being trapped in No 2
hold, he did not seem to mind recounting his experiences in the sea.
I can't remember Tam and Willie ever discussing their experience in
No 2 hold either. What a wonderful, invigorating feeling the sea must
have been for all the men after the humid, dirt-ridden, stinking holds
in the bowels of the *Lisbon Maru*.

❧

"Jack was soon joined by a sailor he knew from Hong Kong who had
lived near him in Nelson. This sailor was one of the prisoners who
had deliberately changed from No 1 hold to No 2 hold. They both
swam a safe distance from the ship believing it was going to sink at any
moment. Jack began looking for his comrades and the rafts, he was too
weak to attempt a swim to an island. He soon found a long piece of flat
timber and clung to it with the sailor from Nelson. Jack said some men
seemed to be swimming out to sea."

❧

Perhaps these men were looking for the submarine that had sunk the *Lisbon Maru*. If successful, it would mean instant freedom; many prisoners on Japanese hell-ships had indeed been liberated this way.

⚜

"Suddenly there was machine-gun fire. Jack could see the bullets hitting the water and coming his way. He dived under the sea as deep as he could manage and watched the bullets zigzag down as they lost power. When he came to the surface he was feeling faint; the sailor who was with him had disappeared.

"It was while Jack was underwater that he saw the shadowy shapes of sharks below him; they looked so small and harmless, seemed afraid of him and darted into the depths. Jack started swimming away from the ship forgetting the sharks. He soon found another kind of raft with two men clinging to it kicking their legs trying to get to the islands. He held on to this raft and tried to help but the raft was too heavy and they made little headway before they were exhausted. The two men on the raft then saw a large plank of timber and swam towards it without speaking to Jack and began to head to the shore. Jack was now alone and decided to stay with the raft in the hope it would drift towards land of its own accord. He did not like being alone and hoped he would soon have company.

"Jack just clung to the edge of the raft, he did not want to make himself a bigger target for the Japanese by being on top; he just rested his head and upper body on the planks while holding on to some ropes with his arms. Many men were swimming past him; the lucky ones had found life jackets or were using blocks of raw rubber [*part of the cargo*] for buoyancy.

"Soon he was joined by an officer from the Middlesex Regiment, who had a deep cut on his head; this officer said he received the wound when he tried to climb aboard a Japanese boat. This man had a pair of nice black patent leather ballroom-dancing shoes hanging around his neck. They began trying to propel the raft towards the land. They made little progress, the strong current was against them; it just seemed to be taking them further out to sea despite their efforts. Jack was soon exhausted by all this exertion and felt faint. His head began to throb painfully; he rested it on the raft and fell asleep. When he awoke, he was shocked to see maggots crawling all over the planks, canvas and his arms. There was only one place they could have come from, his head. He was alone again. The young officer with black patent leather shoes draped around his neck had gone.

"As the wind picked up the waves grew in height and hanging onto the ropes was increasingly difficult so Jack climbed up onto the raft. The salt water had parched his mouth and his thirst returned. In the fading light he caught sight of a man face down in the water. This body was being attacked by small sharks. Although shocked at what he witnessed, he was not afraid as he believed these predators only attacked the dead. Exposed on top of the raft Jack was now feeling very cold. Exhausted, deep sleep overcame him and momentarily released his mind and worn out body from his despair and desperate situation. As he slept it rained heavily and warmed him like a blanket. He drank rainwater trapped in the folds of canvas. When the rain stopped the cold and cutting wind struck him like whip strokes. Jack re-entered the warmer sea.

"Shivering he looked around hoping for company; he was not alone. In the fading light he saw a solitary large high fin slicing through the dark oily surface of the sea near his raft. For the first time the presence of sharks troubled Jack. He looked out for the fin again as if for confirmation; it did not appear and was forgotten."

✣

I find it amazing that initially all the prisoners who were in the sea did not instantly fear shark attack. Perhaps many did believe (like the Sergeant) that sharks only attacked the dead. All warm seas have the attending danger of shark attack for anyone on the surface of the water, especially water that contained blood. As far as the Sergeant was concerned, full fear of sharks would come slowly in stages later while he was still in the water.

✣

"As the day began to fade, he again drank from small pools of rain water caught in the canvas depressions of the raft within reach of his mouth.

These few mouthfuls gave him some short-term relief from his thirst. As soon as one need was satisfied, another took its place; the turbulent sea was making it difficult to hold on to the rising and falling raft. His grip was weakening. All his efforts to get back onto the raft failed. He knew that soon he would succumb to the inevitable when he lost contact with the raft. He craved a last cigarette. Jack began to give up hope as the raft he was on was swept further out to sea. As the raft crested a wave he could see on the horizon an island with trees and hoped to reach land before nightfall. But the next time he saw the island it looked different; he then realized the island was a low lying cloud. Bitter disappointed engulfed him and he began to pray silently.

"As the storm began to grow and the waves grew higher, the sea was now crashing over the wooden raft. Jack's strength was failing and he would not be able to grip the raft much longer. By now he had been in the water for many hours. Then as if by a miracle he felt a powerful surge of warm water on his legs and the raft seemed to have moved into a calmer sea; even the rain and wind felt warmer. Darkness had fallen. Jack had another drink of rainwater. The water gave him strength and he thrashed his legs to propel himself onto the raft. It was while he was doing this that his legs came into contact with something big under the water."

꧁

Whether the unknown object under the water that his foot had struck was a dead submerged body of one of his comrades – or a shark – is difficult to say. From that moment on the fear of sharks took root in the Sergeant's mind. He would soon see his demon.

꧁

"At first he thought he could hear sea birds and hoped he was drifting towards land. It was not long after that he noticed a light nearby; the Chinese fishermen had found him. The birds he had heard earlier on turned out to be the sing-song musical voices of the keen-eyed fishermen. They knew the currents. The fishermen climbed onto the raft and helped Jack onto their junk. Out of the cold wind he was given warm water and a strong Chinese cigarette. He noticed other prisoners on the deck; some were dead, one of the dead had a leg missing. The fishermen were taking the raft in tow. You know, I used to pray every night that he was still alive; I used to pray for a miracle – my prayers were answered.

"Jack had swallowed a lot of sea water and soon felt sick. It was while he was being sick over the side of the junk that he saw a large shark just below his head in the dim light of the lantern. He noticed it had a round, blunt-looking head and indistinct dark stripes over its body. After the war he came to the conclusion that his demon was an adult tiger shark, common in the waters of the orient.

"Back on land Jack and others were carried off the fishing junk and given some clothes, more water and a small bowl of rice. They then slept in one of the huts out of the rain; Jack was too tired to think of escape.

"Tam and Willie had been somehow separated from Jack but managed to reach an island where they joined up with other prisoners who were planning their escape to the mainland about a mile distance across an inlet. But first they needed something to eat, and so headed to the nearest village. The villagers gave them food and water. Sitting around a blazing fire warming themselves, they put off the escape till the following day."

✿

The following morning this group wasted precious time discussing their escape, when boats containing Japanese marines arrived and recaptured them. To the prisoners' great surprise they were treated well by the enemy. Japanese naval vessels took the prisoners to a wharf on the Whangpoo River in Shanghai. Around thirty-six seriously ill prisoners were taken to a hospital in Shanghai; Sergeant Devereux was among their number. After being pulled from the sea his deep neck wounds were open and raw but were free of infection and maggots. All the necessary drugs were available in Shanghai and the prisoners were given adequate treatment there. The food for the sick men also greatly improved due to unknown benefactors.

The so-called "healthy" survivors at the docks were issued with a small amount of rice and given new thin corduroy clothing and put on the *Shencei Maru* bound for Japan. At the docks before boarding, the British Officers and the Japanese took a roll call. Out of the original 1,816 officers and men, 842 were drowned or killed during the sinking, five died on the *Shencei Maru* on their way to Japan and 244 died subsequently in Japan, making a total of 1,091 deaths in total. Just 725 survivors were left.

By this time the sinking of the *Lisbon Maru* was world news, and the Japanese (not wishing the true facts to be known) had allowed representatives of the world's press to be present on the survivors' arrival in Japan. The prisoners had been warned that their answers had to favour the brave Japanese who had risked their lives to rescue them after the Americans had deliberately sunk a prisoner of war ship.

CHAPTER 20

Journey to Tada u

BURMA

࿊

"My mother found a bullock cart driver willing to take us to Tada u for two hundred Burmese rupees. On the morning of our departure, we noticed that Gunso Enoda and his soldiers had already left. We never saw him again. As we now had transport there was no need for the pram. It was so nice not having to carry or push our possession. There were three covered carts in total and their drivers; one with our possessions and the other two with supplies for villages along the way. At night we slept in the cart. Thank God we were no longer travelling on our own.

"We knew that Tada u was a military transit camp for Japanese troops, but the thought of living in a solid house with a tiled roof seemed wonderful. Unfortunately, a nasty shock awaited us. It took us many days to get to Tada u by bullock cart; travelling at the speed of a slow walk and sometimes having to get out and push when the wheels got stuck. At times the bullocks just stopped. On other occasions, if a dead snake lay on the track, they refused to move forward.

"During the journey we stopped at different villages. At night the drivers lit big fires, taking turns to guard their animals. Stopping at a village for water, we were told that a tiger had killed and carried away a man out collecting wild honey the day before. Prior to that, the headman informed us, a local teenage girl was taken by a tiger as she slept against the thatch wall of a hut. The tiger tore through the thin walls of the hut and dragged her away. Her body was never found. I began to worry but my mother said that by the time the tiger was hungry again we would be safe in Tada u. If a spare village hut was available we'd pay to stay in it. I was grateful we had the Japanese document, as some of the villagers looked very fierce and were armed. The Imperial Japanese Army stamp at the top of the document worked wonders as many Burmese could not read the kanji script.

"Sometimes we walked close behind the bullock cart, placing you on the back where we both could keep an eye on you. If we let you walk on the track you always stuck your little hands in the cow dung and played with the wild elephant droppings, looking for big dung beetles. Wild elephants often used the bullock tracks at night and sometimes attacked bullock carts and their drivers who had stopped to rest. Passing some of these sites we could see elephant footprints among the ashes of the old fires. We heard the occasional elephant in the distance, but it was the tiger I could not stop worrying about.

"Fortunately the rains were now just light, the sun grew warmer. Duck and chicken eggs were now more readily available to buy from the villagers. Rice on the other hand was hard to come by. We always ate hot omelettes containing onions, garlic and chillies for breakfast, and then had them cold for lunch with Burmese white bread called palmo. This was where you acquired a taste for stale bread.

Some of the villages we passed had been burnt to the ground by Japanese patrols for being suspected of harbouring insurgents. The Japanese try as they might could not subdue the hill tribes.

"Now we were in the jungle-covered hills the cart drivers became more afraid that their animals could be stolen by hill tribes or attacked by carnivores. We moved at a snail's pace on the uphill climbs. By this time we had eaten all our rice taken from Yu but my mother still had a few small bags of sugar, tins of golden syrup and flour which were vital for making cakes.

"Long before we reached Tada u we could see the pagoda. Before entering Tada u we were stopped at a Japanese check-point and produced our permission to travel document. Moving on, the track led past an overgrown dusty and dilapidated sad-looking cemetery, a large pagoda and a Burmese village, before reaching the brick and wood accommodation built on thick square wooden stilts. We waited under the trees in the shade while my mother went to see the Japanese commander. She told him we came south to escape the Chinese soldiers and showed him our permit to travel given to us by Sergeant Enoda. Several people came out on their narrow balconies to look at us but they did not seem very friendly. At the back of these houses were several large barracks and next to these was the military jail. In the distance and to the left of the row of houses was a big white building which had large barn doors.

"The terraced houses must have been built by the British for a cavalry regiment, as there was space under them for horses. Outside the terrace under a line of trees were many water troughs. On the other side of these barracks were the administration buildings where the Japanese officers lived. The second row of terraced houses were reserved for Indian soldiers and their families. These areas were out of bounds to us internees.

"My mother got permission from the Japanese Commander Major Watanabe to move into an available room. The commander made it quite clear that we were internees, responsible for our own welfare and food and not allowed to go beyond the boundaries of Tada u as we would be shot. When we first got there, many of the small houses were empty; we picked the closest free accommodation by the stairs not far from the well. There were few Japanese soldiers on guard duties when we arrived; the rest had left to fight the Chinese.

"Soon all the rooms on the terrace began to fill up with new arrivals and their children. None seemed to have their husbands with them and they were not Burmese speakers. There was only one man who lived in our terrace with his family who worked for the Japanese in the administration block, an Anglo-Indian called Clive Thomas. Another Anglo-Indian girl in her twenties called Maureen Johnson, who lived with her mother having lost her father during the fighting, also worked in the Japanese admin block; it was the only way she could survive.

"My mother and I prayed you had forgotten all conversations we had had about Jack and our past life; luckily you were never very bright and your head was always filled with all kinds of mischief and useless rubbish. Nevertheless we were always cautious when speaking in your presence. It was only after a few days that we found out from the other internees that the large white building with the barn doors belonged to the Japanese Kempeitai. This building was a prison where the inmates where tortured. Even the ordinary Japanese soldiers were terrified of this building and never went near it, referring to it as: 'the very bad house'.

"Occasionally at night we heard the screams of human beings in mortal agony as they were tortured by the Kempeitai. We were deeply disturbed by these sounds and prayed to God that their suffering would be short. The Kempeitai had been selected for their sadistic nature and were masters of human suffering and despair."

⚜

At Tada u my two guardians stopped teaching me personal details like my birthday and surname, and where I was born etc. I remember being asked the date of my birthday at Alexandra Military School after the war. I did not know; I couldn't even spell or remember my surname. My birthdays were never celebrated, with one exception, my seventh. As I did not know my birthday I did not care. Perhaps my dear mother forgot to re-educate me after the war; if she had, it must have gone in one ear and out of the other, another useless talent of mine.

⚜

"We were told we would receive a pass that allowed us to travel within a specific area around the camp to buy food from the markets and forage in the immediate countryside. Many internees died of starvation and disease, and particularly malaria as we were in a malaria belt. Fortunately we never contracted malaria. Later there was also an outbreak of cholera and enteric (typhoid). The Japanese, who were terrified of cholera and typhoid, asked the Burmese to dispose of these bodies; they refused. Some poor Tamil families including children were brought in and forced to do the job of burning the bodies. These poor people, we heard later, were sent into Thailand to work on the death railway.

"On arrival the new internee menfolk were forcibly removed from their families by the Kempeitai and taken to the Kempeitai building or transferred to Rangoon. Many families could not survive without their menfolk and died quietly in their rooms without anybody knowing. Maureen told us that some of these people had committed suicide. Poor people, the rest of us might have been able to help them if we had only known of their plight. I suppose their fall in position, change of circumstance and not knowing the fate of their men was just too much for them to bear.

"My mother asked for permission to sell cakes, which was granted. These privileges of travelling to find or buy food extended to all who lived in the first row of the terraced houses. The second row where Indian families of the INA *[Indian National Army]* lived, had total freedom and were fed by the Japs. The Indian women and children never mixed with us. Christmas 1942–1943 came and went without celebration it was just too painful to bring back older, happier memories. Around April 1943, my mother returned from the market and whispered to me that the British army had crossed the Chindwin: this would mean liberation. We began to observe the Japanese at Tada u hoping to witness signs of panic; we were soon to be disappointed."

🪷

We lived in Tada u for around three years. Some of my memories of it are still vivid: I can still hear the voices. I don't think Tada u was a prisoner of war camp as such; I cannot remember ever seeing it surrounded by barbed wire or having a daily tenko – again many questions I should have asked Mother. In fact I have never learned of any enclosed civilian prisoner of war camps for women and children in Burma.

🪷

"Our accommodation comprised one small bare room without a fireplace, so my mother had to cook on the narrow sheltered veranda walkway or if it rained, under the stilted terraced house. Firewood had to be gathered from the nearby jungle daily. We had to be vigilant when collecting firewood as a Burmese woman out foraging had disappeared just before our arrival into Tada u. You soon made friends with the Burmese children who appeared and played outside.

"There was a well around a hundred yards from our house. Not far from it grew a line of trees where Japanese soldiers rested on the way to the front. We used to watch them from our balcony. First they would take off their packs and one of their belts and massage their calves; then take turns standing back to back and interlocking arms. One would bend over and jiggle his knees, stretching the other soldier's spine. Unusually, some of these Japanese soldiers had beards. As a Japanese patrol marched past, all you naked children used to follow behind mimicking them until you were bellowed at by their NCO which sent you all laughing and screaming in all directions.

"We visited the well at least three times a day to get water and in the evening to bathe with the Burmese villagers. Towards the end of the war Japanese wounded were seemingly abandoned near the well under the shade of trees. Although racked with fever and thirst, their wounds often septic, they were not a priority and were left untended, while their pleas for help went ignored. These soldiers were too weak to crawl to the well for a drink. They used to beckon you children over to fill their water bottles by flapping their hand from the wrist downwards. You and the other Burmese children were always afraid of these men with their long hair and blazing fever-ridden eyes that gave them a crazed appearance. It was at this well that we witnessed many acts of cruelty, including the brutal way the Japs treated some of their own men. We civilian internees always referred to this well 'as the well of sorrows.'"

⚘

Shaving was not compulsory in the Japanese army and many tried unsuccessfully to grow whiskers. The Japanese soldiers Mum describes with beards must have been Aynu, an indigenous people of Hokkaido, known as northeastern Honshu. One day as we children played, a returning Jap patrol came to the well and began bathing. One of their number was hurriedly drawing water for everyone. Perhaps he was not quick enough, for he was being shouted at and slapped by several laughing soldiers. This beating suddenly got serious when the young soldier began to moan and fell down. The soldiers seemed to get into a rage at this and the beating became more violent; so much so that what we children initially found amusing quickly turned into fear. Some children began crying and we all ran away. I can still see the podgy screwed-up bloody face of the young soldier as the blows and kicks increased.

✿

"Not long after we arrived, another Japanese Regiment appeared from Thailand. They immediately took up anti-insurgent operations in the surrounding countryside often disguising themselves as Burmese villagers. It was said these insurgents were led by British Officers. It was around this time that the screams from the Kempeitai building began to increase. The Japanese patrols would be away for many days and usually returned with prisoners. We could never distinguish the nationality of the unfortunate prisoners before they were handed over to the Kempeitai. The handing over was usually done near the well; the well of sorrows."

✿

We children used to run towards a returning Japanese patrol out of curiosity. Sometimes they brought back wild game they had shot; but mostly it was live prisoners bound in that Japanese way. Knot tying and binding is a daily occupation for the Nipponese soldier, as buttons are seldom used. Most fastenings consisted of tying tapes together; even their helmets were held on by four chin tapes and their packs were held up by numerous tapes all tied with almost ceremonial correctness. The whole of Nipponese life is regimented and orderly, so when it came to tying up a human being, procedures were no different. The prisoner or prisoner's would already have been bound tightly in that excruciating painful Japanese style. First the wrists were tied behind the prisoner's back; then both wrists were roughly forced upwards bending the elbows, stretching tendons and joints to the maximum, until the victims hands were almost level with his shoulder blades; then his elbows would be tied together, and the rope was looped around the prisoner's neck then tightened and taken back to his wrists. This neck binding stifled the prisoner's screams and forced him to look up at the sky which stopped him from running away. The legs were left free for the unfortunate prisoner had to walk long distances. Knot tying to the Japanese seemed to be a kind of art form, like flower arranging.

As yet we youngsters were not fully capable of appreciating the unspeakable physical agony being suffered by the prisoner; yet the pain on the prisoner's face and his pleas distressed our young minds. The prisoner would be brought to the well. The soldiers would then nosily quench their thirst while ignoring the prisoner's barely perceptible pleas for water. The leader of the patrol would then make his way tentatively to the Kempeitai building and would soon return with several stern, scowling Military Policemen. The fierce faces they pulled were all part of their training to frighten everyone including their own soldiers, civilians and us youngsters. The members of the Japanese patrol would then pull back not wishing to be in close proximity to proceedings.

Sometimes before the Kempeitai arrived, passing Burmese women would engage the soldiers in flirtatious conversation and often spit streams of water at the prisoner's face and head in an insulting manner followed by a barrage of what sounded like abuse. However, this could have been an attempt by the women to help the unfortunate victim slake his raging thirst.

The Kempeitai would first question the Japanese soldiers of the patrol with hostility, shouting and face-slapping, if an answer did not please them. One bellow from a Kempeitai was enough to send us youngsters scattering.

꧁

"The Kempeitai policemen were sometimes difficult to spot as they dressed similarly to that of the army soldiers but on occasions wore a strip of white cotton on their arm. On official ceremonial occasions the Kempeitai officers dressed smartly in a light dove-grey uniform with a high-collared tunic, white gloves and gleaming black riding boots. These Military Police were suspicious of everyone. It was never wise to return their blank stares.

"My mother knew a pretty Burmese woman who sold cigars in the market; this woman's husband was a musician. Like most musicians her husband was usually drunk. This pair used to have blazing rows when he came to his wife's stall and pleaded for money. She would then get very angry and insult him by turning her back and lifting her longyi. If he continued to pester her she would then take off her slippers and throw them at him. At this stage he would run. One day we could see this woman screaming and crying at the front of our house. Her husband had been arrested by the Kempeitai. He was spotted flying his fighting kite erratically near the Kempeitai building just as a Japanese patrol was leaving Tada u. They suspected he was sending a coded message to the Karen guerrillas in the hills. The Japanese had many of their patrols ambushed whilst we were in Tada u. They arrested the kite flyer despite the fact that he was blind drunk, then they beat him with bamboo canes in public to sober him up. Looking black and blue he was released. Such was their paranoia concerning the enemies of Japan. Even the innocent sometimes confessed just to escape the physical trauma of torture. Confession meant death.

"Not far from the well was a grassy parade ground the size of a football field. Several incidents were to happen here. Some were impressive, some amusing and others deadly scenes of violence. This parade ground was used for drilling and marching Japanese and Indian troops. All Japanese military were addicted to ceremonies conducted in intricate detail and reverence, wearing grim expressionless faces.

"On special occasions, their ceremonies were impressive, like that of their Emperor's birthday for example. All the Japanese troops would stand to attention in the semi-darkness of dawn before the sunrise and wait as still as stone statues. This parade ground was the perfect place to see the first rays of the rising sun burst above the surrounding hills and flood this field with its golden fingers. This sunburst was sacred to the worshippers of the Sun Goddess. A loud brutal command, 'Kiotski Kerai', would slice through the silence and all the soldiers would bow deeply to their Goddess, holding that position for long seconds, as the subtle yet moving national anthem of Dai Nippon was played. Then shouts of 'Banzai!' – 'Banzai!' – 'Banzai!' would shatter the still morning air; this was an impressive ceremony with a touch of primitive medieval drama, as they saluted their Sun Goddess with naked swords and glinting bayonets.

"We witnessed this ceremony every April as we set out early to catch soft-shelled crabs. We always stopped out of respect, trying not to attract attention. We knew the Kempeitai were present on these occasions, for they worshiped the same goddess. The whole Nipponese culture is built on these various sacred and solemn ceremonies. Once we even witnessed a ceremony dedicated solely to honouring the camp commander's horse.

"Little did we know that before long we were to receive the individual attention of a Kempeitai officer. One afternoon as my mother was preparing the batter for the cakes, a full queue of young Japanese soldiers waited outside the house; the first ones were already on the steps. I had to push past them when your grandmother wanted water from the well. These very young soldiers were heading to the front and full of high spirits, pushing and shoving each other. They used to play all kinds of tricks on each other while they waited. I used to watch their antics from the balcony above. Two Jap officers were passing this queue of young boisterous soldiers. One was well dressed with smart black riding boots while the other appeared unkempt and scruffy. This scruffy officer started bellowing at the young soldiers and began lashing out with a bamboo stick he was carrying. All the young soldiers seemed terrified of this officer. The smartly dressed officer did nothing and just watched. The scruffy Jap officer then lined the men up into an orderly queue, all at a correct distance apart. Then both officers left without a backward glance.

"My mother thought the scruffy officer was Kempeitai despite the fact he was not wearing a white cotton strip of cloth around his right arm. She came to this conclusion because of the soldiers' terrified reaction to him and told me to be careful of him in the future. Later during that same week, this scruffy officer knocked at our door! My heart leapt when I saw him. My mother stayed calm and immediately thought he had come to check if she had permission to sell cakes to the Japanese soldiers. Mother handed him the printed permission written in Japanese. He barely glanced at it then handed it back to her. He spoke in English, asking my mother how long had we been in Tada u, where had we come from originally and had we ever visited Europe. She told him exactly the same as she told the camp commander. No we had never been to Europe and had always lived in Burma as this was our country. The fact that this officer spoke reasonably good English worried us even more. We waited for him to ask our family history, but instead found he wanted to talk to my mother about Rangoon; was he testing us? My mother said she knew Rangoon. It seems he had just returned from Rangoon and thought it was a shame the Japanese Air force had bombed the city so thoroughly. He emphasized that the Japanese had taken great care not to damage the Shwedagon Pagoda as they were also Buddhists.

"While talking he smoked cigarettes from a nice silver case, which he seemed to be very proud of. He came on several other occasions and would stand on the doorstep talking to my mother, always in English. I stayed in our room looking after you. We began to dread his visits and felt he was about to arrest us every time he arrived. He must have known that my mother spoke Nippon Go from the camp commander. Suddenly on one occasion, out of the blue he asked her why she had troubled to learn the Nipponese language. My mother answered diplomatically, without hesitation: 'Because Nippon Go is a beautiful language.' He seemed very pleased at her answer. Every time my mother answered a question he seemed to take a long time considering it. But thank God he suddenly disappeared from Tada u. What a relief it was, we never saw him again.

"We discovered that you were sneaking away with the young village children and playing near the Buddhist pagoda. We had heard stories from the villagers about a large sacred cobra that lived in a hole under the pagoda on the edge of a small path that led to the cemetery. This was certainly true as it was often seen crossing the path and entering the graveyard in the evenings and returning to the pagoda in the mornings. This venomous reptile was only sacred when it was within the boundaries of the pagoda; if it was met outside the boundaries the villagers would try to kill it with no qualms whatsoever. We never saw this snake but it would soon claim a victim. This graveyard was now being used by both

Buddhists and Christians to bury their dead as space for new graves was becoming hard to find."

I remember this pagoda and going to the cemetery with the native children to pick the fallen ripe fruit of the sweet bay tree. This tree was untouched by the Burmese and the Japanese, as they believed the fruit belonged to the spirits of the dead.

"The Burmese loved raw eggs of any kind, including reptile eggs. Egg collecting and the shooting of birds was a favourite pastime for the older village boys who owned catapults and was a welcome addition to their meagre diets during the occupation. The birds would be barbecued and the eggs would be eaten with nutmeg, raw onions and salt. A teenage Burmese boy from the village noticed that several round white cobra eggs had rolled down and were visible at the entrance of the hole that bordered the path. He tried to collect them; he was bitten. He died late that night while unconscious 'when his lungs collapsed,' according to my mother. She knew the boy's mother quite well, and was present at his death. We attended the funeral and joined in the procession with its banging of cymbals and drums; we went as a token of respect to the Burmese villagers. During her life my mother had seen several people die of snakebite including a servant of ours we had in Rangoon, before the war."

Justice Nippon-style

"One day my mother and I were sitting outside when a tribeswoman suddenly appeared along the dirt road. Congealed blood covered her face, neck and her colourful tribal costume. She looked as if she had been mauled by some wild animal (Mother said sloth bears often attack the face). This woman said she had been robbed of her dowry by a Japanese soldier. She asked some Burmese women where she could find the camp commander. They told her to speak to Mr Thomas who worked for the Japanese; he escorted her to Major Watanabe. The Major had lived in Shwebo before the war and spoke good Burmese. The tribeswoman told Watanabe that she was on her way to market when she was stopped by a patrol of soldiers and questioned. One of them demanded the thick gold rings through her nose, ears and around her neck. When she refused he physically pulled the jewellery off, causing her these terrible injuries. These items were her dowry, as was her face, which would now be scarred for life. Her chances of finding a husband were now greatly reduced. Every Japanese, whether he is an officer or a one-star private, inherits an inbuilt tradition of peasant values. This cultural rural logic would pluck at the strings of their code of honour.

"The commander asked the young woman if she could recognize the soldier responsible. She said she could. Waiting until all the patrols had returned, the camp commander mustered all the troops out on to the parade ground. The news had quickly spread and most of the people who lived in the terraced houses, along with the Burmese villagers went to see the outcome of Japanese justice. These curious watchers would soon be shocked. We did not go as it was not compulsory, but heard all about it after it was over.

"The tribeswoman along with the commander and several officers, all carrying their swords, walked along the line of soldiers. The tribeswoman recognized the soldier who had robbed her. He was quickly searched; nothing was found. NCOs rushed to the barracks to search his possessions and the gold was found. The soldier was then disarmed and his face slapped in public by Major Watanabe, who then drew his pistol and shot the Japanese soldier dead. That was the first time many of the onlookers had seen a man killed. The gold was returned to the tribeswoman.

"One day we heard wonderful whispers: the British were counter-attacking in the Arakan, and the Chinese Army together with the Americans were pushing down from the north. We were so excited at this news and watched the Japanese with interest. But they carried on as normal and looked unconcerned. We heard that British soldiers who had been captured would soon be arriving at Tada u. We were all very curious to see them and waited in anticipation. A lorry arrived with the prisoners who looked very tired and thin in their tattered uniforms but did not seem to have been tortured. Their hands were tied at their sides with rope around their waists. They had to be helped off the trucks because when they fell over they could not get up again. They were lined up and several Japanese officers arrived with swords. Oh my God, I thought they were going to be beheaded in public and we would be forced to watch.

"These British prisoners looked apprehensive and blinked in the sunlight. They were all given water and then led away to the Kempeitai building. We all dreaded hearing their screams that night. The following afternoon Maureen, who worked for the Japs, said the prisoners were given food and were then taken to Rangoon. I prayed Jack was still alive and not being ill-treated wherever he was.

"The Allied ground attack never came but Allied planes began flying over Tada u. Then one day a pilot who had been shot down was brought in to camp. He was to be decapitated and everyone was ordered to attend. I did not want to go; my mother said that if we did not attend the Kempeitai would suspect us of having anti-Japanese feelings. I was determined to close my eyes when it happened."

❧

I remember this gathering as we young children wanted to see a man's head being cut off, or so we thought. We were fascinated by the Japanese swords and the reverence their owners afforded them. We were led to believe they were magical weapons and could cut through iron; these swords could win battles on their own when in the hands of the Japanese.

❧

"A large crowd had gathered; army to one side, civilians to the other. Most of the people from Tada u and surrounding villages were present and seemed to be looking forward to the event, although they remained very silent. I believed they all changed their minds after. I was almost in tears; my mother told me to pull myself together, she said the pilot would have been drugged with opium, he would not know what was going on. In fact, that afternoon there would be two beheadings. All the Japanese soldiers stood around smoking and chattering until two Jap officers appeared smartly dressed in white shirts and white gloves: both carried swords. Now the mood of the watching Japanese troops changed and everyone fell silent while they went about their rituals."

♧

Beheading was almost conducted with solemn reverence a mixture of Bushido and Shinto Buddhism. The more sensitive of the Japanese watchers may have felt a twinge of sympathy for the prisoner if he died bravely. I did not see this beheading; perhaps I just heard the faint sigh of expelled breath from the watchers after the blade flashed downwards.

♧

"When we got there, I stood behind my mother; I couldn't see anything, and neither could you, thank God. Even so, I closed my eyes during each beheading. We did not know who the second man was. We were told of another beheading a few weeks later that had taken place behind the Kempeitai building, witnessed only by some Burmese men who had climbed nearby trees for a better view. The execution was carried out crudely without skill; at each failed attempt the victim's screams could be heard by the spectators. This upset them, as the man was locally known."

"Every morning we would go out foraging to collect firewood and various wild plants that were safe to eat. There were small soft-shell crabs to be found in a swampy area; these would be fried in peanut oil with onions and garlic. In this swamp we had competition in the form of a very large monitor lizard that used to hiss at us. When it realized my mother was intent on killing it for food, it kept its distance. I was terrified of it; it could run and swim extremely quickly. Every time we went out foraging in this area, I thought about the woman who had mysteriously disappeared.

"On our way home from our foraging trip, we passed the large sports field and noticed a group of Burmese had gathered and were intently watching something in the middle of the field; they appeared ready to bolt, young legs nearest, old legs further back to ensure a good head start. As we moved closer, we saw the object of their interest to be two large male hamadryads in ritual combat. This titanic battle had been going on for some time. These were the first wild king cobras I had seen."

꧁

I can still see in my distant mind's eye, the two massive venomous snakes with their large oval hooded heads raised high off the ground. The two king cobras were fighting for the pleasure of mating with a female; I presume she was watching the contest with amorous interest. When these aggressive snakes are fighting for a female, they become oblivious to the presence of nearby humans.

꧁

"A young junior Japanese officer happened to be passing by the field at the same time when he was called over by some pretty Burmese girls. Curiously he approached and the two fighting snakes were pointed out to him. At first he could not believe his eyes – the two snake heads were five to six feet off the ground and you had to look closely to see they were indeed snakes. The Jap officer's mouth fell open and he grimaced like a monkey. We would later get to know this officer quite well as he and his men were in charge of the pack ponies that used to be tethered under the trees outside our terrace; he reminded my mother of a startled frog.

"The watching Burmese, especially the pretty young women, encouraged the Japanese officer to kill the snakes. They conveniently neglected to inform him that there was a female hamadryad nearby. If bitten the massive amount of venom injected [*the bite of a king cobra can inject over 500cc of venom at one time which can kill an elephant*] would have rendered him unconscious before he reached the army barracks. The Jap hesitated, but Nipponese manhood was at stake. He drew his sword and pulling a face only a Jap could pull, slowly approached the two preoccupied reptiles in true kendo fashion legs apart. As soon as he was in range, his sword flashed and two large decapitated heads fell to the ground while their bodies coiled and uncoiled like giant corkscrews. All the pretty girls clapped and commented on his bravery. The Jap stood distracted and basked in the adulation. It was only when he turned to inspect the two heads that he saw the female hamadryad approaching; head high off the ground charging down on him with great speed. Without further ado the terrified Jap bolted, dropping his sword in the process. Deprived of revenge the female hamadryad returned into the jungle. On seeing the female snake's departure, the Japanese junior officer returned grinning and with sign language, asked the watching Burmese to retrieve honourable weapon. They declined his generous offer. Slowly with an eye on where the female snake had disappeared, he picked up his sword and after skewering both heads on his blade, made for the army barracks to show his comrades. The disappointed Burmese disbanded.

"One day, I remember, you stole a ping-pong ball belonging to a Japanese soldier who chased you as you ran back home with it. You were hiding behind your grandmother still holding the ping-pong ball when the angry Japanese soldier appeared at our open door only to be confronted by my mother. The enraged soldier was surprised when my mother spoke to him in Nippon Go. When she found out what you had done she grabbed you by the arm and gave you a good beating on your naked bottom with her leather slipper watched by the smiling Japanese soldier. You were still loathe to give up the ball, so your grandmother had to wrestle it out of your hand. The watching Jap soldier then requested an extra whack on your backside for good measure. This you got. You were balling your eyes out."

🪷

I remember this well; me and other naked Burmese children were sitting on chairs watching the Japanese soldiers play a game of ping-pong in one of the army barracks. I was fascinated by the ping-pong ball; it seemed like a magical round egg that didn't break and as soon as it fell at my feet I picked it up and scarpered with the Jap in hot pursuit. It would be several years before I owned my own ping-pong ball that would lead to a far more frightening experience.

※

"Several days after you stole the ping-pong ball, you came running in the house crying. A Japanese soldier who was giving out slices of watermelon to the village children shouted at you to go away. Your grandmother got angry and went straight out to buy you a watermelon. When she came back and cut the watermelon open, you refused to eat it because the flesh wasn't as red as the Jap's melon. We could have murdered you. My mother and I ate the melon."

※

I remember this incident clearly. I joined the queue for a slice of melon but an Indian boy spotted me and said something to the Japanese soldier. I was bellowed at – "Kurra!" – and legged it home crying. Perhaps the Indian boy had told the Japanese soldier that I was the notorious ping-pong ball thief?

※

"It was around this time that we heard rumours that the Japanese were running out of ammunition and that they were now using bamboo machine guns that made the same noise to fool the enemy. This turned out to be true."

※

CHAPTER 21

The Cherry Blossom Islands

JAPAN

The 724 fit survivors of the *Lisbon Maru* reached Japan without incident on the *Shencei Maru,* which docked at Moji harbour on the 10th October. To the surprise of the prisoners, representatives from the world's press were present and wished to speak to them regarding the sinking of the *Lisbon Maru.* Before this could happen, the prisoners were warned not to divulge any of the details that would compromise the reputation of their captors. Knowing there would be severe reprisals, the survivors were forced to comply. This enabled the Japanese to sanctimoniously announce that all the rescued prisoners were eternally grateful for the kind and generous treatment they received from the Imperial Army and Navy. Tokyo Rose (Iva Toguri D'Aquino) had another field day praising Nipponese gallantry while criticising the American submarine arm as heartless barbarians for deliberately sinking a prisoner of war ship.

However, soon after, the Japanese Army Headquarters in Tokyo issued an order concerning all prisoners being shipped to Japan: "Recently during transporting prisoners of war to Nippon, many prisoners have died and many have been incapacitated due to their treatment on board. In future the prisoners should arrive at their destination in a condition to perform work for the good of the Nipponese war effort." The next part of the order was typical of the Japanese when dealing with non-Japanese: "If the present conditions continue [concerning prisoners] it will be impossible for us to expect world opinion of us to be what we want it to be!" Despite this order, conditions for prisoners at sea did not change for the better; perhaps this order was "belly talk"; you had to guess what it really meant.

The remaining prisoners (the so-called "fit" men) were then split into two groups. I have no exact information regarding where Sergeant Devereux was at this time, perhaps he was still in Shanghai with the seriously sick or in the hospital at Kukara where another twenty-two prisoners died.

At Moji the prisoners were surprised to be loaded onto comfortable trains and provided with regular meals of good quality and quantity. The prisoners were taken to Hiroshima; from there they were split up and sent to various work camps, mines and dockyards in Nagasaki, Osaka, Narumi and Nagoya.

Sergeant Devereux, when classed fit for work, spent some time in Narumi, Tateyama and Nagoya POW camp. Nagoya camp was situated in the middle of the town where he was in charge of a working party of Royal Scots. He was later transferred (according to Mother) to Nagasaki before the war ended. This may well be true, as he often talked of the Australians (there were no Australians in Tateyama as far as I know) who were the greatest risk takers, thieves and saboteurs of Japanese war production, despite the regular bashings they received from the guards. He and other men of the Royal Scots used to cringe as an Australian whose surname was Diamond used to nosily puncture drums containing oil with a hammer and spike late at night.

One thing I do know, wherever the Sergeant was, he would be exchanging his midday rice and small pickle for tobacco. The weather in Japan can be colder than Britain, as the islands are situated not far from Siberia. The biting cold wind cut through the thin uniforms of the half-starved prisoners.

✿

"Jack said that the winds in Japan where colder than those that came off the Pennines in winter. In Nagoya Jack began to learn Nippon Go from a member of the Hong Kong Volunteer Force who spoke it fluently. Many of the elderly businessmen serving in the HKVF spoke Japanese and Chinese in their line of work. Their presence was one of the reasons why this POW camp ran relatively smoothly. Much of the troubles in POW camps were caused by misunderstandings."

✿

Tam and Willie finally ended up in Nagasaki. At the beginning the food and the daily quotas of work expected were reasonable and this continued throughout the first year, however, the following year when Nippon no longer ruled the seas, the food situation grew steadily worse for all the people of Japan. The submarine embargo enforced on Japan by America was biting hard. Japanese civilians were hungry and were forced to go out at weekends to forage for wild greens in the countryside and collect seaweed.

One day at Nagoya POW camp, the volatile veteran guard Sergeant Kanamura presented Sergeant Devereux with a small satsuma as if it was the most rare and mythical "All Seeing Eye." The grateful Sergeant quickly swapped it for three cigarettes. Sergeant Devereux was Kanamura's favourite prisoner because of his honesty and military bearing while taking his punishment, and perhaps because he survived an attempted beheading. He considered himself an expert on decapitation after his long service in China and had many photographs to prove it. Using his cane, Kanamura often used Sergeant Devereux to demonstrate the correct way to behead a prisoner. It must have entered the Sergeant's mind that one day a warrior-god would use a real sword instead of a stick.

CHAPTER 22

Typhoid and Cholera

BURMA

꧁

"Cholera and typhoid were bought to Tada u by some poor Tamil slave workers who had escaped from the Three Pagodas Pass, on the Burmese side of the Siam death railway. They left several of their dead companions behind near the Buddhist pagoda and water well. To our consternation, you contracted typhoid. If it was not for your grandmother's care and attention, you would have died. I didn't know what to do or how to cope keeping your illness a secret not only from the Japs but everyone else that lived in our terrace. The Japanese were terrified of typhoid and cholera, which could kill in twenty-four hours. They walked around wearing white masks and gloves for many days keeping away from everyone. All the bodies had to be burnt in the jungle. My mother said we had to isolate your drinking water from ours as typhoid is spread through water.

"After a week or so you began to recover, but we didn't allow you to play with the other children until you had gained weight and looked relatively healthy. We used to go to all kinds of lengths to get you to eat and look normal. Luckily just before you fell ill you had caught a serious parasitic disease called mec-a-lau. You broke out in boils on your bottom, each containing parasitic worms that would have eventually burrowed into the skin and entered your vital organs, killing you. This was our excuse to keep you indoors for this infection was also very contagious. My mother had never heard of this disease before and did not know how to treat it. The Burmese women told her to contact a tribal shaman woman who could cure the infection with a native remedy. The shaman, an old tribeswoman, arrived.

"We had to hold you down on your tummy while she put some white powder on the boils on your bottom; she then placed something in her mouth and began chewing, then puffed on her big cigar until it glowed red. She then dabbed the red hot cigar on each boil and burst them while you screamed the place down. I felt so sorry for you, but the female shaman just laughed and spat some brown liquid on each wound. This quietened you down a bit and you soon fell asleep. My mother said the shaman had been chewing opium.

"One day I was overjoyed to hear that the De Souza family had moved into the end house of our terrace in Tada u. I quickly rushed over to see them and was shocked to learn that since we last saw them at Yu, only three females of the family had survived and they had lost everything. Only Maria De Souza left the house to visit us every day; she was such a lovely girl; it was now our chance to help them find food and give them money."

☙

I am not sure what misfortunes had befallen the De Souzas since we last saw them, as I was always told to wait outside whenever my grandmother or mother went to visit them. I only ever saw the oldest daughter, Maria; she looked after me sometimes and came foraging with us. I can't ever remember seeing the younger sister or their mother and Mum never mentioned what tragedy had befallen them. Grandmother was happy to repay their generosity and cooked their evening meals, cared for their mother and gave Maria money.

☙

"Many of the internees who arrived in Tada u died of hunger and disease once their money had run out, as they were expected to look after and feed themselves. It was not long after the De Souzas' arrival that my mother received news from people who worked on the railway and were travelling through Tada u. She heard that her youngest son Victor, my brother, was seriously ill with malaria. She went to see the Japanese commander immediately to get permission to go and bring her son back to Tada u. How my mother got this permission I do not know; perhaps she bribed him as she was still carrying some rubies. Written permission was given in Japanese.

"My mother made the journey to get Victor firstly on foot and then caught a train at Shwebo; many people she knew still worked on the railway. Eventually Mother found Victor and paid porters to carry him on a bamboo stretcher. They also travelled by bullock cart and boat. The return journey was a great strain for a woman of your grandmother's age. She used all the money she had to hire and bribe Burmese officials and porters wherever she could.

"One night a tiger was heard roaring as they sheltered in an old dilapidated hut in a deserted village. It seemed to be approaching their hut. My mother sat with her unconscious son cradling his head. She was sure that, had it not been a dark moonless night, the terrified porters would have deserted her. The roaring stopped at the outskirts of the village. Exhausted she fell asleep. The following morning when they resumed their journey they passed a dead bullock that the tiger had been feeding on during the night.

"The whole journey took over two weeks. It was late one night when Mother arrived back at Tada u with Victor. She was so upset; poor Victor had somehow contracted cholera on the journey and was now dying. Victor died in my mother's arms a few days later. It was the only time I saw my mother weep; her one consolation was that she was able to grant her son's last dying wish: a glass of sugar water."

❦

I remember Uncle Victor lying on the floor hidden behind a waterproof ground sheet screen. I used to sit just out of reach of his long bony fingers and stare at his shrunken face framed by long blonde hair until he opened his blue-grey eyes; I had never seen such eyes before and they scared me. Victor would call my name as if wanting me to move closer; I would quickly scuttle away. I had been told never to make contact with Victor. Grandmother and Mother always sat with him when he was conscious. He would say "Mother, get my guns – I will go shooting later."

༄

"In moments of consciousness he recognized Mother and me. We found out from Victor that after we were separated on the Myitkyina train he went on to Maymyo on his own while Cyril returned to the hills and stayed with the Shans. Lucy returned home to her family. The night my brother Victor died the Banshee was calling from the trees nearby. My mother told the Japanese that Victor had died of malaria.

"The following day Mother wrapped Victor's body in some cheap cotton cloth. He was so thin, only skin and bone; he used to be such a tall strapping young man. We had to bury him quickly. The coffin was only a wooden box; too small for my 6ft 2in brother. Mother struggled to get Victors body into the makeshift coffin. I could not bear to watch. We took Victor straight to that grim, overgrown graveyard in a covered bullock cart. My mother had paid some Burmese men who were grave diggers to have the pit open when we arrived. Maria De Souza, several Christian families and some of the Burmese villagers accompanied us. Halfway to the graveyard we were joined by two Japanese soldiers who were armed; they may have been ordered to keep an eye on us, or perhaps they were Christians. Many of the Japanese soldiers from Nagasaki were Christians. These two soldiers just watched proceedings from a distance.

"When we got to the overgrown graveyard we found to our horror that the grave had been dug in the exact spot where another person had been recently buried. The woman's body was laying not far away, her long luxuriant black hair partly covering her scull. My mother was so angry with the two grave diggers; she called them all kinds of names in Burmese. Some of the Burmese women joined in the insults. The two grave diggers looked sheepish and said that a fresh grave was too hard to dig so they had to dig up the woman's grave because the earth was much softer there. Mother got them to move the woman's body further away but the smell still lingered.

"My mother conducted a short service in Latin and Victor was buried. I just could not help balling my eyes out – what a waste of such a young life. My mother told the grave diggers that she would visit the grave of her son every day, if she found it had been disturbed she would then report them to the Japanese commander. We cleaned around the grave and placed wild flowers on it. It was such a lonely, dry and barren graveyard almost completely surrounded by jungle; it was not a place where a Christian soul could rest in peace."

⚜

I can distinctly remember the dead women the grave diggers had unearthed. Her black hair was long and thick and firmly attached to her skull. Her whole skeleton was still in one piece, held together by tough dark sinews and cartilage. Her mouth was wide open as if she was screaming, her perfect white teeth clearly visible beneath strands of her long black hair. Her bones were still in that black stained stage and her fleshless and naked pelvis could be glimpsed through her rotting longyi. The smell of the woman's earthly remains dominated that sad and humid Burmese afternoon.

My grandmother visited that lonely graveyard every day to make sure her youngest son's grave was undisturbed. After a while I and some of the younger boys (hearts racing) sneaked past the pagoda and rushed in among the graves to pick up fallen bay fruit, then rushed out again. By that time the woman's bones had been scattered and splinted by hyenas; only long wisps of her black hair remained.

⚜

"Somehow news of the war *[be it out of date]* filtered into camp. We never knew where it came from but the local Burmese were now becoming disillusioned with their new allies. In 1944-45 Allied planes began attacking targets in and around Tada u. To add to our worries, people who lived in our terrace began to disappear during the night; no one knew what had happened to them as often their meagre possessions were taken away. We began to suspect the Kempeitai. Our dread of them grew.

"We were so excited when we heard rumours that British troops had crossed the Chindwin and some time later had crossed the Irrawaddy River. There were also rumours that the American and Chinese Armies were still pushing the Japs back. We waited expectantly to hear the sound of fighting. We were so happy at the possibility of being liberated and watched the behaviour of the resident Japs, expecting them to start running around jabbering in that excited way of theirs. But they did nothing and carried on as usual with their parades and patrols into the hills. It wasn't long before our hopes were dashed by the Japanese, who boasted that 'the American and Chinese Armies had been defeated and pushed back with severe losses.' They also claimed that the British Army had been beaten and had retreated back across the Irrawaddy and Chindwin rivers, leaving behind many dead and wounded men, equipment and pack animals. The most heartbreaking news of all was that the Japanese Army and Indian forces were attacking India and would soon be in Delhi. It seemed that Burma was still totally occupied by the Japanese. All the same, the amount of Japanese troops passing through Tada u increased and captured British tanks, together with Japanese tanks, were parked on the playing fields."

❧

These could have been the smaller Jap 94 type tankette or the bigger Type 95. Both tanks were obsolete but had reliable air-cooled engines. Captured British tanks were often used by the Japanese.

❧

"They were very proud of these tanks and had them constantly guarded and covered in cut branches. Curious children were chased away.

"Although we could not see the Indian families, we could hear them celebrating the march on India. But I think most of these poor Indians knew by now that India would end up like Burma, part of the Japanese Empire."

❧

It was generally believed that the Japanese were natural jungle fighters and had gone through extensive jungle training. This was a myth. The fact is the Japanese had conducted no such general training; the climate in Japan, China, Formosa (Taiwan) and Manchuria did not provide the right environment. Their successes lay in the fact that they were tough, disciplined and conditioned to hardship. In truth, many Japanese were afraid of the jungle. To emphasize this, the Japanese did not succeed in subduing the hill tribes who were masters of jungle warfare. A group of Chindits had been captured by the Japanese in dense jungle. At night, the Japanese guards ordered several large fires to be built around their bivouac then arranged the prisoners into a perfect circle, in the middle of which the Japanese guards slept. Their logic was simple: if a tiger appeared it would help itself to a scrawny prisoner rather than a nice plump Jap.

After the war many people looked on the British Major General Orde Charles Wingate, who created the Chindits, a long-range jungle penetration unit, as some kind of eccentric genius and the master of jungle warfare. This was not the general opinion. Eccentric he certainly was; a genius in jungle warfare, perhaps not. Wingate had no previous jungle experience, having served in North Africa against the Italians. It was said by many that he sometimes briefed his officers in Africa lying stark naked on his camp bed.

The brave Chindits were usually marched until they were too worn out to fight. Long range penetrations, it is said, did the enemy little harm; yet they gave those at home a great boost to moral. However the Chindit defensive blocks were with one exception a total success. It is said Wingate asked too much of his brave soldiers. Many were left behind. The Burmese jungle is a dangerous place for a man who had the misfortune to become separated from his comrades. A guest (ex-Chindit) staying at my hotel during the late seventies recounted an event during the Burma campaign concerning a personal friend of his, a lance corporal. The column of Chindits reached the top of a hill and decided to brew tea before descending. The lance corporal walked a short distance to check the route of their descent. He never returned. Despite a search by his comrades, no trace of him was found. I have sometimes pondered this man's fate on that far off humid Burmese afternoon. Suicide perhaps; but no shot was heard. Did he just walk away? Was the soldier's death natural, falling prey to a predator? Was he being intently watched by the golden malevolent eyes of a feline? Or had he attracted the attention of a large Burmese python? If it was the former, death would have been instantaneous; a single bite to the neck severing the vertebra. He would then be carried away. There would be no tell-tale blood to indicate such an encounter. Death in the coils of a large python would be slow and traumatic once a thick muscular coil encased his ribcage, allowing just one soft groan perhaps before suffocation. We shall never know.

When Wingate was killed in a plane crash in India in 1944, Brigadier Lentaigne was chosen to replace him. Mike Calvert, an excellent soldier and leader, would have been a more popular choice. Brigadier Lentaigne adopted the Grand old Duke of York tactics and marched his men up the hill and all the way down again, until they were exhausted.

The Japanese invasion of India caught out the top brass. Despite reports by the Karen and Gurkha levies that the Japs were crossing the Chindwin in battalion strength, little or no action was taken. It seems a few of the high and mighty had short memories. When it was established that the enemy was about to attack, regiments were ordered to dig in then received new orders to change positions at the last minute: shades of 1942. The enemy only just failed to reach the massive dumps at Dimapur. If they had, the battle of Kohima would have been lost. If it was not for the brave defence of Shanshak by the Indian Parachute Regiment led by Hope Thomson, the enemy would have arrived several days earlier while nervous commanders were still shuffling their defences. The successful defence of Kohima and Imphal were due to the bravery of men and officers in the badly prepared defences. General Slim reshaped Allied tactics.

⚜

"News of the campaigns to the west and north flooded in to Tada u. For us there was nothing worse than first receiving good news, only to have our hopes of liberation dashed a few days later. News of the Japanese advance into India sent many into despair. We all expected India to fall quickly considering the situation there, but after weeks of fighting the monsoon broke and many Japanese sick and wounded began arriving at Tada u. This gave us hope. Some soldiers brought back parachutes of different colours and sold them to the Burmese; cloth was difficult to obtain during the war but unfortunately the parachutes were not made of silk. The Japanese now began telling the Burmese that the war would last a hundred years. Then one day we heard a name whispered: Iwo Jima."

CHAPTER 23

The Lost Japanese Patrol

BURMA

"One day a group of Japanese soldiers set out from Tada u in a lorry on an anti-partisan patrol; with them was a Burmese tracker. Only the Japanese driver and Burmese tracker returned. The Karens were now coming down from the hills and ambushing Japanese convoys. According to the single Japanese survivor, the patrol had been a victim of an evil Outosan. He claimed the patrol was driving along a lonely jungle flanked track when they passed a large banyan tree and saw a beautiful naked Karen girl standing at the side of it while combing her long black hair. As the Japanese approached the girl, she turned into a large python and attacked them. Seeing this, the rest of the patrol ran into the jungle. We all laughed at the Japanese soldiers' cock-and-bull yarn to hide a very successful ambush by the Karens. We had also been told previously that a Jap pilot had beheaded an enemy pilot with his sword while flying his plane.

"The ambush was the talk of Tada u for many days; the Burmese believed the story and that it signified the end of Japanese rule in Burma. The Karens under British leadership were now coming down from the hills and attacking Japanese outposts. The Japanese made up the most ridiculous lies and repeated them to us with stony faces. My mother said the Japanese were among the most truthful and polite of

races *[amongst themselves that is]* and that they were only just learning
how to lie to non-Japanese."

☙

The naked girl was probably a decoy, knowing the Japanese love of
beauty. The Japanese had a healthy respect for the hill tribes and their
skill as jungle fighters. These hill tribes inflicted enormous casualties
on the Emperor's troops and as a result they suffered terrible revenge.
These hill tribes were badly let down after the war by British politicians.

☙

"One day a Burmese boy was playing with a metal object that fascinated
you; it was full of small coloured wires and taken from a crashed British
plane. You wanted one and asked me and my mother to come with
you. My mother said it would be very dangerous and forbade you
to leave the house despite your bawling. Some days later we thought
you had forgotten about the metal object and let you out to play. My
mother then noticed that you were missing. We searched everywhere
until a neighbour said she had seen you walking in the direction of
the Kempeitai building. This was dangerous. After a long search we
returned home hoping to find you there; you were not. It was while we
were deciding what to do next that you returned, crying your eyes out."

☙

On my way to find the plane, I was forced to pass the Kempeitai building.
As I walked past, the big doors were closed. I carried on along the track
until the camp was out of sight. Stories I had heard about the dangers
of wild animals began to worry me and I decided to go back home. On
returning again I passed the Kempeitai building. The big doors were now
wide open and I could hear the angry bellows of the Japanese soldiers
accompanied by high pitched animal-like screams of agony.

I moved nearer to have a look through the big open double doors. A
naked man was suspended from the wooden beams by his arms, which
were tied behind his back. He was being tortured by two Japanese

Kempeitai policemen. One of the torturers was holding a long length of pointed bamboo which he was pushing into the prisoner. The prisoner was pleading, wailing and screaming for mercy. This sight and the sound of the desperate pleading shocked me and I froze into a numb silence until one of the torturers turned and saw me. He screamed "Kurra – Kurra!" This sent me running home crying. Although much sand has passed through the hourglass since that day, I can still picture the scene vividly, and the glistening pool of blood below the victim. It was the first time I heard a human crying out in mortal agony. What nationality the man was I could not say, but screams of pain must all sound the same regardless.

🪷

"British planes began attacking Tada u and the surrounding area. We could feel the vibrations of the bombs and hear the machine guns. Anti-aircraft guns were erected about a quarter of a mile from our terrace. Because of these guns, the Allied planes began to bomb the whole of Tada u camp.

"Then one day bombs fell on the terraces. Luckily our terrace was not damaged as the planes concentrated on the barracks and administration buildings. We no longer felt safe. There were two air raid shelters not far from our house; one used by the Japanese, the second, which was smaller, situated under trees and used by the internees. If we stood up, there was room enough for all."

🪷

This was Mother's favourite story, she was so proud of being British. Being British, she was convinced, saved both our lives that day.

🪷

"At midday, you were not allowed to go out and play because of the heat. At this time my mother and I used to tie thick string around your waist to stop you sneaking out when we were asleep. To keep you occupied we got you to massage our feet; first you massaged my mother's feet till she fell asleep and then massaged my feet. One day my mother was out so you massaged my feet until I was fast asleep. Out of mischief you tied my two big toes together with string. Suddenly I was woken up by the Japanese air raid siren. I got up quickly and immediately fell over – you began laughing and hopping around, while I called you all the names I could think of. By the time I untied my toes, the siren had stopped. I grabbed and pulled you down the stairs. We were only halfway to the shelter when I saw a British fighter plane flying very low firing its machine guns. It was coming straight towards us. My God, we were totally exposed! A bomb exploded nearby and took our breath away; my ears were ringing. We were caught in the sharp painful blast of sand and white dust which made our hair stand upright. Later we suffered with stomach pains. I was still holding your hand. Stay still Brian, look up and smile, I said, the pilot will see we are both British and stop attacking. The British pilot must have seen us as he did not drop any more bombs or use his machine guns again, he just flew away. Standing still and being British saved our lives that day, you know."

⚜

Mum always smiled with pride when she told this story. She was so convinced that we had been recognized by the pilot as British citizens. When older, I never had the heart to tell Mother that what the pilot probably saw was a mad-looking woman and her naked imbecile child, their faces smeared in ashes, hair standing up on end, staring up at him and grinning whilst being bombed and shot up. We must have looked as if we had just escaped from a lunatic asylum. I can remember this incident vividly; the shattering sound of the machine gunning and the compression of the bomb took our breath away and blasted our bare skin with stinging sand particles. The reason the pilot concerned stopped the attack was probably because he had run out of bombs and bullets.

⚜

"Despite the war going badly, the Japanese still conducted their sacred ceremonies with such reverence on the big playing field near the camp.

They seemed to have a solemn ceremony for almost every occasion. The haunting melody of the Kimigayo *[Japan's national anthem]* was always played at the end of each occasion. We civilians often used to watch out of interest or for fear that any Kempeitai present would take our non-attendance as proof of anti-Japanese feelings. If any passers-by neglected to stop when their sad and lilting anthem was being played, they would get their faces slapped. Face slapping was part of their much loved culture. They were very sensitive about their rituals and expected everyone to worship their emperor who was related to the many Gods that favoured Nippon.

"Due to the increasing number of casualties, dead Japanese body parts, usually fingers, were being burnt en masse at the edge of the playing field. The Japanese – or Nipponese, as they preferred to be called – were very meticulous in this ceremony and always wore white gloves. This state of affairs would not have been accepted at the beginning of the war. All the same despite the fact that the war was turning against them, they continued to perform these time-consuming sacred rituals with great devotion. That is, until they were on the run and starving. My mother was told by a Japanese soldier that once his parents had received his ashes, which were duly placed in the family shrine, a black flag would be flown from their dwelling place to show everyone that their son had died; it was an honour to give a life to the Emperor."

※

Allied soldiers were mystified by the amount of fingers and ears found in the knapsacks of the dead Japanese soldiers, and wrongly believed that the Japs were so hungry they were beginning to eat their own dead. In fact these fingers and ears of dead comrades were to be burnt and the ashes sent home to their families. However in the Pacific Islands, Tokyo was informed that some of their starving soldiers, who had been bypassed, were eating slices of meat taken from their dead comrades' thighs. Tokyo was disgusted and sent back a strict order: "If you are starving it is still inexcusable to eat your dead comrades. However if you have to eat human flesh try eating the Americans." Even before this order, some Japanese officers seemed to have acquired a taste for executed American airmen in the Pacific; they were encouraged by the much disliked Lieutenant Colonel Tsuji Masanobu, who recommended the liver, medium rare.

۞

"Very soon Tada u was becoming overcrowded. Jap troops were coming up from Thailand while many Japanese wounded were being brought from the front which was in the opposite direction, poor men they were just left with a few of their medical orderlies on the playing field to fend for themselves. Other Jap soldiers from different units completely ignored them and were deaf to their calls and requests for food and water.

"These men were starving and some were eating jungle greens raw. It was said by the Burmese women who gave them water that some of the deliriously wounded soldiers were picking live maggots out of their wounds and eating them with chopsticks in the belief they were eating grains of rice.

"Unfortunately we had to pass these poor soldiers when out foraging; many were so young. The Burmese helped these unfortunate men get water, as they were forbidden to visit the well for fear of polluting it. Most of the soldiers where suffering from gangrene; we had to cover our noses because of the terrible smell. Many, feverish, would call out to women passing by, mistaking them for their own mothers. Thank God these men only stayed on the field for a few days before they were taken by train to Thailand. I often wondered what happened to them. But after a few days the field was full of wounded soldiers again, ignored just as their predecessors were. Being badly wounded and not able to fight was considered a disgrace and a burden on the army.

"As the war continued the Kempeitai at Tada u were becoming more paranoid and suspicious of everyone. All internee houses were regularly searched. They would just appear and begin shouting. We dropped everything we were doing and went straight down the stairs and waited below without speaking until they had finished. Any delay in leaving the room was considered suspicious. We only had a few possessions so the searches did not take long. Even the Burmese were under suspicion. The Burmese did not take kindly to these searches; they still had not achieved their independence as promised. They felt that they had jumped from the frying pan into the fire and their leader Aung San was becoming disillusioned with his new Asian allies. All the wealth of Burma was disappearing into Japan and the Pacific Islands. Despite the vast amount of rice grown in Burma there was now a shortage, and this soon applied to most local food items. Burma also had to support the occupying army with all its needs. The villagers said the Japs were now trying to get them to grow a different type of rice from Japan; this they refused to do.

"Christmas came and went without celebration. However, one of the Jap soldiers in the barracks owned a gramophone and instead of playing carols, played his two favourite songs over and over again. One was called 'Don't fence me in' by Cole Porter and the other was 'The Good Ship Lollipop' sung by Shirley Temple. We all prayed for liberation. The bombing increased and the Japanese began digging tunnels in and around Tada u. It seemed they intended to fight to the death. Frightening news began to circulate that the Japanese intended to kill all the internees and a mass grave was being dug. My mother's thoughts once more turned to escape."

CHAPTER 24

Froggy Comes a-Courting

BURMA

"The Japanese used to spread ridiculous stories. They claimed they were bombing America and Britain, and Thailand had entered the war against the allies and were sending troops to fight with the Japanese in Burma. My mother said it was time to escape. I was terrified that we would be caught and handed over to the Kempeitai.

"The bombing by British planes had increased. All the air raid shelters had been taken over by the Japanese to store food items. The air raid shelter near to us was filled with the best quality Brahmin rice and cases of Tate and Lyle white sugar. At first there were sentries posted outside the entrance, but later, as the sentries joined the soldiers who were being sent to the front, the shelters were left unguarded despite having no door. Although there was a shortage of food, none of the internees dared enter these shelters. Mother was still selling small cakes to the young Japanese soldiers in the afternoon, but now she was using gram flour, jaggery and palm nut oil; this small income helped us survive and enabled us to save money for our escape. It was also vital that we bought new traditional Burmese slippers.

"There was a swamp within the boundaries of Tada u where we often foraged. We started to carry all that we owned on these trips in preparation for our escape. By now the guards at the checkpoint had become used to foragers. They were always interested in what we had found and wanted to know how it was prepared. These soldiers had to live partly off the land and cook for themselves. When the Japanese military kitchens arrived in camp, they looked like small locomotives with wheels and long funnels.

"The Japanese in general did not like spicy foods but loved all things sweet; they even put sugar in their vegetable stews. My mother's cakes tasted very sweet. One day while she was mixing the batter for the cakes a new regiment appeared from Thailand with many small pack ponies that were tied up under the trees opposite our terrace. Soon the pack ponies were joined by big mules. The animals were under the charge of a young Japanese officer based at Tada u – the one who had killed the two king cobras. My mother said from now on we would never get a good night's sleep, as mules were very noisy animals. But fortunately for us, they did not make a sound.

"One day as we were standing on our balcony watching the pack animals being fed, a group of working elephants ridden by their mahouts began passing by below us. As soon as the elephants smelt the pack animals all hell broke loose and the animals bolted, scattering their feed all over the sand. The Japanese soldiers went chasing after them. My mother and several other women immediately took their rice sieves and began sieving out the sand from the fallen grains before the Japanese returned. We now had some extra food for our escape.

"Many years after the war I developed beri-beri. Water collected in my legs just below the knee and my legs began to swell. Every time I pressed my legs it left a visible deep indentation. It was the consequence of not getting enough vitamin B during the war."

✿

We youngsters were frightened of the big pack mules and had seen them lash out at any village dogs that went too close to their hindquarters. But the small ponies were very mild and we could stroke them. The Japanese troops seemed fond of these small ponies. It is written in the Japanese soldier's hand book: "Look after your pack animal, it cannot complain." These animals attracted many wild birds like bulbuls, pigeons and sparrows that came to eat the fallen grain. The older boys used to shoot these birds with their catapults; small birds were part of the local diet. Whenever the working elephants passed by, we children always ran under the houses for safety. Elephants seemed to hate dogs, horses and quick-moving children.

"We got everything ready to escape. I was so nervous. Then something happened that nearly spoiled our plans. The following day the officer in charge of the pack mules started talking to my mother. He would stand at our doorway in his shiny boots nervously clicking his sword hilt up and down. You were always interested in his sword. One day he lifted the hilt just high enough to show you the chrysanthemum symbol embossed on the blade. He was not good looking like some of the Japanese, and your grandmother thought he looked like a startled frog. His name was Lieutenant Kobayashi. He wanted to improve his Burmese and would ask how to pronounce certain words. My mother would be listening to every word and answer his awkward questions sternly in Nippon-Go. My mother did not think he belonged to the Kempeitai, as they would not lower themselves to clean up after pack animals. I think he was just lonely and wanted to educate himself. Everything we told him he would write down in a small book and ask us to check it. He always wrote very slowly and had beautiful handwriting. He smelt of Pears soap. We had no soap left and had to scrub ourselves with coconut husks. He told my mother he did not like the war and was glad he was in a supply unit. He said how hard it was being a recruit and how the other soldiers had forced him to climb a smooth wooden pole in the barracks and ordered him to chirp like a cricket, 'yipe – yipe – yipe,' they would beat him when his feet touched the ground. He would also miss his rice.

"This young officer used to visit two or three times a week and because of this we could not escape. One day he gave my mother a bar of Pears soap that had been half used. Sometimes he would give my mother an aluminium container full of henjo or henko, a kind of vegetable stew, which we were very glad of. My mother would give him any leftover cakes. She used to say when she saw him coming towards our house: 'Look out, here comes young Lochenvar to court you.' One day he came to say goodbye, as he was leaving for the front. We never saw him again."

⚜

Being young herself my mum must have been flattered at the attention of this Japanese officer. *"He was always a gentleman,"* she would say. All Japanese equipment was stamped with the sixteen-petal royal chrysanthemum, as they belonged to the Emperor. Fine swords that were made by craftsman for the samurai class only had a fourteen-petal chrysanthemum on the hilt. Initially many Allied soldiers collecting samurai swords wrongly believed that the swords with the sixteen-petal chrysanthemum were more valuable than the fourteen-petal versions.

⚜

"News kept filtering in; the British Army had crossed the Chindwin and Irrawaddy and the Chinese army were now approaching Bhamo. We never knew if these rumours were true or not. We watched the Japanese closely. They said that the British were using black cannibals *[East and West African soldiers]*. This really appalled and worried the Japanese soldiers in Tada u: how could they join their ancestors if their bodies were incomplete? It was also said that black soldiers mixed their cornflakes with Japanese blood. We had never heard of cornflakes!

"The area was now being shot up by American and British planes on a regular basis. Thank God it was mostly the other side of the barracks the planes concentrated on; all the same people were being killed including internees. Despite the British and Chinese being so near, the Japs were still conducting anti-guerrilla operations against the British-led Kachins.

"The day finally arrived when, to our surprise, the majority of soldiers left for the front line. Tada u was now almost devoid of troops. This was our chance to escape before more troops arrived so we gathered together all our meagre possessions without telling a soul and headed off on our last foraging trip: we would not be returning. My mother decided we should head in a westerly direction towards the British advance. Apart from soldiers building new tunnels there were only a few Jap soldiers guarding the road block. We went to the small river first *[that fed the swamps]* to collect water spinach and found several Burmese men in the river collecting big fresh water prawns off the bodies of dead pack horses. We never touched these prawns *[tiger prawns]* as we knew they also ate dead human bodies. We had seen it with our own eyes.

"While the men collected these river prawns, their women fried them in a pan over a fire on the riverbank. We approached them so as not to look suspicious. As we drew nearer we were shocked to see several Japs dressed only in their fundoshis *[traditional Japanese undergarment]* also in the river working with the Burmese men, turning over the carcasses of the dead animals to reach the clusters of prawns underneath. We could smell the dead animals. Dead animals smelt different from dead humans.

"My mother stopped and talked with the Burmese women, who she knew. We then moved away along the edge of the river to the swamp pretending to look for soft-shelled crabs; there we would be hidden from view. By now we could no longer smell the dead animals, just the delicious aroma of the big prawns frying in garlic and ginger. As we were now out of sight of the checkpoint, we slowly made our way to the main road beyond, pretending to look for edible plants; the road was our boundary. My heart was thumping in my chest as we crossed the road: we could now be shot. Instead of running around you were very quiet, even though we had not told you we were escaping. Now in the lantana scrub, we began walking as fast as we could between the dense bushes. My mother roughly knew the direction to take to the Shwebo plains. The monsoon would soon begin again.

"We continued walking as fast as we could to place as much distance between us and Tada u. It was now about midday and we were pushing through the lantana bushes when we came to an open space full of dead bodies. They had just been thrown there. Animals had been tearing the bodies apart. Thank God we could not see their faces. We often wondered what happened to the poor people from the big white house after the Kempeitai had finished torturing them. Perhaps some of the internees living in our terrace who disappeared during the night were lying here unburied. We hurried away from the smell and the clouds of flies.

"Planes often flew over us but it was difficult to distinguish who they belonged to as the bushes were so thick and they were past us in a split second. After a mile or so the lantana began to thin out and before long we were walking on the edge of cultivated fields in plain view. Unusually there were no Burmese in the area and we would soon find out why. We had now run out of water and were very thirsty. Following a path that led us under a line of trees we were now in the shade out of the blazing sun; water dominated our thoughts. Suddenly my mother whispered ... 'My God Kate ... don't look up and don't turn around, there are Japs in the trees above us ... just carry on walking.'

"My mother's words coincided with me looking up and seeing the face of a young Japanese soldier holding a rifle. He was staring down at us with that quizzical yet sad look they have. I was almost paralyzed with fear. I was holding your hand. This Jap had been tied to the tree and was covered in small branches. There must have been others but we dare not look up again. My mother stopped right below them and began to collect small sticks of kindling. I was on tenterhooks. I bent down and whispered to you, 'we need sticks for a fire,' you always liked that job. I think you realized our fear and the urgency in my voice; for once you did not disobey me. This was a terrifying moment; walking beneath the snipers seemed to take forever. Having progressed through the trees, we were now out in direct sunshine out in the open. My heart was in my mouth, I expected to hear a shot ring out at any moment. The Japanese snipers were facing in the direction we were going. I worried they might shoot us as we were now heading towards the British advance and could give their position away. My mother continued picking up small kindling sticks and I followed suit.

"Turning onto a well-worn path Mother led us towards a village. I prayed that these snipers would think we were retuning to our village but we dreaded reaching it, as there could be more Japanese soldiers garrisoned there – or Burmese who could betray us for reward. My mother's face was red, something that always happened when she was afraid for our lives."

␬

I remember this incident; I had heard my grandmother's warning, looked up immediately and saw a Jap soldier looking down from a tree directly above us. I can still see his face through the mists of my distant memory. Looking back as an adult, the sniper's expression was probably anxious resignation to his coming fate. Not all the sons of

Nippon believed that death was as light as a feather. I did what all children did when first making contact with any Japanese soldiers: grin. I don't remember him grinning back. Thinking back, the snipers had probably been ordered to kill British soldiers and not foraging Burmese villagers (both my guardians wore Burmese longyis). Japanese soldiers followed orders to the letter; however it must have been a terrifying moment for my guardians. In these kinds of desperate situations logic remains elusive: it hides behind panic.

🪷

"The trauma of our situation added to our thirst, and the energy drained from our legs. We were so tired. Finally we reached a screen of trees that would hide us from the snipers. Quickly leaving the village path we cut through some tall grass and headed for a grove of bamboo. Continuing we came to another path that crossed a small stream via a palm trunk bridge. We could hear the water. The temptation to drink water was too great. Placing everything on the ground, using the side of the log bridge to support us, we made our way down to the water through the thick undergrowth praying there were no snakes lurking there. We began drinking the clear water, filled our vessels then quickly continued on our way. We kept following this small stream stopping to drink every now and then until it turned and headed back in the direction of Tada u. It was then that we suddenly saw a group of people in the distance walking towards us so we were forced to re-cross the stream and hide in the tall reeds on the other side. Looking back I could see our passage through the reeds was obvious. We crouched in the reeds and waited, our hearts thumping. The group of people passed by noisily laughing and talking in Burmese, but we weren't sure if they were dacoits or Burmese villagers. Once they had left, we carried on until we reached dense bushes where we slept for the night not daring to light a fire to prepare food. Waking early the following morning, we continued our journey in the direction of Shwebo hoping to meet up with the British Army, only stopping in the afternoon by a small pool fed from an underground spring. We were so hungry."

🪷

I can remember this vividly. For once I was also hungry and thirsty, despite being given most of the water carried by my guardians. I watched my grandmother holding on to the long reeds as she struggled to enter the pool. With the hem of longyi in her hands she began to catch tiny fish in the shadows of the bank, while my mother sat down and husked handfuls of gram and I watched large metallic green glazed dragonflies darting above the reeds. Within half an hour Grandmother was frying the small fish and boiling gram.

⚜

"We ate our food and moved on, hidden by a screen of trees. The sun was slowly sinking in the west and we searched for a place to sleep for the night. Under the dense tree canopy, we bedded down while listening to the frogs calling for rain. Early the following morning we walked towards the sound of the big guns in the distance. Passing another stand of bamboo my mother saw a stem of rare male bamboo; she needed a stick to protect us from snakes. Male bamboo is thinner than female bamboo, but is solid and does not split. She began to cut it. I was so nervous that the sound of her cutting would bring Japanese soldiers to investigate. We reached open dry ground before nightfall. My mother chose a deep soft sandy depression to sleep in, first laying down the waterproof sheet and then the blankets. We were now out of sight. As usual jackals began calling as the sun went down. I was exhausted and went to sleep as soon as it got dark, but woke up later because of a strange noise that penetrated my dreams. It sounded like someone gasping for breath. I woke my mother up. She said it must be some kind of nocturnal lizard or bird and told me to go back to sleep and not disturb her again. I could not sleep. I could hear whatever it was stealthily approach then stop. I was too afraid to stand up and investigate. I was exhausted and finally fell asleep only to be woken up with a start. Looking up I saw a dark face with light rings around its eyes staring down at me. The face was on a long neck. I screamed and the face quickly disappeared.

"My mother woke up clutching her large dah. I was trying to describe what I had seen when the face reappeared again. My mother threw a stone at the animal and said it was a hyena. I was worried it was going to sneak in and grab you, but my mother said it must have been attracted by the fermented fish paste that we had brought with us. I still could not sleep though because not long after I noticed bats flying low above our heads.

"After several days of travelling, the countryside became more open and dry; again water would become a daily problem until the mango showers began. In the distance lay the Kachin Hills. Ahead we saw a village enclosed by a cactus hedge that had been partly destroyed by fire. We knew it would have a well, but where were the people and the village dogs? If it wasn't for our raging thirst we would have bypassed this village, but we were desperate. We approached cautiously but stopped when we saw faces peering at us through the cactus screen. It was then that a group of men holding long dahs approached us. We anticipated danger from these unsmiling villagers. Your grandmother greeted them politely in Burmese and asked for water. We noticed that most of the men had some kind of eye disease. One of the men also had a large goitre; this man began asking my mother questions. She said we were from Tada u and the Japanese there had informed us that we could find water here; she also added that a party of Jap troops were following not far behind us.

"The mention of Japanese seemed to alarm these men. My mother showed them the out-of-date official form written in Japanese that allowed her to travel and collect Victor. Not wanting to enter the cactus-enclosed village, my mother gave the man with the goitre a few coins that she had at hand and our tin water container to fill at the well. All the men returned to the village talking amongst themselves. Sensing danger we began to move away but the men quickly came out again with the water demanding the rest of our money, which my mother gave them. Thank God she had hidden the majority of our money elsewhere. As we hurried away through a gap in a cactus hedge, we saw a black shrivelled body of a man hanging from a tree by a hook through his jaw. The lips had shrivelled, exposing the man's teeth, and he looked as though he was grinning at us. These men must have been afraid of cutting the corpse down which was forbidden by Japanese law.

"Once we had placed some distance between us and the village we quickly changed direction, in case we were followed, and drank the water as we walked; we dared not stop to boil it. Despite being exhausted, we travelled as far as we could. I lost track of the days but my mother always thought she knew when it was Sunday and we said our prayers. Sometimes it did not feel like a Sunday. We both missed attending church. One afternoon, as we sat resting in the shade of a big bush enjoying the cool breeze and birdsong, my mother suddenly stopped talking mid-sentence. I knew something ominous was about to happen. Time hung suspended, the breeze and birdsong ceased abruptly. A complete silence then descended over us. We were paralyzed with fear. Suddenly a shimmering fleeting haze and a rush of air swept passed us. The spell only lasted a few heartbeats; then the spell was broken and the faint breeze returned followed by the sound of birdsong: an Outoasan had passed."

🪷

This occurrence is widely accepted throughout the east, and is thought to be a spell weaved by a spirit as it passes unseen. This spirit, called a Sherrill in India, and to the followers of the Prophet in Malaya an evil Djinn, is part of eastern folklore. Since then I have met others who have had the same experiences. It is possible at that time of day when the heat is at its most overpowering, the brain is distorted, allowing our vivid imagination to short-circuit, and turn superstition and hearsay into reality. Although I don't remember this occasion, this sensation is real enough. I have heard several people talk of it and it is not restricted to Burma. This occurrence often happens when certain circumstances and conditions prevail prior to the monsoon, for example, on hot still afternoons between 12pm and 2pm in quiet lonely places away from human habitation. Perhaps it is a natural phenomenon that occurs at certain latitudes in the east where heat hazes are more visible. The shimmering fleeting haze could just have been that, a distorted heat haze; the rest of the illusion could be the fruit of a vivid human imagination.

🪷

"We were now running out of food, but water was all we could think of. In the distant hills we could see dark clouds and sometimes rain, but the clouds always dispersed by the time they reached us. We knew there would be water in the jungle-covered hills but this would take us in the wrong direction. As our energy levels were low, we only walked in the early mornings and late afternoons; during midday we just sat in the shade and listened to the distant sounds of war. The countryside here was open and gave me the sense of being safe. I was beginning to get used to sleeping on the ground again. At night we just spread our ground sheet and blankets on the clean soft sand and slept.

"We woke up the following morning demented by thirst and could think of nothing but water. Even though we were very weak we had to carry on. About an hour before nightfall we came to a deserted village which had been burnt to the ground, but we knew there would be a well there. The water in the well was very low and there was no bucket. We took items of clothing and tied them together, and then tied them to my mother's bamboo stick and lowered this into the well. By doing this we were able to reach the water. By squeezing the end of the material we managed to fill a tin pot. This was only enough for one good drink each. I prayed there were no dead bodies in the well. That night we slept on soft sand well away from the village; it was now cool but our throats were still parched and speaking was difficult.

"The next day we saw Burmese people in the distance. We were so desperate we tried to call out to them, but our throats were too dry. We followed them as quickly as we could and finally arrived at their village. Alerted by the dogs, curious people appeared from their huts and watched our approach. We were given fresh well water immediately. Mother told the villagers that we had walked out of Tada u because of the bombing and showed them the Japanese document with the official stamp. Of course, like other Burmese, they could not read Japanese.

"This village called Pelubum [*spelt phonetically*] belonged to cattle herders. We got the feeling these villagers had once been part of the Burma Independence Army as many of the men guarding the cattle were armed. Sun-flags and Burmese national flags were on display. These men must have helped the Japs on their sweeps against the hill tribes. Perhaps they were now in fear of retribution by the British. But like many other Burmese they were quickly willing to change sides.

Some even began killing small groups of retreating Japanese soldiers. The Burmese National Army led by Aung San was now attacking its former allies. The villagers told us the British were now fighting the Japs near Mount Poppa *[Cobra Mountain]* a sacred place to the Burmese. The villagers were worried that the retreating Japs would requisition their cattle. We also found out that a large body of Japanese troops had been camped nearby only a few days ago. These Japs had been ordered to reinforce Meiktila and fight the British on the Shwebo plain and told the villagers that they would return. This worried us.

"Mother informed the villagers that we hoped to travel around Meiktila and head towards Yinday then Pagan to avoid the fighting. They said Pagan was no longer deserted and was full of Indian National Army troops who were robbing the surrounding Burmese villages and raping their women. Pagan was now out of the question. The villagers announced that the men who had asked payment for water at the village where the desiccated mummy was hanging, were escapees from the civil jail in Meiktila which had been bombed by the British. The headman agreed that we could stay the night and sleep on his bamboo platform porch a few feet off the ground. This village had plenty of chickens. It would have been lovely to buy and cook a chicken but we were starving so instead my mother bought eggs and made us a big omelette with tomatoes, pimentos, a little chilli and garlic.

"Lying down on the open platform that night we prayed the Japanese would not suddenly arrive; they can be so brutal when angry. Getting up the next morning we noticed all the sun flags had disappeared. The villagers could never be trusted completely and like blades of grass bent with the wind. We decided it would be too dangerous to stay. We bought a chicken and a few supplies with the last of our money and made a lovely chicken curry before we left in the afternoon. We were given a dried hollow vegetable gourd filled with water and told that a small stream could be followed to the outskirts of Meiktila. This stream did not completely dry out, as it was fed by rains in the hills.

"On the second day after we left the village it suddenly grew dark and began to rain. We sheltered under our waterproof sheet in the overhang of low bushes huddled together for warmth. A heavy storm was coming from the hills and forked lightning began to fill the sky. I placed our big tin pot outside our shelter to catch rainwater. Just as night began to fall, I reached out to retrieve the vessel to fill the gourd and place it out again when I saw several men in capes coming our way; only Japs wore these rain capes. My mother ordered me to retrieve the empty tin pot quickly, which was making a noise as the raindrops hit it. My heart was in my mouth as I reached out again. Pulling it in I looked in the direction of the Japanese soldiers, they were keeping to the contours of the ridge we were on; they were sure to see us. We froze at their approach and listened as they chatted with excited voices. Watching their shadowy figurers pass we could see they were driving a bullock. Shivering and cold we stayed in our hideout until the next morning. Mercifully, you slept throughout.

"After another day's travel we found the stream. The flow was not continuous despite the rain storm; water was collecting in small pools that looked relatively clean except for the small frogs and mosquito larvae. We boiled the water. Where there are frogs there are snakes, but thank God we saw none. It crossed my mind that having survived the war all these years then have one of us die from snake bite at this stage of our escape to freedom would be tragic."

✿

Our journey to get behind the fighting by bypassing Meiktila must have continued without incident, as Mother did not speak of it and I can't remember any significant events. We just followed the line of trees along the trickling river to keep in the shade and near cover.

✿

"After many days of travelling we must have been somewhere near Meiktila, for the noise of fighting grew louder. We stopped near a pool surrounded by trees that provided us with shade. Here, we waited to ponder our next move. Not long after we were joined by a group of people who had come from Thazie, which was also being bombed by Allied planes. Among them were a mother and son, an uncle and his Burmese wife; they had been on their way to the oilfields where they worked. Their Burmese escort had abandoned them. They were an Anglo-Indian family and their name was Rawlings; the woman had a son your age. She told us that their lives had been saved by her husband being an expert in oil extraction. They were all well dressed compared to us and had bags full of food; they gave us some rice. Before we knew it, you and the Rawlings boy were rolling around in the dust wrestling. We had to prise you apart before they moved some way from us and settled down. The rest of the group carried on their journey."

❀

I remember these people and their son. Together we collected dry sticks for the fire but after cooking and eating, these people kept away from us. We must have looked like down and outs.

❀

"We stayed here for a while as there was nowhere else to go and the country ahead looked very dry, despite the mango showers. One afternoon we were discussing moving on when suddenly we heard the heavy mechanical noise of tanks and saw plumes of dust. To our horror, the tanks were coming from the wrong direction. Instead of coming from the west as we expected, they were approaching from the east. These had to be Japanese tanks – we would be trapped. There was nothing we could do as the noise grew louder. The tanks stopped near to us and several dusty men climbed down stretching their legs. To our joy, we heard English voices.

"'Are there any Japs around here?'

"'No,' we answered, 'but there is a garrison in Tada u many miles away.'

"'They would have been dealt with by now', answered a man in a Jeep. The man took off his cap and introduced himself. He was a Major and his first name was Frank. Many other transport vehicles began to arrive. I told the soldiers that my husband Jack was in the Royal Scots. They said the First Royal Scots were now fighting in Burma. It was a wonderful feeling to know that finally we had been liberated and our wanderings were over. We were now protected by the British Army."

❀

I remember this occasion well. When my mother, grandmother and Mrs Rawlings realized the tanks were British, they began looking into small mirrors and running around titivating themselves as best they could. The man in the Jeep (Frank) had a bald head and seemed to have taken a fancy to my mother; he was always trying to get her on her own but this was difficult as she was carefully watched by Grandmother and me. I was given a tin of jam and more sweets than the other boy because I was barefoot and dressed in my mother's old torn chemise (the other boy was well dressed and shod); his mother was quick to complain. Later that day I punched him.

I also remember the soldiers stopping to brew some tea. My grandmother and mother were standing nearby eating jam out of a tin watching a soldier prepare to light a fire. He then proceeded to instruct grandmother on the correct way to light a fire, "never use green wood," he knowingly added, "it will give your position away, is difficult to light and provides less heat." He was lecturing the queen of firemaking. My grandmother said nothing.

CHAPTER 25

Winter's Bite

JAPAN

"Jack always told me after the war that the winters in Japan were substantially colder than those of Britain – even colder than winters in the north of England where he was born. The freezing winds in Japan came from the Russian artic and Siberia. All the prisoners were underweight and their clothing was far too thin. Their footwear was falling apart, despite having an ex-cobbler who belonged to the Hong Kong Volunteers; he did his best to mend their worn boots. Canvas had to take the place of leather, which was hard to come by in Japan. Some men with small feet managed to squeeze into the Japanese Tabi, rubber and canvas boots. Prisoners were given mining helmets made of cardboard. Often men went barefoot. Jack said standing outside while waiting to be counted in the sleet or rain was far worse than the beatings they occasionally received for minor offences. But Nagoya was not a brutal camp compared to others, and the work quotas were not excessive. Jack was in charge of a small group of Royal Scot prisoners.

The Japanese were always disgusted at the amount of swear words available to the Anglo-Saxon tongue. Their race had to be content with just two much repeated exclamations: 'Buggero' and 'Damme' both meaning basically fool, idiot and no good. We constantly heard these words bellowed when the young Japanese soldiers were being trained at Tada u.

"Jack said the worst offenders for bad language were the Middlesex Regiment *[Cockneys]*; the Scots tended to swear less. Once the Japanese guards at the camp understood what English swear words meant; they would shake their heads and walk away disgusted or clout the offender. Their verbal culture was strictly moral and their taste in Japanese female beauty refined.

"Some of the Jap guards soon realized that there was no love lost between the Scots and the English and used this to get more work done. At one camp *[Tateyama]* the Japanese guards and civilian workers were always interested in a prisoner's marital state and how many children they had; over three offspring usually earned them a cheap Japanese cigarette. A way to gain a little kudos with their guards and foremen and have a rest at the same time was to ask them (at the right moment) if they were married. This would usually make them proudly produce photographs of their families. Another way to prolong a conversation and rest periods was to admire the guard's handwriting."

❧

According to the Sergeant, the prisoners soon learnt that while looking at their po-faced wife and their grim-looking children, who stared back at the camera with intent hostility (it is almost impossible to find a smiling photo of a Nipponese family of that era), it was advisable for the prisoner to gently suck air through the teeth in admiration of his wife. But a prisoner had to be careful; too much sucking in of breath when looking at the guard's wife could easily be mistaken for carnal lust, earning the prisoner a clout around the ear.

❧

"I believe it was here that Jack and the men from Tateyama met the veteran wrinkled faced guard called Kanamura known to the prisoners by a rude name. Sergeant Kanamura was well-respected by the other guards and even the officers and NCOs in the POW camp because of his long service. Kanamura took a liking to Jack. Perhaps it was because Jack took his punishment without flinching; also both soldiers had been seriously wounded in battle and had the visible scars to prove it. Kanamura spoke a little English, he was also an accomplished mime actor and would use this talent to describe past battles against the Russians. The veteran guard had seen active service in Manchuria, China, the invasion of Burma and was seriously wounded in the face and neck at the Sittang River by a Gurkha's knife.

"Sergeant Kanamura often appeared from the gloom of the mine's tunnels the worse for drink and had to be handled carefully; he was usually in the mood to boast of his past battles or to beat a prisoner who caught his attention. At such times the civilian foreman and other workers quickly made themselves scarce because of Kanamura's unpredictability; this surprisingly included the owner of the mine. They all had a healthy respect for the veteran, so strong was the army grip on the civilian population.

"Jack was always a good listener when Kanamura wanted to talk. The better he listened the longer the tale, the longer the tale the longer the rest from the back-breaking work. The right side of Jack's face was paralyzed and his lower eye lid drooped significantly causing tears to trickle down his cheek at regular intervals, giving the impression he was crying *[this problem continued after the war despite two operations at Roehampton]*. Perhaps these tears gave the impression that he was moved by Kanamura's tales. Japanese men were not ashamed of tears when occasion beckoned. They have been known to cry at the beauty of a butterfly's wing. Jack's crocodile tears added a touch of sincerity and bonhomie, especially when brave deeds were recounted and photos of family were produced. A few tears and just the right amount of sucking in of breath at the beauty of his scowling dame and her plump-faced children could end in a small gift or a cigarette."

During the above the POWs in Jack's work detail remained silent leaning on their picks and shovels in the dim shadows of the tunnels, conserving their limited energy.

✿

"On other occasions, the deep sword cut on the back of Jack's neck fascinated the sword-loving Kanamura, who it seems was quite an expert at the art of decapitation, having honed his skills to a high degree in China."

✿

The Japanese soldiers often sent pictures home of these events; a "wish you were here" kind of thing. Sergeant Kanamura would often produce photographs of these events, showing Chinese people being used for bayonet practice and beheadings. As manpower in Japan decreased, more women were conscripted to work in the mines.

Tam and Willie often laughed at the thought of Nipponese Annie, an attractive Japanese woman they named after a female Glaswegian music hall entertainer. "Nipponese Annie" sometimes came to the mine to work for reasons unknown. It seems that any exertion Annie made, even bending down to pick up a small object, caused her to have loud flatulence. At first all the prisoners thought Annie was mimicking the sound orally to amuse them. But by closely watching her baggy trousers every time she bent over, their hypothesis was proved to be incorrect. Scrotum-face, the old crinkled skinned guard, used to walk away disgusted: "this woman no good-a" he would announce bringing a handkerchief to his nose.

✿

"Jack admired the Japanese ingenuity when working in the mine in Nagasaki; not having the proper tools or equipment did not seem to worry them, they always improvised. The Japanese were on the lookout for skilled workers. All the prisoners were given forms to state their previous occupations and skills. Jack claimed he was a 'steak and kidney pudding tester'. This was the food he missed the most during his imprisonment; I used to make it every week for him in England when I had learned to cook. I remembered my mother's recipe; it was also my father's favourite."

✿

These steak and kidney puddings were my favourite too. Mum always used the best steak, cutting away all the fat. She used lambs' kidneys, boiling them first to remove the strong taste and cutting out all the small ventricles. She would beam with pride when dad said "That was lovely, Mrs D." But by far the most popular pre-war occupation claimed by the prisoners was "Brothel Inspector", or "Chief Gooseberry Shaver" at Hartley's Jam Factory.

Little did the Sergeant realize that after the war when he was promoted to RSM of the 2nd Battalion Royal Scots that prisoner and guard roles would be reversed. Under his control at Fort Dufferin were over two hundred Japanese troops including officers. Some Japanese were awaiting the death sentence by hanging. RSM Devereux and other soldiers who were former prisoners of Nippon would be present to watch them die. They all went to their deaths with a resigned composure and dignity. Occasionally, some diehard would shout "Banzai" just before the trap door gave way. To deny them this last gesture of defiance, the Sergeant Major made sure the trap door was opened as soon as the prisoner stood on it.

Some of these soldiers, consumed by an overwhelming shame at being alive, chose not to return to their cherry blossom islands on release. As far as their families were concerned they had become "non-persons", the greatest insult to any Japanese man. Many chose Thailand as their new home. Others found ingenious and sometimes extremely painful ways to kill themselves. The most popular method of suicide in Fort Dufferin was cutting the jugular vein with glass during the night while their comrades watched with vague interest. When a shard of glass was not available, one Japanese soldier bit through his own wrist to sever his artery.

I sometimes accompanied the RSM on his tours of the British Military Jail and then the Japanese jail on Sundays while Mum entertained friends and relatives. He used to stride into the jail with his swagger stick under his arm and me following behind. As soon as the Japanese prisoners saw him they would jump off their beds and stand to attention. It was compulsory that the Japanese prisoners wore only their traditional fundoshis which made it difficult for them to conceal weapons to harm themselves. All prisoners would stand stiff upright and bow deeply to the RSM. I would stand with the two armed guards of the Royal Scots while he made a quick inspection, poking here and there with his baton. He would then order them (in Japanese) to stand at ease. His Japanese was quite proficient by then. I never witnessed any violence by the RSM or the guards towards the Japanese prisoners. Bullying was commonplace by the senior Japanese NCOs. Murder was also suspected among the Japanese prisoners although it was often passed off as suicide by their comrades.

In their leisure time they kept themselves busy making various ingenious items. I was given some beautifully made toys by the Japanese prisoners including a semi-automatic pistol made entirely out of different kinds of wire and a spring. It fired nine small perfectly made cylindrical hollow paper pellets (made from Players packets). Once the magazine was loaded and the firing mechanism cocked it fired a pellet by way of a spring, while another pellet was loaded into the chamber ready. It was excellent for killing flies at the range of two feet. This toy weapon was as reliable as the Belgian .22 semi-automatic rifle I later owned.

CHAPTER 26

Liberation

BURMA

❧

"Before long we were boarding military lorries with our pathetic possessions. According to Frank, this fighting force was hoping to reach Meiktila and then Prome, but we would be dropped off somewhere suitable on the way. The next day we entered greener country and finally found ourselves on a metalled road. In the afternoon we crossed a shallow river in a duck *[DUKW – an American amphibious truck]* and came to a residential area with nice looking brick and wooden two storey houses that had overgrown gardens. Here the convoy stopped for the night. Frank asked me if I fancied stretching my legs by the river; before I could answer, my mother said 'no.'"

❧

The bald Major, I remember, was always trying to get rid of me when Grandmother was not around. But I stuck to my mother like glue to a blanket. Grandmother was not slow to notice this and openly disapproved of the Major's attentions.

〰

"We were dropped off with all the tinned food we could carry and told to occupy any house of our choice. Frank came with us. We were so tired we took the first house in the street; it looked nice from the outside. There was no water in the taps but finding water would no longer be a problem as the monsoon had already started. This house actually had a double bed and a ceramic bath filled with small round Japanese beer bottles. I think it had previously been used by Japanese officers as there were some round wooden bathing tubs in the back garden. This was a big overgrown space with nice fruiting fig trees in it. Even though it was still light we all went straight to bed. It was wonderful to sleep on a soft sprung mattress again. Frank came around late that night but my mother would not let him in Poor man – he had been so good to us. It was so nice to feel safe again. When we woke up the following day you were missing; you had sneaked out while we were sleeping. We could have murdered you. We were told by the British soldiers before they left that there were still many explosive devices lying around the area like grenades and live ammunition.

"Running outside we found you playing in the rain with some Burmese children. Later we met their families, who had been civil servants before the war. They informed us that the Japanese who had been stationed here had gone to defend Meiktila. The sounds of fighting could still be heard in the distance; the war was not as yet over.

"I hoped Jack was still alive somewhere. I never gave up hope and prayed we would soon be together again.

"The gardens of these big houses were so overgrown, and as the monsoon rains came down in sheets it was a dangerous time for snakes. Following the afternoon rains, at dusk, the whole street became alive with fireflies of all different colours. All you children used to run up and down chasing them – even my mother said that she had never seen such a wonderful display of colour. You were a little bugger and always disappeared at mealtimes hiding sometimes in a big rain barrel full of water with just your eyes sticking out. One day we were surprised to find you playing with a pretty little blonde girl called Rosemary. She wore plaits in her hair and a flowered dress. Rosemary looked sad and was always hungry. She usually appeared at mealtimes; Mother thought she had worms but she was a sweet little thing and we always fed you together. Rosemary never spoke much. I noticed when she left our house she climbed into the overgrown garden next door and disappeared among the trees and bushes. I always thought she was looking for some fruit to eat and the next time she visited, I told her to be careful. We never did meet her parents or relatives; we did not even know exactly where she lived. My mother thought she was Dutch.

"I only heard the sad story of Rosemary later. Her father was dead and her mother worked for the Japanese in the local club. Rosemary's mother was usually drunk and had little time for her daughter, who lived off scraps given to her by the Burmese staff. One night Rosemary's mother killed herself in the garden next door. This little blonde girl was climbing the fence to visit her dead mother's unburied remains. Poor little Rosemary – if only we'd known ..."

🪷

I remember Rosemary well – with her blues eyes and fair hair she was just like my uncle Victor. She would try to eat anything I said was edible. We both used to get into the big rain barrel and look out at the world. During the day someone's white albino rooster used to strut around the overgrown street as if it owned it. For some reason he always took exception to Rosemary's presence and would attack her on the way to our house. Both my guardians used to laugh as Rosemary came screeching towards us with a bright red face, just like the rooster who was close behind. One day Rosemary did not appear.

🪷

"The war was still raging in Burma; refugees came and went trying to escape the fighting and the retreating Japanese Armies. The Japanese troops were still in Meiktila and as far north as Shwebo. Large groups of Japanese were escaping into the hills and jungle trying to regroup. This would be a dangerous time to meet them. Around a fortnight later some British army trucks appeared and we were told to board them quickly with all our possessions."

🪷

Mother was very proud of the fact that we were now classed as British Military Personnel and we would no longer be responsible for feeding ourselves and finding our own accommodation. We were moved another four times because of the fighting. I can still remember the varied accommodation. Each new location had an incident that sticks in my mind. Some of these incidents were rather painful.

The second house we stayed in consisted of one single room and a cooking area. These terraced houses built of timber and brick stood on brick stanchions. The area under the houses had previously been used as a toilet by its former occupants. The stale smell of desiccated human ordure dominated the surroundings and hung like an invisible shroud over these lonely buildings on hot still afternoons. The whole area was in a sea of dry thorn scrub jungle. The only other occupants were a Christian Anglo-Indian family with a daughter older than me. This girl, Teresa, believed in water-babies (or so she said). Noticing I was gullible and that my grandmother always gave me a good slippering for "leaving the shadow of the house," this girl would approach me (making sure I was alone) and tell me she had just seen water-babies playing in the stream about four hundred yards away along a wide dusty road bordered by thick scrub. I desperately wanted to see a water-baby and intended to catch one and tie a string around its waist.

She would walk with me to the gin-clear pebbled stream telling me how wonderful water-babies were, then exclaim "look there's one ... it's hiding just under the water ... catch it." As I did not know the difference between a water-baby and a bush-baby I was not sure what to look for. Excited I would climb down the bank by the concrete and iron bridge. While I was searching, Teresa would quickly leg it back and inform my grandmother that I had "left the shadow of the house." Running back on my own always scared me as hyenas lurked in the scrub. Gran was waiting with her slipper with the girl waiting to witness my punishment. Yet I always fell for this trick: idiot!

﷐

"Our next move was to a large grand house called Lambert House, situated in the middle of a dense area of lantana bushes except for the dirt track driveway. The lantana was in full bloom. If you pulled a floret you could suck the sweet nectar from the ends. The fruit, when ripe, could also be eaten. A quiet Indian family had a single room in this same house; we hardly saw them. One day my mother returned from market with a young pet lamb for you. Soon after the lamb disappeared, you were so upset. My mother said she suspected a leopard was responsible."

﷐

I always believed that to be the case. I never suspected the quiet Indian family … until now.

A basha camp on the banks of the Irrawaddy was our next accommodation, and it was here that I saw my first working water tap. It was also my first opportunity to closely inspect a freshly dead Japanese soldier lying on his back on the white sand. He was in full uniform with the usual two belts, from which hung a small lucky charm corn dolly and a tiny bag of rice. His helmet was still attached to his head with four tapes; his eyes were open and he seemed to be looking up and smiling at the sun. I noticed some of the adult male refugees kick this body when they passed. Every morning this dead Jap was my first call of inspection.

The water tap dripped. We were told that the Japanese used this tap to torture prisoners by forcing a hose into their mouths and down into their stomachs then turned the tap on until their stomachs distended. Another torture was to tie a prisoner under this tap and let a single drop of water drip on their heads until it became too painful to bear.

I always pondered that if I was given a choice, would I prefer the slow dripping tap. I often sat under the dripping tap waiting for it to become painful, until I became bored or somebody dragged me out from under the tap with a few choice words in order to get their water.

🪷

"We then moved nearer Meiktila to a brand new refugee 'basha' camp and were informed that we would be joined by many other former internees. This never happened so we remained the only ones there. The basha huts comprised two sleeping platforms about a foot off the ground divided by a central walkway leading to a back room, which was used for cooking. Every evening, you would watch quick-moving snakes dart from underneath one platform to the other and would scream to your grandmother to kill them. 'They are only young rat snakes,' she would say."

🪷

It was here that we suffered the strong monsoon winds again forcing my mother and grandmother to pray to God and all the saints they could think of as they pushed against the palm walls to stop them collapsing.

🪷

"Despite having tinned food and army rations, we still went on foraging walks in the surrounding area. Evidence of striped hyena was everywhere. It was on these occasions when the light showers occurred while the sun was still shining, that my mother would say: 'Sun and rain – jackals' wedding.'

"Our last temporary move was into Meiktila itself, well after the fighting had ceased, where we observed some soldiers repairing their vehicles and other soldiers painting stones white at the side of the road. When the war with Japan was finally over, we were taken by army lorry to a large house on Edward Road, Maymyo.

"We waited for news of Jack then heard the terrible reports of a new weapon: the atom bomb. I prayed Jack had not been near it but on this occasion my prayers were not answered. I was overjoyed when we finally learned from the authorities that Jack was alive and had been liberated in Nagasaki. I also learned that he would not be coming straight back to Burma from Japan, but would be taken to America along with many other Allied prisoners; we were to wait for his return in Maymyo. We were told all the prisoners in the US would get the best food and medical treatment America had to offer. Poor Jack, he was just skin and bone when he was liberated, as he always exchanged his midday rice for a few cigarettes. Tam and Willie did not go to America, as they were in better health.

"Life slowly returned to normal. Many people came around to see us, including our first cousins Willie McPherson and his two sisters. Willie was a small, jolly man with a bald head and always wore Japanese cloven-hoof rubber boots. Everybody wore all kinds of clothes and shoes just after the war.

It was here in Maymyo that we were invited to a wedding at a hotel just down the road from our house. My mother and I waltzed together; we had such a lovely time and were given a piece of wedding cake as we left.

"One day when we were in town, shopping at the market, we saw an Indian woman and her small son being taunted by other Indian stall holders. She was trying to exchange an item for some food; she looked half-starved. My mother took pity on her and invited her and her son to come home and live with us. She was the wife of an Indian soldier who had fought and died alongside the Japanese. She became our cook, sharing our army rations until she was able to return to her homeland with her son, after we left Maymyo for Mandalay. Before she left she was visited by her young brother called Lucas, who had come from Mandalay. Lucas had worked for the Japanese in the officers' club as a waiter. He was a Christian and had just got married. Later on, Jack promised Lucas and his wife a job working for us in Fort Dufferin, Mandalay."

It was in Maymyo that I first tasted lemonade. The bottles did not have stoppers, just a marble held against the opening by the gas within.

CHAPTER 27

Bed Bugs

JAPAN

❀

"Lower-ranked guards in Japan had problems with the counting of Allied prisoners; they usually counted them several times. On a cold day with an icy wind whipping the prisoners' scrawny bodies, this fiasco taxed the weaker prisoners to the point of collapse. On the other hand, the prolonged tenko on warm summer mornings wasted time and made the long day of back-breaking work a few minutes shorter. It also added a little entertainment when the guards began slapping each other's faces, believing some of the prisoners may have escaped.

"Escape would have been impossible in Japan. As far as Jack knew, no prisoner made plans to escape and there were no illegal radios in Tateyama Camp. The prisoners had learned to keep a straight face and find another point of interest when a Jap slapped Jap. One guard used to count up to ten and then extend a finger as a kind of abacus. This worked till he was forced to salute a passing superior officer and had to start again. He would then bare his teeth at the prisoners and snarl. God help any prisoner who laughed or made eye contact. This guard was known to the prisoners as 'Mad Dog'.

"There were only a handful of Royal Scots at the Osaka Camp and they all worked together just like the other regiments tended to do. But in general everyone did their best to help those who were too ill to work. The senior officer at Nagoya Tateyama was a Dr Riley, whose calm disposition and medical knowledge greatly helped the sick and weak. But Dr Riley left the camp's discipline to the senior NCOs, as he was a very mild and modest man.

"The freezing winters in Japan killed off all the flies and kept the bedbug population down in numbers. However during the summer months, the Japanese insisted that the best way to control the numbers of flies and parasites was for each man to kill fifty bedbugs and flies a day. This number was difficult to sustain on a daily basis despite Mad Dog's demonstration on the correct way to sneak up on unsuspecting flies. Nevertheless, the prisoners were forced to find different substitutes to pass off as bedbugs or cut the bugs in half; this did not always work with the sharp-eyed guards. Strangely they were never beaten for this attempt to cheat, but given a lecture on the benefits and virtues of honesty."

🪷

Other prisoners collected large numbers of live and ravenous bedbugs and sprinkled them in the guards' quarters or in the civilian coats hanging in the mine. The result gave these prisoners pleasure as they watched their guards scratching themselves.

I believe the men at Tateyama POW camp had been transferred there from the Narumi POW camp at Osaka due to the bombing by the American Air Force (prisoner of war camps were not marked in Japan). Usually the massive B-29 arrived during the day when the prisoners were out working.

Tateyama POW camp was also attacked soon after. The number of civilian victims in the town must have been high, however, according to the guards, the American bombs were selective and only killed non-Japanese. All Japanese casualties were quickly removed from the prisoners' sight. As usual the Japs kept to their practised doctrine when dealing with non-Nipponese: never admit anything, even the obvious truth; admitting the truth is admitting defeat and losing face to an inferior race. A good example of this was a story that circulated among prisoners in Japan after the war, which my father found amusing. He had heard that when Japan surrendered, a British Captain approached a Japanese Captain and inquired:

"I believe the war over?"

"Yes."

"Who won?"

"Nobody, it was a draw!" the Japanese Captain replied, looking his counterpart straight in the eyes.

The number of American planes shot down (according to the guards) on each raid beggared belief. One good thing: the bombing produced was to help uncover the hundreds of Red Cross parcels and warm clothing that had been hidden in a camp building. The presence of these parcels and clothing had long been suspected by the POWs when some of the guards were seen smoking Red Cross cigarettes and civilian camp workers started wearing warm clothing that was far too big.

The existence of Red Cross parcels at the camp the Sergeant was in, had always been denied by the honourable gentlemen while they secretly helped themselves to items that suited their taste. The camp interpreter was asked to explain the sudden presence of torn and damaged Red Cross parcels scattered over the camp. He said he would find out and went to the Japanese commander. He returned shortly afterwards sporting a wide grin and bearing an explanation.

"After the American bombers had run out of bombs they decided to throw out their personal Red Cross parcels in the hope of injuring some innocent Japanese below."

The above explanation was ridiculous, even humorous – that is if you were not a starving, freezing prisoner.

Red Cross parcels began to be distributed to the men at the rate of one parcel between six men. The Red Cross parcels were months old and many items were missing. But, to the Sergeant's delight, the last men to receive their Red Cross parcels found that, because they were at the bottom of the pile and out of reach, the cigarettes were untouched. Two of the Royal Scots were non-smokers, so that left enough cigarettes for the Sergeant and the rest of the men to indulge their craving.

Initially, due to the heavy civilian causalities of the US bombing raid, the men were confined to their huts and given their yasumi (rest) while the bodies were taken away. Not that the prisoners managed to get much rest. The Japanese were convinced that all Allied prisoners were capable of constructing a radio and transmitter. On two consecutive days the guards, wearing white masks and gloves (the prisoners were considered un-hygienic), came in and searched the huts. Nothing incriminating was found, though one of the guards complained that his packet of cigarettes had been stolen. He lined up all the prisoners and reported this to his superior officer (a suspected Kempeitai officer). The prisoners anticipated trouble and ordered the culprit to discard the cigarettes. The grim-faced officer appeared and studied each prisoner's "holier than thou" face for a good minute; he suddenly burst out laughing and left. Nothing more was heard of the incident.

۞

"Jack said later, as the bombing increased, prisoners were ordered to board lorries and help clear the streets of Osaka. The first lorry was having trouble starting up. A Jap NCO approached and gave the driver a slapping. Furious, the driver took a bamboo stick and laid into the bonnet of the lorry, watched by the NCO. Believing that the driver was beating the wrong part of the lorry, the NCO snatched the bamboo and proceeded to beat the petrol tank. The lorry started first time to the cheers of the prisoners. We had seen vehicle beating at Tada u. The prisoners were always happy to get out of camp and considered it another opportunity to find food. It was also a chance for an outing and change of scenery. Cleaning up operations was also a chance to steal useful items found in the ruined houses. Fresh meat soon became available in the form of stray dogs and cats that often roamed the ruins. Some of the prisoners who had an affinity with animals befriended both species. When the deed was done the animals were quickly skinned and hidden.

"Jack never liked cats. He said that in Japan, when clearing up after the American bombers, he noticed that cats, when trapped in confined spaces with their dead owners, would readily eat them, beginning at the face. Dogs preferred to starve. Cat and dog meat became very popular with the prisoners and all agreed cat was far tastier than dog.

"It was clear that the whole of Japan was becoming short of everything; it was a common sight to see civilians searching for small amounts of coal amongst the debris. This shortage had a beneficial effect on the prisoners, as the guards could be bribed to turn a blind eye to the pilfering. These Japanese were terrified of directly stealing themselves; the Kempeitai treated all thieves with the same brutality."

✿

After several months at Tateyama 8B, the prisoners were moved to different camps in Yokohama and Nagasaki. At these bigger camps the work was far more strenuous and the guards more brutal and watchful. It was here the men of Tateyama first came in to contact with the Australians. Many of the Diggers went about life with a total disregard to the strict rules set by their captors, despite constantly being caught red-handed. Some Americans were present and because of their far superior American Red Cross parcels were doing well in trading. Some Yanks were bribing the Japs in charge with cigarettes and food to avoid work. But it is fair to say every man had to do his best to survive; it is also fair to say the Americans and the Australians were able to buy and get drugs into camp for the seriously ill; this helped save the lives of hundreds of POWs.

✿

"It was important to learn the rudiments of Nippon Go and Jack soon became quite proficient. He also learned to ascertain the likes and dislikes of his captors. For example, it was important for tall men to make themselves look smaller by stooping; it was never wise to tower over the Jap bashing you. To fall down or make eye contact when being beaten or to make a noise was a mistake. Standing to attention and bowing correctly after the beating was very important etiquette. We had noticed this at Tada u when young Japanese soldiers were disciplined. The Japanese disliked prisoners with red hair, especially those who also had green eyes *[not that they were fond of blue eyes either]*. Jack had black hair and brown eyes. It was wise for a redhead to pretend to be simple-minded, for the Japanese were not comfortable dealing with prisoners who they believed were mentally unstable. A red-headed Scot in Jack's team would place a piece of coal in his mouth and pretend to eat it, prior to a beating. This would often cause the Japanese soldier concerned to walk away.

One day while working near the surface of the mine in Nagasaki, Jack and other prisoners felt a single tremor; earthquakes were not uncommon, and together with the guards, they rushed outside to see the damage. Jack did not go with them."

⚜

Early on the morning of August 1945 the B-29 super fortress piloted by Major Charles Sweeny took off from Tinian in the Marianas. Onboard was a plutonium bomb called "Fat Man". The arsenal town of Kokura was the intended target but due to low cloud, the bomb was dropped on Nagasaki instead. Fat Man exploded five hundred metres above ground creating a force of twenty one kilotons of TNT and a searing heat wave of 7,000 degrees Fahrenheit followed. Not knowing exactly where the Sergeant was working in Nagasaki, it is hard to say when the heat wave reached the guards and prisoners outside.

The Sergeant for some reason remained in the gloom; perhaps he was too tired or perhaps the instinct to survive warned him to remain below ground: it saved his life. The white heat wave of the atom bomb followed shortly after the tremor. Faint shadows and small piles of human ash were all that remained of the men who had gone up into the sunshine. It would remain forever their cremation site in the Cherry Blossom Islands of Nippon.

CHAPTER 28

The RSM Returns

BURMA

One day in Maymyo I woke up to find my grandmother missing; she had deliberately left while I was sleeping. I frantically searched the whole house without success. Grandmother had left to seek out her other children. Unbeknownst to me, my mother had received Army mail: my father would be arriving that day.

The Sergeant had been promoted to Regimental Sergeant Major of the Second Battalion Royal Scots. Mother was delighted that they would finally be reunited after all these traumatic years. Her prayers had been answered. I remained unimpressed. The word "father" meant little to me; I did not even understand the implications of it. I was brought up and looked after by two women who had loved and disciplined me: kisses and cuddles interspersed with good doses of the slipper and a sprinkling of Burmese swear words. I was happy with the situation.

I was not impressed when the RSM arrived later that day, his face badly disfigured. I did not like him, especially when I learnt he intended to stay. Hearing stories about him in the third party was one thing, but vacating my mother's bed for him was another; I had never slept alone before. My attitude to Father did not help our first meeting; I suppose it was natural for him to react to me negatively from then on. All the same, there were times that he tried, but the initial bond of father and son was missing. The birth of my cute sister Glenis later made up for this shortfall, and she was his pride and joy. Despite my mother's best efforts, we never had a very strong relationship. His efforts to physically discipline me often caused friction between them.

My parents were curious about their house in Taunggyi, although they must have had a good idea that it was no longer a hill station paradise. Besides, I think my father knew or had a fair idea that Burma would soon be given independence. I think he also knew by then that the 2nd Battalion Royal Scots were being posted to Singapore where his army career would come to an end. It was Dad's intention to move back to England eventually. Mother was not happy about leaving her mother and family behind in Burma. England was on the other side of the world and did not appeal to my mother and me, as we had just seen the film *Great Expectations*. Our concept of England was based on the scene when Pip and the convict met in the cold foggy graveyard. To us England was a frigid country, a mass of swirling damp mists, fog and cold rain; a land devoid of warmth and sunshine. One evening my dad asked my mother what special gift would she really like. She told him she wanted a Singer sewing machine. I was then asked what special gift I would like. My answer was simple: a ping-pong ball.

⚜

"We returned to Taunggyi in a Jeep with an armed military convoy that was taking stores and equipment to the Shan States. My heart broke when I saw Taunggyi; it had changed so much. Everyone we knew had gone, and only their ghosts remained. When we pulled up outside what was once our lovely home, I cried. I could not recognize it. The fence and gate were missing and only a glimpse of the foundations could be seen through the tangle of jungle. I did not want to leave the Jeep. Taunggyi would never be the same again; I wanted to remember it as it was before the war.

"Before we left Burma, we stayed with my sister Grace, who lived near the Shwedagon Pagoda. I will never forget what happened when you realized that your grandmother was leaving. She was trying to sneak away in a gharry when you noticed what was happening. You were determined to go with her. We could not catch you, you were running through the legs of the horses and finally climbed up onto the roof of the gharry like a monkey, screaming and bawling your eyes out. Even my mother could not stop crying. You had to be dragged down and held while my mother left. We would never see her again."

Cyril, Lucy and Harry survived the war. After we had left Burma, Aunty Lucy's entire family were viciously attacked by one of their servants, who turned out to be a dacoit. All members of this family suffered terrible injuries inflicted by a Burmese dah. Though badly mutilated, all survived the brutal attack but carried the terrible scars for the rest of their lives. My uncle Cyril, who escaped capture, lived with hill tribes and married a Shan chieftain's daughter. They had many children.

The RSM died in the winter of 1962. I tried to give him the kiss of life. He was only 52. Mother joined him in 1988; she was 76. They are both content now.

Appendix

A brief history: My family and their prejudices

Grandmother's mother was Anglo-Burmese and her father Portuguese. They owned a ruby mine. Her father disliked the French but favoured the English. Her first husband James Talbot, an Irishman, disliked the English, preferring the French. Her second husband – Herman Unger, a German businessman – also disliked the English and believed they were allowing the Indians to dominate the markets; he favoured the Japanese. My mother Kate Devereux was so proud to be British but disliked the name Devereux as it was a Norman name. My grandmother, being half Portuguese, disliked the French. Napoleon and the Grand Armée were as popular in Portugal and Spain as Oliver Cromwell and the roundheads were in Ireland.

❧

"My mother was multi-lingual and spoke five languages including Nippon Go. My father Herman Unger had Japanese clients who he often entertained at home. Mother also used Japanese professionals as they were skilled, reliable and polite. She soon picked up the Japanese language and its delicate intonations from the wives of his clients."

❧

Jack Devereux was from Nelson, Lancashire. His siblings did well in life; one of them owned the Devereux Private School for Girls. Dad's father sang in operas and his younger brother Brian was a successful businessman. Dad was proud of his sensible nieces and nephews. He told me once I should emulate them, but I was still wayward and could only see through a light glass darkly.

The two main characters of this struggle of survival are my matriarchal grandmother Harriet Unger, formerly Harriet Talbot, and my father RSM Jack Devereux, formerly of the 1st Battalion Royal Scots (The First of Foot). The 1st Battalion saw action protecting the flanks at Dunkirk. Later, they were posted to Burma where Father met and married Mother before the battalion was sent to Palestine.

Throughout the book I spell Burmese names phonetically as Mother pronounced them. I cannot find Tada u, our internment camp, on any map, despite it being a substantial British barracks pre-war. I asked Mother about the location where we joined local Burmese as they looted warehouses; she said it was near Yu. Looking at various maps (some Japanese) I can see a town called Yeu, a village called Yu, and a town called Ye-u. There are also rivers called the Yu and the Mu, so the location of the warehouses is still uncertain. The only spelling Mother corrected (when she noticed it was incorrect) was "Tada u" which was where we were interned for three years. I had initially spelt it "Dada-u" as Mum pronounced it. However, the publisher has researched the subject thoroughly and proposed a location for the camp, indicated on the map at the front on the book.

During the war, Esme and Olly, who lived in a nunnery, were saved from starvation by Japanese officers. Esme, a nursing sister, did her best to care for Patrick, Aunty Lucy's oldest son, who was a doctor when he became ill with cancer. He died young despite the care of his aunt, Sister Esme McPherson and Olly her sister. They now live in Harlow.

Glenis was my father's pride and joy. At two years old while living in Johore we nearly lost her. Now walking, Glenis never missed an opportunity to escape. A large black cobra (Malayan sub-species) lived in our front garden. Every evening our dogs would harry the snake as it left its lair. One night we were having a dinner party, and my mother went to check on Glynis. "Jack!" she screamed, "Glenis is gone!" Dusk was falling. A sharp-eyed guest spotted Glenis running down the driveway. Jack chased after her and brought her back in his arms. Entering the house, the dogs began barking. Glenis had missed the cobra by seconds …
Glenis is now a successful sculptress.